What God Wants for Your Life

What God Wants
for Your Life

➤━◆━➤

Changing the Way
We Seek God's Will

Changing the Way
We Seek God's Will

➤━◆━➤

Frederick W. Schmidt

HarperSanFrancisco
A Division of HarperCollinsPublishers

HarperCollins books may be purchased for educational, business, or sales promotional use. For information please write: Special Markets Department, HarperCollins Publishers, 10 East 53rd Street, New York, NY 10022.

HarperCollins Web site: http://www.harpercollins.com
HarperCollins®, 👪 ®, and HarperSanFrancisco™ are
trademarks of HarperCollins Publishers.

FIRST HARPERCOLLINS PAPERBACK EDITION PUBLISHED IN 2006
Designed by Joseph Rutt

Library of Congress Cataloging-in-Publication Data
Schmidt, Frederick W.
What God wants for your life : finding answers to the deepest questions / Frederick W.
Schmidt. — 1st ed.
p. cm.
Includes bibliographical references.
ISBN-10: 0–06–083449–8
ISBN-13: 978–0–06–083449–4
1. Christian life. 2. Title.
BV4501.3.S35 2005
248.4—dc22 2004060874

06 07 08 09 10 RRD(H) 10 9 8 7 6 5 4 3 2 1

For Lindsay,
the graduating class of 2007 at Southern Methodist University,
and all those, younger and older,
who long to be free to do the will of God

CONTENTS

Foreword   xi

Introduction   On Opening an Invitation   xv

One   I-Questions and God-Questions   1

Two   Triage Theology   31

Three   Signs and Wonders   63

Four   Proving the Will of God   99

Five   Listening for the Voice of God   129

Six   We-Questions   163

Seven   Gifts and Graces   189

Eight   Putting It All Together:
Envisioning a New Life in God   205

Acknowledgments   223

Notes   227

At a higher altitude with flag unfurled
We reached the dizzy heights of that dreamed of world
Encumbered forever by desire and ambition
There's a hunger still unsatisfied

David Gilmour and Polly Samson

Every existing thing is equally upheld in its existence by God's creative love. The friends of God should love him to the point of merging their love into his with regard to all things here below. When a soul has attained a love filling the whole universe indiscriminately, this love becomes the bird with golden wings that pierces an opening in the egg of the world. After that, such a soul loves the universe, not from within but from without; from the dwelling place of the Wisdom of God, our firstborn brother. Such a love does not love beings and things in God, but from the abode of God. Being close to God it views all beings and things from there, and its gaze is merged in the gaze of God.

Simone Weil

FOREWORD

For more than one reason, I am pleased to write the Foreword to this book. Friendship is a factor, as I have known its author, Fred Schmidt, for almost two decades. And beyond friendship, I feel that the subject matter of this book—the practice and life of discernment—is vitally important.

Fred and I met almost twenty years ago. We spent time together when he lived and worked at St. George's College in Jerusalem and at the National Cathedral in Washington, D.C., and professional meetings have brought us together in other places. Our friendship has included conversation and correspondence about many things, including matters of vocation, profession, and discernment.

Over the years, I have come to know Fred as a first-rate writer, a fine theologian, and a person who lives the life he writes about. Fred's intellect, wisdom, and Christian orientation are all apparent in this book.

The subject matter of this book is central to our lives. It concerns the question of discernment, the most important question of the Christian life as it grows and matures. As the title of this book puts it, discernment is about "What God Wants for Your Life." For people who take God seriously, it is the most important question there is.

As Fred develops the notion, discernment invites us to reflect on what God is doing in the world today and how each of us, with our particular histories, gifts and graces, may discern how to live in relationship with God and God's purposes. He begins with the "God" questions, moves on to the "we" questions, and concludes with the "I" questions. This book thus provides a theological framework for discernment, as well as practical guidance for the process of discernment.

If "theological" is a negative word for you, let me put it another way. This book provides a "thinking" framework for discerning the will of God for our lives, for theology is about thinking; it is the reflective task of the Christian life. What is God like? What is God's character? How do we live our lives life in relationship to God? How do I live my life in relationship to God? Said differently, how do we live our lives in relationship to *what is*?

What is is my most generic and secular expression for "what is all around us." When I speak of *what is* in religious terms, I speak of it as "the sacred." When I speak of *what is* in Christian terms, I speak of *what is* as God as known in the Bible and Jesus.

We are all in a relationship to *what is*, however we name it. Importantly, how we see our relationship to *what is* matters greatly. Does how we see *what is* lead to a fearful and anxious relationship, to self-preoccupation and self-concern? Or does how we see *what is* lead to a trusting and liberating relationship, to the self-forgetfulness of faith and the freedom of the children of God?

Depending upon how they think of *what is*, of God, Christians bring different questions to their life with God. For some, the question is, What must I do to be saved? Or, How do I measure up to what God requires of me? These are anxious questions, and they suggest that life with God is an anxious task.

For other Christians, including the author of this book, the questions are not about "me" and my salvation but about God. What is God doing in the world? And how do I live my life in relationship to God's intentions for the world, and thus for me? These are the questions that Fred treats as a framework for the more particular question, "What God wants for your life."

This book is not only helpful and insightful, but an interesting read. Several features contribute to its worth and interest:

- Illustrative stories drawn from Fred's own life and the lives of people he has known
- A theology shaped by a transformational understanding of the Christian life
- An appreciative engagement with the Christian tradition
- Reflection questions for personal and small-group use
- Solid grounding in contemporary scholarship, with footnotes for readers who want to know more
- An appreciation of other religious traditions (though written primarily for Christians)

Discernment is a practice and a process. There are times in life when the need for discernment is greater. To be autobiographical for a moment, I recently turned sixty and am now "doing sixty," as I sometimes say. And on some highways, that's over the speed limit.

For me, turning sixty was my first serious encounter with my mortality. Of course, like all of us, I have known for a very long time that I will die. I would not have gotten that wrong on a true-false test. Nevertheless, only the advent of sixty made my mortality compellingly obvious to me.

The issue is not primarily death. I don't think I am afraid to die, though I will miss this life. Rather, the issue is the awareness that the future holds increasing limitations and decline, and that I cannot take for granted the health and vitality and mobility that I, gratefully, have been blessed with.

Thus the sharpened awareness generated by a big number has involved me in a process of discernment. There are "I" questions involved. How do I balance my life between vocation, family, friends, and leisure? Given that I can't count on being active indefinitely, what do I still want to do that requires a reasonable degree of vitality? What do I want my next year to be like? My next five years?

This book puts these questions in the larger framework of "God" and "we" questions. What is God doing in the world today? What is God doing in the communities in which I live? What is God doing in my life? This larger framework is very helpful.

As Fred describes discernment, it is more than a practice and a process. It is also a way of life. It is not simply a practice to turn to when faced with a life-changing decision or crisis. Rather, it is a way of living all of our days in an intimate relationship with God. Discernment is not only for "crisis time;" it is also a way of living in "ordinary time."

The life of discernment is marked above all by listening for God in the dailiness of our lives. As contemporary author Frederick Buechner puts it:

> Listen to your life. Listen to what happens to you because it is through what happens to you that God speaks. . . . It's in language that's not always easy to decipher, but it's there powerfully, memorably, unforgettably.[1]

This book suggests how to listen for God as part of the life of discernment. Such listening involves "the kind of reflective and prayerful space that makes (our spiritual) maturation possible."

This is a wise book. Wisdom is quite different from knowledge and information. From antiquity to the present, wisdom has treated the largest and most important questions of life. What is real, and what is reality like? How then shall we live? How then shall I live?

I commend this wise book to you with pleasure, conviction, and confidence.

—*Marcus Borg*

———◆———

ON OPENING
AN INVITATION

When you receive an invitation, do you automatically check for a return address or the identity of the host or hostess? I do. Invitations gain or lose significance for me depending on a variety of considerations.

Personal relationships usually figure prominently in piquing my interest in attending a particular event. Invitations from relatives and close friends get my attention instantly. I also respond positively to invitations from people or organizations whose work I recognize, and I am inclined to accept invitations from people who share common goals and values. But if an invitation fails to meet these criteria, my motivation to respond positively drops pretty quickly.

So what kind of inducement do I offer you to accept an invitation from a total stranger to discuss the subject of God's will for *your* life? After all, it is a pretty intrusive invitation, and it is issued with little or no risk to the author!

The best possible introduction, I suppose, is to note that this particular invitation comes from one whose struggle to live as a son, husband, father, citizen, employee, adult, and disciple has never been without its challenges. My own attempts to do the will of God have been marked by fears and misgivings, moments of success and moments of failure. There have been times when I have been spiritually grounded and times when I felt grounded in another, not particularly positive or spiritual sense of the word.

In spite of the unevenness of that experience, I am convinced that most of us *want* and *need* to know God's will. I see that desire and need in the ready interest of people when the spiritual life is mentioned. I hear it regularly in conversations with people about the almost pilgrimlike character of their life stories. And I hear it in conversations about the effort to give life meaning and significance.

The complexity of our lives also lends urgency to that quest. We live increasingly unreflective lives, consuming minutes, hours, and days without savoring them. We rush from encounter to encounter without asking how those experiences might modify or challenge the way in which we live. And we move reactively through the events of a day, making incremental and unrelated decisions that shape our lives without our being aware of it. Then one day we find ourselves saying, "This is not the life I intended to live."[1]

Yet, for many of us, the effort to find the will of God only makes matters worse. Many of the people I have met who thought they could avoid a sense of frustration, emptiness, or isolation by looking to God have instead compounded their misery. Unsure how to find the will of God and afraid of "getting it wrong," they are tormented by their doubts about a process that was meant to give them a sense of peace and belonging.

The good news, however, is that this sense of frustration is largely rooted in misunderstandings and not in the search itself for God's will. For myself, this realization grew out of my own effort to find and do the will of God.

For years my effort to find and do the will of God was framed by two extremes. On the one hand, I engaged in a fearful search for *the one right answer*—with all that those words imply. On the other hand, I have wondered whether some of what I have labeled "the will of God" included things I would have done anyway.

My own struggles with those extremes have led me to believe that there are many who need more than either extreme can offer. For those who look for the one right answer, it needs to be said that there is rarely a choice of that kind to be made, except perhaps in the case of some moral decisions. For those who fear that they have masked their decisions from themselves and from others by describing them as the will of God, it needs to be said clearly that we really do make choices. It is nonetheless profoundly important to grapple with what it means to make those choices rooted in faithful, creative attention to the will of God.

I remember well the decisionmaking process that took me and my family to Jerusalem some years ago when I assumed responsibilities as the dean of St. George's College. To say yes to a position of that kind was no small matter. Inside the walls of St. George's Cathedral, the college had for years provided theological education for Arab Christians. Then, five minutes into the 1967 Six-Day War, homes and institutions that had been in the country of Jordan were suddenly in the country of Israel. Pockmarks from small-arms fire still punctuate the cathedral tower, and the so-called Green Line that marks the original boundaries between Jordan and Israel continues to serve as the unseen barrier that divides an ostensibly undivided city.

For years following the war the college floundered. Arab students were not able to attend, and the future of the college was in doubt. Then, in a stroke of genius, leaders hit on the idea of reinventing the college as a place for continuing education and pilgrimage with a dominantly expatriate student body. A small but steady stream of people from around the world began to travel to St. George's to study and pray. But that hardly meant that it was an easy place to be.

The Israeli Court of Justice was adjacent to the college, and for that reason a contingent of armed, uniformed eighteen-year-olds was stationed outside our gates. One block away was Orient House, head-quarters of first the PLO (Palestinian Liberation Organization) and then the Palestinian Authority.

Inside the walls of the cathedral close (or compound), where we would live and I would work, things were no easier. A history of tribal behavior and political machinations had created tensions among the clergy and their families, lending a conspiratorial air to life. To make matters worse, predictable religious differences had strained the relationships between Christians and Muslims on the staff.

As you can well imagine, my family gave prayerful attention to the will of God in attempting to make our decision about this move. We carefully weighed the nature of the distinctive professional contributions that both my wife and I could make to the communities for which we would be working. We considered the impact that moving abroad, to a very troubled country, might have on our daughter. We talked at length about the decision with people in both the United States and Jerusalem in an effort to understand the needs that the college faced, and we made lists detailing the arrangements we would need to make. With enormous care we probed and prayed about the prospect of moving, and when we were finished, we were confident that we were making the right choice. We thought this was God's will for us.

Some of the dislocation we experienced during the first few months after our move prompted the kind of misgivings that almost always accompany a choice of this kind. Saying good-bye to close friends and selling our home prompted feelings of remorse. Moving to a country in which people lived in close proximity to one another, and in such obvious tension with one another, made us instantly wary. New sights and sounds reminded us at every twist and turn of just how far we were from home.

Guilt, too, was a frequent companion. We celebrated my wife's birthday in an open-air café near a restaurant that was attacked by armed gunmen just an hour or two later. We had dinner with friends living on the West Bank just an eighth of a mile from a village where, on the same evening, commandos attempted to free a soldier who had been kidnapped. And I can remember calling my wife during an extended trip back to the United States:

"How are things?"

"Oh, all right. We needed to bring the children inside. There was too much tear gas in the air."

How, I thought, could I expose my family to so much danger?

We grappled with the kind of what-ifs and if-onlys that all of us experience hard on the heels of momentous, life-changing decisions. Then, in the first few weeks of my tenure as dean, I found myself dealing with questionable practices in one of the institutions upon which my own work deeply depended.

At first blush, the issues I faced were straightforward. The harder I tried to get to the bottom of the issues involved, the clearer it became that the answers I sought would not be forthcoming. Given what information I could gather, from my point of view, the choice was obvious. I instructed the officer who was responsible for the institution to take the necessary corrective measures.

It was a significant decision, and I still feel that it was the right one. But it was also a decision that placed me squarely in conflict with some of the people with whom I worked most closely. As a result, in a matter of weeks after moving to Jerusalem what had seemed like the right choice suddenly felt like the wrong choice. And the months that followed were marked by the effort to work in a disciplined, creative fashion, knowing all along that the growing conflict was likely to negate the efforts we made. Overnight the anticipation and excitement gave way to sheer effort, and as we expected, things ended badly. A fact-finder studied the situation and discovered that the problems with which I was dealing were long-standing and intractable. His efforts to resolve the situation met with resistance, and I eventually resigned.

Had the experience simply been part of a professional calculus, then it might have been possible to view it with a bit of detachment. But because my family was so deeply affected by the experience and because the decision to go to Jerusalem had been part of a conscientious, prayerful decision, the crisis was also part and parcel of a much deeper struggle with the extremes I mentioned earlier. I revisited my motivations for accepting the position, wondering whether some dimension of my attraction to the job had clouded my judgment. My wife wondered out loud how God could have led us into something so deeply broken from the start. And the deep satisfaction we had experienced in saying yes to what we perceived to be the will of God gave way to feelings of isolation and repeated attempts to process the seeming hypocrisy we had witnessed within the Christian community.

Even my nine-year-old daughter had her own struggles. Hearing the word *fraud* on a television show, she asked my wife, "Mommy, what does 'fraud' mean?"

My wife responded, "Sweetheart, that's when someone pretends to be something in order to take advantage of other people."

Lindsay observed, "Oh, like the church."

Inevitably, we also struggled with the practical challenges of the aftermath. Moving back in just a year meant moving back into the same community, but not to the home we had loved so much. It meant returning to huge uncertainties around the issue of employment and the prospect of moving yet again. And it meant living at length with a sense of having been abandoned.

The questions that arise from an experience of this kind—mine and yours—tumble over one another in their demand to be answered. In reflecting on our time in Jerusalem, I questioned whether I had failed to hear God clearly. Did the fact that things ended so miserably mean that I had missed or misread the signs from God that might have guided me? If this was what I was supposed to do, then why didn't things turn out well? Or did God use my limited understanding of the job's demands to get me where I needed to be, in order to do what I needed to do? Were there steps I could have taken that would have ensured that I could find the will of God?

The questions themselves really don't matter, except as they illustrate the kind of inner interrogation that we all experience from time to time. But the answers I would give to them today are different from those I might have given at another point in my life—and they are certainly at odds with the kind of answers I was taught to expect.

No, I don't think that things ended so miserably because I had failed to hear God clearly. I did not miss or misread the signs. In fact, I am convinced that the depth of our relationship to God and our capacity for spiritual insight determine what we can see of God's presence in the world. Events themselves are more or less neutral in character. I don't believe in signs and wonders, as such. But I do wonder at what God is able to do, and this requires that we look at the world in a new way. The fact that sometimes things do not turn out well has no bearing on what you and I should choose to do. Some of what is really important for us to do is in fact bound to fail.

Did God use my limited understanding of the job's demands to get me where I needed to be, in order to do what I needed to do? The answer again is no. I am not a fatalist, baptized or otherwise.[2] The future is open, and the shape of it depends on the decisions we and others make. The only "reasons" for going to Jerusalem were the ones that motivated our choices as a family, and those were reasons we weighed in conversation with God. If what transpired defined the nature of our time there in unexpected ways, that, too, was shaped by the choices we and others made. My faith in God's guidance does not lie in the conviction that God has *scripted* everything that happens to us, but in the confidence that God *is with us* no matter what happens.

God can and does speak to us—even in times when things go terribly wrong. What often troubles and torments us are the assumptions that shape what we expect and how we listen. Thus, much of the conversation that follows is an effort to redefine what it means to find and do the will of God. My prayer is that in the course of that conversation you will find freedom, meaning, and direction—maybe even a bit of adventure and the courage that adventure requires. Together, we will think anew about a number of issues:

- The kinds of questions you should be asking as you look for the will of God

- Your motives for asking those questions

- The place of "signs and wonders" in your quest

- What we expect when we talk about "proving" the will of God

- How we go about listening for the voice of God

- The role of listening with others in our search for God's will

- The significance of our own gifts and graces

- The relationship between doing and being

- The importance of asking questions in community

In spite of the struggles I have encountered along the way, I am more confident than ever that life's deepest rewards lie in finding and doing the will of God. At the heart of my spirituality is the conviction that God is relational, straining every fiber, risking existence itself, to love us, care for us, and nurture us, and that God's desire for us is inseparable from the freedom, creativity, and risk that characterize our lives. The one cannot be had without the other.

Shaped by an open-ended, inner dialogue with God about the choices you and I really do make, finding and doing the will of God is not a baptized fatalism; God is not the puppet master who orchestrates every twist and turn of our lives. Finding and doing the will of God is an adventure in which, hand in hand with God, we define what it means to live as people of faith.

If there is something in the return address on this invitation that commends reading further, it is the fact that, in spite of my struggles, I continue to have the confidence that this adventure is possible and deeply rewarding. It is not a confidence that grows out of a carefree, happy-go-lucky romp through life, bolstered by heavy doses of denial. It is a confidence defined, shaped, and sharpened by setbacks and failures, and then reexamined with as much honesty as I can muster and—fear not—with joy as well. If that strikes you as a place worth living, then I hope you will accept the invitation. No RSVP necessary.

---◆---

I-QUESTIONS AND GOD-QUESTIONS

When you fathom the life of things and of conditionality, you reach the indissoluble; when you dispute the life of things and of conditionality, you wind up before the nothing; when you consecrate life you encounter the living God.

Martin Buber[1]

Tradition holds that in the deserts of Egypt a small group of men sought out Anthony the hermit, who was widely regarded for his sane and sensible approach to life. They wanted to know how to achieve spiritual perfection. Their conversation began in the evening and, it is said, lasted most of the night.

Anxious perhaps to demonstrate their own wisdom, they quickly offered answers to the question they themselves had raised without allowing the old hermit to speak. One argued that fasting and the keeping of vigils would accomplish the desired goal. Another recommended abandoning attachments to this world. Some thought that the key to achieving perfection lay in solitude and secrecy. Still others urged the opposite, recommending that perfection be sought in engagement with the world and the practice of charity.

Finally, Anthony spoke. "All the things that you have spoken about are necessary and helpful to those thirsting for God. But those who have been most zealous have often suddenly fallen prey to illusion. Discernment is that which above all else leads to God. It keeps us from presumption and excessive fervor on the right and from carelessness, sin and a sluggishness of spirit on the left."[2]

I am convinced that we ourselves are much like Anthony's interrogators. We are anxious to know the will of God and yet far too anxious to supply the answers without listening. What should I do? What am I able to do? How can I prepare? Where will I go? Moreover, in our fast-paced ADHD world we want answers to these questions *now*.

So, as we seek to find God's will, instead of turning to the anxious questions that we so often ask and answer without listening, let me suggest that we begin by asking different, deeper questions. In doing so, I am convinced that we can find a greater measure of spiritual balance and a way to nurture lives marked by greater significance. When we come back to the questions about ourselves—and I promise you that we will—I am also hopeful that we will have better answers. To get there, however, I want to do four things:

1. Introduce a basic distinction between "I-questions" and "God-questions"

2. In light of that distinction, define what I mean by the practice of discernment

3. Give you two basic strategies for asking your own God-questions

4. Illustrate why the distinction matters

Distinguishing Between I-Questions and God-Questions

Twelve of us had been asked to serve on the senior staff of Washington National Cathedral. The number, I think, was a fluke. Besides, we all reported to a thirteenth member of the staff who served as our immediate supervisor.

In those early days we did lots of team-building exercises. We jumped off a tower, each of us strapped into a harness hanging from a zip-wire, and went hurtling down a mountainside—okay, hillside—one by one. We went on trust-walks, blindfolded and led by another member of the staff. And we took the Myers-Briggs Inventory to discover a sense of how each of us responded to the world around us. We were a diverse bunch, and we came from a variety of work worlds, including not just the academy and the church but the worlds of advertising, nonprofit work, accounting, business administration, social work, and public relations.

But almost all of us also shared a frightening common denominator. Out of the twelve, eleven of us were firstborn children, and the one who was not was an only child. When he discovered the ugly truth about our team, our supervisor dropped his head into his open hands and wailed, "I don't believe it! I'm working with a group of people who have spent their entire lives asking, 'Can I do extra credit?'"

First children may be particularly bad about it—I know that I am—but we all live in an increasingly first-person-singular world where questions about extra credit dominate. We value and celebrate individual enterprise. We reinforce it in the way we market higher education, and we surround ourselves with the language and consciousness of personal initiative. We live in a world of applications, aptitude tests, and examinations designed to test our preparation for the solitary achievements that lie ahead, and we are ushered into a world that is deeply shaped by asking and answering I-questions.

I remember it well. At times the succession of challenges issued by parents, teachers, and others felt like an invitation to adulthood—a well-meaning welcome to the world where decisions were made and problems were solved. At other times those challenges felt like a gauntlet with unidentified traps nestled among the ones that were already clearly labeled. The effort to graduate from high school gave way to the task of finishing an undergraduate degree. Finishing that degree gave way to applying for graduate programs. Finishing a graduate degree gave way to anxiety over finding a job. Through it all the first-person-singular dominated, and far from seeming selfish or self-absorbed, overachieving, action-oriented lives and good answers to first-person-singular questions seemed to be the measure of responsibility.

For many of us, by midlife what seemed like preamble or preparation has taken on a life of its own. I am not a psychiatrist, so I cannot account for everything that contributes to the legendary midlife crisis that we all anticipate. But I am convinced that much of what leaves people feeling strangely at odds with the lives they are living is the product of I-questions asked and answered in ever greater isolation from deeper conversations with each other and with God.

It is little wonder, then, that as we begin to reflect on the shape of our spiritual lives, the I-questions are often simply transposed into a new key. Instead of asking, "What am I going to do?" we begin asking, "What am I going to do for God?" The new question may reflect a basic change in spiritual *allegiance*, but it doesn't necessarily reflect a change in the spiritual *logic* of our lives.

That is why the lives of some otherwise very sincere people often appear self-serving or self-absorbed—in spite of their interest in the will of God. They may focus energy on spiritual concerns in a way that they never have in the past, but the first-person-singular is still there, deeply at work in their spiritual DNA.[3] The result is dissonance: spiritualized conversation about self-seeking goals, self-actualization disguised as service, lives that lack everything except the appearance of piety, and relationships that lurch between affection and abuse.

The inability to move beyond the first-person-singular is particularly acute in parts of the West, and it has its own peculiar shape in our "post-postmodern" world.[4] But the struggle between I-questions and God-questions has far deeper roots. There is ample evidence of the same struggle, for example, in the ancient literature of Jewish prophets and leaders.

Moses, when called upon to represent the people of Israel before the pharaoh of Egypt, complains that he is not eloquent enough (Exodus 4:10). Saul, when called upon to serve as king, has second thoughts about his tribal bloodline—"Am I not a Benjaminite from the least of the tribes of Israel?" (1 Samuel 9:21)—and David simply protests, "Who am I?" (2 Samuel 7:18). One of my favorite stories, though, is that of Jeremiah's call to prophetic work.

> Now the word of the Lord came to me saying,
> "Before I formed you in the womb I knew you,
> and before you were born I consecrated you;
> I appointed you a prophet to the nations."
> Then I said, "Ah, Lord God! Truly I do
> not know how to speak, for I am only a
> boy." But the Lord said to me,
> "Do not say, 'I am only a boy';
> for you shall go to all to whom I send you,
> and you shall speak whatever I command you.
> Do not be afraid of them,
> for I am with you to deliver you," says the Lord.
> Then the Lord put out his hand and touched my mouth;
> and the Lord said to me,
> "Now I have put my words in your mouth.

See, today I appoint you over nations and over kingdoms,
to pluck up and to pull down,
to destroy and to overthrow,
to build and to plant." (Jeremiah 1:4–10)

Jeremiah had ample reason for asking I-questions. For starters, there was the complexity of the task. It would be a mistake to think of prophets as the equivalent of ancient clergy, with whatever (dubious!) clarity that designation might carry. The ancient prophet played the role of spiritual leader, to be sure, but the nature of the task overlapped with a number of other modern roles as well: social critic, editorialist, student of foreign affairs, policy specialist, and public intellectual — to name a few.[5]

In addition, according to Old Testament scholars, most Jewish prophets were motivated to address their own nation. They challenged the people of Israel, focused on issues of national significance, spoke to its leaders, and goaded its people to listen for God's leading. They occasionally "spoke" to other nations, but these were occasional, tangential oracles. As far as we can tell (not all of the prophetic oracles were recorded or survived), Jeremiah was the first of the prophets moved by God to speak as a prophet "to the nations."[6]

To make matters worse, Jeremiah became particularly active as a prophet in a year during which the throne of Judah changed hands three times. The first of the kings was Josiah. A charismatic reformer, Josiah had galvanized the nation around a cleansed and revitalized Temple, centralized worship, and instituted public readings of the Torah. He advocated the reunification of Israel, which had been split north and south, and he gave rights of citizenship to all landowners in Judah. Because Josiah had been king for thirty-one years, Jeremiah had never known another ruler, and Josiah's presence had that givenness that we all take for granted until it suddenly disappears.

Caught in a battle between the Assyrians and the Egyptians, Josiah was killed by the latter. Josiah's younger son, Jehoahaz, assumed the throne for three months, but when the Egyptians finished their conquest, they sent him into exile and placed his older brother, Jehoiakim, on the throne as their vassal. Thirty-one years of stability had been followed by three months of chaos, and it is not hard to imagine Jeremiah's reeling under the impact of it all.

Then there was the issue of age. All of this chaos took place when Jeremiah was probably only eighteen years old.[7] He lived in a culture that valued age, experience, and wisdom, and clearly he could bring none of those traits to bear on the task. Small wonder that the young prophet felt overwhelmed by all his I-questions, and said so.

The enormity of Jeremiah's task, the demands inherent in making himself heard, and his position in the society around him are all reminiscent of the same complaints we ourselves have lodged with God from time to time:

I am . . .

only a boy.
only a girl.
only retired.
only trained to do this.
only capable of doing that.

This doesn't mean, of course, that Jeremiah's I-questions were asked with quite the same import as ours are today.[8] Our I-questions are often driven by the need for self-actualization and a sense of entitlement. For us society is often little more than a collection of individuals. In addition, the engine of our anxieties is undoubtedly different from those that shaped the prophet's world. For example, modern Western cultures often value youth over age. Ancient Near

Eastern cultures did not. But in spite of such differences, the spiritual logic is the same. The first-person-singular dominates.

God, however, does not respond to the prophet in kind. There are no answers given to Jeremiah's I-questions. God does not attempt to reassure him about his innate abilities ("Jeremiah, you underestimate your gifts!"). God does not attempt to address the issue of his age ("Don't worry, Jeremiah, by the time you have completed the training program, you will be old and venerable"). Nor does God attempt to modify his estimate of the task ("Don't worry, Jeremiah, we'll take it one nation at a time").

Instead, the spiritual logic of the encounter shifts from I-questions to God-questions, from a preoccupation with Jeremiah's capabilities to the question of what God is doing: "I knew you. . . . I consecrated you. . . . I appointed you. . . ." The emphasis is on divine initiative, intimacy, and the covenantal bond between the young prophet and his God.[9]

The intimacy of God's calling is not, however, a private catering to Jeremiah's need to feel cared for or coddled. What is emphasized instead is the depth of God's activity in the world and in the prophet's life. Jeremiah's sense of adequacy is beside the point. The work to which he is called is not his in the final analysis. It is God's, and by virtue of that intimate initiative, Jeremiah is able to claim not only the title of "prophet" but the title of "prophet to the nations." There is a basic shift in the spiritual logic and DNA of his life.

Defining Discernment

It is not surprising, for that reason, that some of the earliest references to the search for God's will focus on the ability to "separate," or "distinguish," the presence of God's influence from the presence of other influences in the world. The practice of discernment is not—in the first place—the task of identifying your role or mine. Nor is it a matter of asking or answering I-questions, although there is a time and place to ask those questions. Discernment is the task or process of distinguishing the spirit or presence of God at work in the world from other, competing spirits in an effort to determine where the spirit of God may be moving.[10]

This is a very different task from the one we typically describe as discernment. Discernment is—by definition—theological, ethical, and critical. It forces us to think about our understanding of God and the ways in which we see God at work in the world. It compels us to make decisions about the moral implications of our lives and the lives of others.[11] And it requires a critical capacity to navigate our lives—individual and collective—guided by the light that our spiritual traditions provide.

Truth be told though, asking God-questions is not a familiar practice for most of us. We may ask I-questions from time to time, and we may ask ourselves moral questions in a narrow fashion, weighing whether it is right to do this or that. But we are unaccustomed to asking ourselves: What is God doing in the world? Where is God moving?

Naming God

How do we begin? One way is to ask: "What are the names that I give to God?" I am not talking about the politically or theologically correct names that you might be tempted to give in response to a question of that nature—the names drawn from sacred literature, creeds, hymns, or theological works. I am talking about the names that are deeply formative for you—the names that shape your prayer life, the names that shape what you expect from God, and what you don't expect. What are the names for God that shape where you expect to see the presence of God, and what are the names that shape where you don't often see God?

Some of those names derive from our cultures and from the issues at debate in our societies. The controversy that marked the life of Jesus could be seen in this way. Occupied by a foreign power, Roman-controlled Israel debated the names given to God and, by inference, what it meant to be the people of God.

The Pharisees' answer to that question was, "God's name is 'holy,' 'separate.'" And in an occupied country, where other kinds of borders had been compromised, a "holy" God was followed by a "holy" people whose lives manifested borders of a more complex kind: borders delineated by a cycle of worship in the Temple, prescribed sacrifices, foods that were permitted and foods that were prohibited. The Pharisees of the first century were not hypocrites but rather people of deep faith who named God in one way and saw God at work in ways that were deeply consonant with that name.

The Zealots, on the other hand, gave God very different names: "conqueror" and "king." They were inclined to see God as someone who could restore the hard political borders of Israel. At odds with the pharisaical option, they were inclined to believe that a God who expressed holiness or separation only in terms of worship, conduct, and food laws was, at best, not enough and, at worst, a serious compromise with their Roman overlords.

Jesus did not hesitate to engage the same debate, and the vocabulary he used to describe God was not completely different from the language his contemporaries used. But because he associated the "father" and "king" of first-century Judaism with a ministry to sinners, outcasts, and Gentiles, the descriptions resonated very differently. As a result, it became clear that, for Jesus, God was "Abba," a contagious compassion, moving across both literal and behavioral borders, embracing people who were not considered either holy or a part of God's people in any other sense.[12]

Similar dynamics shape every community's thinking. Both the best and the worst of every culture and religious tradition either enlarge or constrict our ability to discern the presence of God in the world. The desire to live faithfully names God in one way, galvanizing spiritual communities and challenging their members to live lives marked by sacrifice and humility. But press too far and the desire to live faithfully can lapse into a xenophobia that sees God at work in a single nation, race, or religion. Press even further and a person of faith can also be a person of violence.

The faith of the medieval church gave us both Saint Francis of Assisi and the Crusades. Judaism gave us not only the work of Martin Buber but a brand of Zionism that built the refugee camps of the West Bank. Islam gave us the poetry of Rumi and the jihad of September 11, 2001. We cannot avoid the influence of the cultures in which we are reared, and it is difficult, if not impossible, to completely escape their formative influence. But similarly, we cannot afford to blithely adopt the vocabulary they give us. The names given to God by them can just as easily mislead us as guide us.

On another level, of course, the names we give to God are shaped by much more personal experiences. How we were parented, our earliest formative spiritual experiences, the people who shaped our thinking, and the larger forces of nationality, race, gender, and social standing—all of these factors and others shape the ways in which we name God in more private ways.

For my own part, I grew up thinking of God as the-one-who-moves-goalposts. My understanding of God revolved around expectations: the need to be a good person, a good son, and a good student. Once I was within ten yards of life's goal line, I would look up from the huddle to discover that the goalpost had been moved— another ninety yards down the field. For that reason, I tended to look for God in the lives of people who worked hard and measured up. Oh, I was relatively gentle with those who didn't—after all, a good boy should be gentle. But that did not mean that I could easily see God in their lives—or in mine when I struggled.

Then, en route to an invitational debate tournament during my senior year in high school, our coach lost control of the car in which our team was riding, and on snow-covered roads we fishtailed into a head-on collision with a two-and-a-half-ton truck. The impact killed our coach and injured the four of us on the team. I spent twenty-eight days in the hospital and the better part of six months in various stages of recovery.

In the months that followed I revisited the names that I gave to God. In a world where doing good could end so abruptly and so much that is precious could be lost, a God who simply moved the goalposts and demanded more struck me as empty. During that time and in the years that followed, those names changed. A God of relationships, in love with us, straining to remain close to us, became far more important in my own prayers and thinking. I also began to appreciate the significance of a God capable of embracing us unreservedly in the midst of our imperfection.

You have your own names for God. The God who is "in control," the God who "has to be in control, because *I* don't feel in control." The God who "loves others, but can't quite love me." The God who "can't be a father, if being a father means being like mine." Some of those names arose from dark moments in our lives, born of relationships that strained or distorted our view of life.

Other names—thankfully—are life-giving, the gift of grace-filled relationships. One friend from New Orleans observed: "My first image of God is of a mountain, sitting solidly on the earth, rising majestically into the sky, all-powerful, all-seeing, immovable. Its presence speaks of ancient things and knowledge far beyond my comprehension. There is patience in its stance, and I am reminded of an old woman, an elder in the Choctaw tribe in Jena, Louisiana. I met Ms. Mary recently at a folklife festival. She was demonstrating how to make necklaces from chinaberries. Her hair was steel gray and hung in a braid to her waist; her face was deeply lined, her skin a weathered mahogany. She sat like a mountain with an aura of patience and authority about her. Her gaze penetrated the veneer, her expression hinted at experiences and memories beyond the present, and her bearing elicited obedience. God is like that for me."

The names still others give to God change with time. One student told me that there were three images at work in his life, "God the Good, God the Bad, and God the Ugly." Growing up in a minister's home gave him a strongly fundamentalist background. The God of his childhood "was a God of vengeance, persecution, and eternal damnation."

"This God followed me," he said, "wherever I went, waiting for me to do something wrong . . . so He could flick me on the back of my head with His thumb and middle finger. . . . I was in a perpetual state of fear." This, he said, "is the 'Ugly God' of my life."

"At the age of nineteen," he recalled, "I rebelled against this 'Ugly God,' a God I found I couldn't please. I joined the army and discovered that a life of sin was much more fun than a life of 'holiness.' It was at this point that I discovered the 'Bad God.' I'd put myself in situations where I knew God could strike me dead. . . . I just didn't care anymore. . . . Guess what? Nothing happened. God didn't strike me dead and didn't flick me on the back of the head with His thumb and forefinger. God didn't do what he was supposed to do. . . . I went out of my way to prove His absence in my life, and therefore His absence in the world. If there was a God, I didn't know Him. If I didn't know Him, He didn't exist. If He didn't exist, for me, He was absent and unknown. If He was absent and unknown, He had to be a 'Bad God.'"

"Many years passed," he said, "and then one day I looked back on my life. I looked back on the temptations and the challenges. I came to a very shocking realization. I was still alive. . . . As I reflected on those times when death surrounded me, shoved at me, tugged on me, I realized that there was a hand on my life. . . . To make a long story short, in that search I found a new God. This was the 'Good God.' Like a magnet, He began to draw me closer. . . . I found the Forgiving God."

The names are there, active, formative, shaping what we can see but, even at their best, obscuring some part of God's presence in the world. One participant in a retreat I was leading observed, "I have never even considered giving God a name. . . . How interesting now to crawl deep inside myself and request three images of God that are entirely my own, shaping my life and faith."

This is not to suggest that a single set of names, let alone the names that are deeply formative for us, will capture a large enough vision of God's presence in the world. That is why the capacity to listen for the names that others use is so important. That is also why the politicized debates over how we describe God have tended to both enlarge and constrict our capacity for finding and doing the will of God. An older generation of fixed and stereotyped ways of naming God has, in some religious traditions, obscured the richness and learning that arise out of differences in gender, race, and culture.

At the same time, unfortunately, many of the efforts to make those voices heard have employed zero-sum rhetoric that excludes established names in favor of enthroning new ones. When this happens, whether the advocates of tradition or inclusion triumph, the politics of the debate triumphs over the need for spiritual awareness. Exclude feminine images to describe God and the image of a nurturing mother eagle who wraps her wings around her young is lost to us (Deuteronomy 32:11), as is the God described as wisdom, crying to us in the streets (Proverbs 1:20–23a). Exclude the male images used to describe God and the image of a kingdom that grows from small beginnings like a mustard seed is lost, as is the intimacy of the prodigal son and his father (Mark 4:30–32; Luke 15:11–32).

In times of dispute and debate, the loss of such images may seem like a small price to pay in order to carve out a space where influence is sought or protected. Seen as a means of describing the movement of God among us, a victory by either side constitutes a tragic diminution of what might be understood about the nature of God's presence in the world.

The practice of naming God is just one means of discerning the presence of God in the world, and indeed, names fail at some point to be enough. Ted Loder writes:

> Holy One, untamed
> by the names I give you,
> in the silence
> name me,
> that I may know
> who I am,
> hear the truth
> you have put into me,
> trust the love
> you have for me,
> which you call me to live out
> with my sisters and brothers
> in your human family.[13]

The mystical traditions of many faiths have long witnessed to the silence in which God is finally and most palpably present. Shams-ud-din Mohammed Hafiz, a Muslim, spoke of "pulling out the chair beneath your mind."[14] Bodhidharma, the Buddhist monk who is credited with introducing Zen practice in India and China, describes the marks of that practice as

> A special transmission outside Scriptures
> Not relying on words or letters
> Pointing directly to the human mind.[15]

In my own tradition, the unknown author of a work called *The Cloud of Unknowing* observes:

> Although it can sometimes be beneficial to think carefully about the kindness and excellence of God and although this can be both a revelation and a part of contemplation, nevertheless in this work it must be thrown aside and covered with a cloud of forgetting. And you must step over it resolutely and gladly and with a dedicated and pleasurable impulse of love try to pierce the darkness that you seem to encounter above you. And beat upon that thick cloud of unknowing with a sharp dart of yearning love. And never for a second think of giving up.[16]

That said, however, surfacing the names that we give to God allows us to see patterns of God's presence in the world and gives us a place to begin asking God-questions. It is important to avoid jumping too quickly into "namelessness" lest we fail to understand the God we actually worship.

Heeding the Law of Love

Another way of beginning to ask yourself where and when you see God active in the world is to look to the needs of others. One of the great struggles that many of us face in attempting to find and do the will of God revolves around the search for what seems to be the otherworldly and ineffable expectations of a God who is beyond us and unseen. When God is viewed as hovering above us, we are driven by the conviction that God's will is an exotic and unknowable thing.

But the best of spiritual traditions identify the love of God with the love of others. As such, the will of God is, on one level, reducible to the love of others. For that reason, finding and doing the will of

God is as immediate and concrete as loving one's neighbor. Jesus in Matthew's gospel teaches, "Truly I tell you, just as you did it to one of the least of these who are members of my family, you did it to me" (Matthew 25:40). The prophets of ancient Israel observe, "What does the Lord require of you but to do justice, and to love kindness, and to walk humbly with your God?" (Micah 6:8b).

Already a postmodern saint long before the term "postmodern" was applied to the world in which we live, Dag Hammarskjöld, secretary general of the United Nations from 1953 to 1961, understood this well. Considered an unlikely candidate for his post, he served an institution that scarcely commanded the respect of its member nations. He traveled widely, negotiated disputes, and confronted the hope and ugliness of a very real world. Keeping a spiritual journal in which he could write only a few lines at a time, the young secretary general knew that doing the will of God was intimately connected with a life of service and of love. Reflecting on his work, with the journalist Edward R. Murrow, Hammarskjöld observed:

The explanation of how man should live a life of active social service in full harmony with himself as a member of the community of the spirit, I found in the writings of those great medieval mystics for whom "self-surrender" had been the way to self-realization, and who in "singleness of mind" and "inwardness" had found strength to say Yes to every demand which the needs of their neighbors made them face. . . . Love—that much misused and misinterpreted word—for them meant simply an overflowing of the strength with which they felt themselves filled when living in true self-oblivion. And this love found natural expression in an unhesitant fulfillment of duty and an unreserved acceptance of life, whatever it brought them personally of toil, suffering—or happiness.[17]

Hammarskjöld discovered that in expressing love to others we transcend the I-questions that dominate our lives and find the answers to the God-questions far more readily. What seems mysterious and ineffable becomes obvious and tangible. The apparent rift between the realities of life and the demands of the spirit dissolve. And it becomes clear that much of what is entailed in finding and doing the will of God lies immediately at hand.

Even when we "know" better, it is difficult for us to learn this. The quest to find and do the will of God can so easily take us back to I-questions that the renewed preoccupation with our own needs can be obscured by the seemingly spiritual nature of the quest. We can quickly become our own favorite topic of conversation, and it is only the thin veneer of our religious vocabulary that is new.

We need only listen to the shape of our conversations with one another to see this. How often do our sentences begin with "I" and end in "me"? How often do we ask others about the shape of their lives and the condition of their souls? Loving others requires thoughtful attention to their needs, long silences, the discipline to avoid "fixing" other people in order to move beyond our own discomfort, and the ability to hear the echo of deeper longings behind the words that people use. The capacity to respond to what we learn as a result can be tedious, domestic, and demanding—all at once. By contrast, the effort to find and do the will of God for our lives can be endlessly romanticized, and when necessary God can be kept at arm's length.

That is, in large part, why the deep relationship between the disciplined and unconditional character of love has been severed from its romantic dimensions. We revel in the romantic dimensions of love and delight in re-creating the warmth and light of it all. The other dimensions often require more of us than we are willing to give. Far too late in life we learn that the one cannot be had without the other or that in giving love to another human being we can worship God.

What is important to remember about this approach to exploring the God-questions is that we do not need to travel across the world. The opportunities are as close at hand as the people with whom we live and work on a daily basis. We need not worry about the scale of the effort or about where to begin. Here and now, with the people who are already in our lives, is an appropriate place to begin.

J. C. Irby taught me that secret years ago. J.C. worked as an "escort orderly," ferrying cancer patients in wheelchairs and on stretchers between their hospital rooms and radiotherapy. As a young volunteer, I was often at his side, and I also had the chance to compare his behavior with that of other hospital employees.

Even now what strikes me is the disciplined attention he gave to others. He asked how they felt. He moved them gently from their beds to stretchers or wheelchairs. He lightened their day with cheerful banter, and he treated everyone with dignity—hour after hour, day after day. He treated patients with a selfless love that never seemed forced or artificial.

Some, I am sure, thought that J.C. was simply a good-hearted, simple man, and perhaps that is exactly what someone lost in love for others appears to be. But as the years have passed I have realized that it was love of others that gave him the strength to be that attentive.

I-Questions and God-Questions: Why the Distinction Matters

So why is asking God-questions of so much spiritual significance? In part the answer lies in the nature of the quest to find and do the will of God. On the surface of it, that quest appears to be motivated by a simple need for direction. We want some indication that we are doing the right thing with our lives, and we are more comfortable having a set of "marching orders," a to-do list. Our questions are much like those I was regularly asked by undergraduates: "Should I go into business or teach in the inner city?" This is an understandable kind of question.

But it turns out to be of very limited value. Flat, one-dimensional questions about *my* life or *your* life are questions asked in a vacuum. What we need is not a word *about* us from a God whom we may or may not know, but a word *to* us, spoken in a relationship in which we know God and we are known by God. And we can neither ask that kind of question nor get any kind of useful answer to it without asking how, where, and to what end God is at work in the world.

Once we have surfaced this deeper reason for finding and doing the will of God, it becomes clear that it is not just direction for which we are looking (as much as we need it). We are attempting—intuitively perhaps—to address a far more subtle constellation of needs that are even more basic to us as spiritual beings: the need to have a sense of belonging; the need for the courage and conviction that come from living with purpose; and the need to have the experience of oneness with God that the ancient Hebrews called *shalom*.

These three needs are basic to our nature and become more acute with time. There is a great deal in our world today, for example, that erodes a sense of belonging. Oh, to be sure, we've made a spiritual virtue out of a cultural necessity by celebrating the speed and pace of the world in which we live. In fact, those of us who live in the Western world spur ourselves on with cultural self-talk that revels in a thirst for change and the glories of seeking. My wife and I have made eight major moves and another six minor moves (if there is such a thing as a *minor* move). We have traversed state lines, national boundaries, impermeable and semipermeable cultural barriers, and two oceans. In the spring we instinctively look for moving companies and cardboard boxes the way birds think about migrating. In that regard we are typical of the ADHD world in which we live.

But none of us has lost the need to belong. It has simply disappeared further underground where no one can see it. And like an underground aquifer, our need for belonging is growing, like a vast, unseen ocean. We pass through experiences with so much speed that we hardly have time to process their significance. Rituals of celebration are fast disappearing. Retirement parties I have attended recently are held in the middle of the workday and last not much more than an hour. "You are only as good as your last performance," we tell one another, and when we are through performing, we are through.

We labor under an ever more fragile set of connections with the places where we live and work. We use our jobs as stepping-stones to other opportunities. Our communities have become places to camp out between workweeks. The ubiquitous chain stores in major cities have begun to function like commercial umbilical cords, promising a sense of belonging to people who don't belong.

We are no longer where we were yesterday, and we are not where we will be tomorrow. That is why when we seek the will of God we are looking for something far harder to name than a list of divine marching orders. We are looking for a place to stand, a place to dwell in a world where no one can find a place to rest—and no one is allowed to admit it.[18]

The same could be said of our quest for a sense of purpose. To seek the will of God is to seek a wedding of heart, mind, and soul— the reintegration of lives lived out in a society that promotes disintegration. Heart, mind, and soul are those enduring words that ancient people used to describe our innermost passions and motivations, our capacity for relationships and the wellspring of our being.

Modern life insists on pulling those passions apart and demands that many of them go unexpressed. The places where we work, for example, often demand enormous energy and focus, but they are not necessarily places that nurture a deeper connection with the work itself. Employers are interested in our skill set. It is not as clear how interested in us they are. Still other workplaces demand that we "check our values at the door."

Taken together, the pace and fragmentation of modern existence can force us to live a series of discrete lives that have little or no connection with one another. That pressure has been so strong, in fact, that we scarcely recognize the ways in which we have reshaped our lives to meet the demands made on us. We are like the young man in the fable who is presented with an ill-fitting suit that the tailor insists is actually a fine piece of work. Convinced that the tailor is right, the young man is persuaded to drop one shoulder, hold his arms akimbo, and walk with an uneven gait. We have accommodated ourselves to the world around us, scarcely aware of the eccentric shape of our lives.

A good friend who works as a successful defense attorney observed, "I have one vocabulary that I use to talk to my clients in jail, another I use with their families, a third that I use with my colleagues and with judges, and another that I use at home. At first, I justified the differences as a practice analogous to using a foreign language. I speak Spanish with Spanish-speakers, German with German-speakers. But I've begun to wonder if the differences are more profound, differences in my way of being and not just my way of speaking."

And therein lies the need for that sense of oneness or wholeness that the ancient Hebrews called shalom. It is a part of what we intuitively look for when we seek the will of God, but we scarcely recognize it. In part, the problem lies with the English language. To capture the meaning of shalom, you need more than one word. But the problem is not simply linguistic, it is cultural as well.

The two words most frequently used in English to capture the meaning of the Hebrew illustrate my point. In English, if one is living out of a sense of oneness or wholeness, we often say that he or she is living *authentically*. That person's actions and convictions possess a certain congruity. They are in harmony with one another. "What you see is what you get," we say about someone who is authentic. To some degree that word captures a piece of what shalom is all about.

The difficulty, however, is that in our culture authenticity is, more often than not, an achievement. We talk readily about *self-actualization* and about *working hard* at therapy. But shalom is not an achievement. It is a gift, and a divine gift at that. As such, shalom flows out of us when, in God's presence, we recognize that oneness as a gift from God. We set aside the alternatives that we have fashioned for ourselves—alternative personalities, alternative voices, addictions, and distractions—and we begin to live with freedom the lives we have been given.

The other word we use in English to capture the notion of shalom is *peace*, and on the face of it, that word also conveys something of what the Hebrew means. It is in fact the word most often used in English translations of the Old Testament. But we have confused peace with the absence of conflict—or even more superficially, with getting the lighting and music in our lives properly adjusted. As a result, peace has become a fragile commodity, governed almost entirely by our emotions. It is felt or lost depending on the things that happen to us and on our ability to preserve some sense of equanimity in the midst of conflict or struggle.

All of this might seem purely academic, but the absence of both a vocabulary and a culture that comprehend the fullness of shalom drives us to look for alternatives, to which we then cling. A friend who is a high-functioning addict commented that her success at work and her ability to keep pace with the debilitating effects of her addiction made it possible to evade the sense of fragmentation and lack of oneness that she experienced for years. Only after she destroyed two marriages and alienated her children did she begin to look for something deeper.

True peace and a sense of oneness—shalom in all its fullness—comes with the embrace of God. Like a walk hand in hand with someone you love, some dimensions of the experience have a shape and texture confined to the moment. There are moments when a sense of authenticity is almost palpable and emotional highs bear us along. But like a walk along the beach with someone you love, the sun will set and the tide will erase the footprints from the sand. In those moments it is important to remember that there are other dimensions of the divine embrace that endure, and they are rooted in the conviction that shalom is first and foremost a matter of being embraced by God, whatever our circumstances.

At first blush, one might think that needs of this kind can be met on an ad hoc basis—adding them to our lives in much the same way that we add a certification for a particular skill set or augment our diets with a vitamin supplement. We have commodified spirituality, dispensing spiritual practices and gifts as if they were products. That approach, however, is misguided. A sense of belonging, singularity of purpose, and an experience of shalom cannot be amended to lives shaped by other forces. They are not dispensed as discrete answers to discrete prayers. They are the fruits of a life lived in a particular way and shaped by a specific understanding of God. And because that understanding is formative, God-questions serve as a starting point.

This is not to say that a desire for direction isn't also an important reason to look for the will of God. On the contrary, we desperately need it. Viewed from the outside, the business of becoming an adult looks like the business of *arriving*—or more accurately, of *having arrived*. Not long ago my daughter, Lindsay, echoed that conviction in one of those obligatory family moments over dinner that I've heard called "the table of accountability." As we checked in with one another, the subject turned, as it so often does, to the question I've asked her for years: "Did you learn anything today?"

"Yes," she replied. "We are studying human development in psychology."

"And what stage are you in?" inquired her mother.

"I'm differentiating," she responded.

"And what stage are your father and I in?" her mother asked.

(*Thin ice*, I thought.)

"Oh, you're through developing," she quipped. "You're adults."

But far from having arrived, becoming an adult is a growth experience, and the specific moments of that experience have prompted us all to look for God's will as a key to navigating its challenges.

In my life Lindsay has been a catalyst for at least part of that quest, as children and others we nurture in classrooms and at work often are. When my daughter was born, she was so fragile and quiet that my wife and I wondered whether she was healthy. We felt the full weight of what it meant to assume responsibility for her well-being and development. Now, at age seventeen, she is a verbal maelstrom, ready to talk from sunrise to sunset—the perfect example of the sins of the father visited on the father.

As she meets new challenges, so do I, and the immediacy and practical shape of those challenges have forced me to scramble, looking for a means not only to respond to the demands of the moment but to think about the ways in which those responses will shape her. I have weighed my words, modulated my voice, relented and resisted, pleaded and cajoled. I have succeeded and I have failed. At every juncture—or as often as I could remember to do it—I have asked myself, how can I respond from a deep sense of God's guidance? What response will be not only the "right" response but a response that will nurture a deep sense of God's guidance in her life?

My performance has been uneven. I've been brave. I taught her how to drive, calmly inquiring, "Can you tell me why we are up on this curb, dear?" I've also chosen the coward's way out. Yes, I confess that in the third year of Lindsay's life I secretly chose to replace her first dead goldfish on the morning of December 26. Preferring to sidestep the subject of death, I put "Goldy" in a margarine container, rushed to the pet store while my daughter slept, purchased a look-alike, placed him in the goldfish bowl, and gave him a false identity. (She wanted to know why he had changed so much overnight.)

In retrospect, though, as much as I have attended to her needs, parenting has also forced me to revisit my own values, to stretch and to grow. I have struggled to distinguish realism from cynicism, and idealism from naïveté. I have sought to balance the value of goals and the need for grace. I have leaned heavily on what I have learned, and I have learned to question the assumptions that shaped my own childhood. I have looked into my daughter's eyes and seen something of the world that lies ahead for all of us, and I've also remembered dynamics that shaped my life and are likely to shape the lives of the children she may have. I have experienced moments when the distance between my own adolescence and adult life has seemed negligible, and there have been other moments when the distance seems almost impossible to calculate. In short, I've looked for guidance from God in a process that has been a little bit like teaching someone to fly—while learning how to fly myself.

As with so many other adults, however, the business of seeking God's guidance in "learning how to fly" has been neither easy nor the source of comfort that I had hoped. Instead, it has introduced an added layer of struggle that I have often wished I could shed. I have read books, sought the advice of trusted mentors, and looked high and low for spiritual secrets. I've also revisited the subject time and again as I've advised students, counseled parishioners, listened to retreat attendees, and spent privileged moments with pilgrims on two continents. Those experiences have convinced me that the search for direction cannot be amended to lives that otherwise are lived on their own terms.

Asking God-questions ushers us into another way of being, a new way of seeing the world. As important as the I-questions might be, it is necessary to set them aside initially. If we focus on the I-questions, our search for the will of God becomes myopic and self-centered. God becomes enslaved to our needs, our program, our concerns, and our vision. What we think we can or should be doing is fashioned with little or no awareness of what God is doing in the world. If we don't pay attention to the God-questions, we court the temptations to self-sufficiency and pride. Our prayer life becomes dominated by the narrow world of our own self-interest, and our spiritual life becomes little more than the quest to find a life that we can find gratifying. The world dominated by I-questions is a burdensome world in which ever more resources, spiritual and temporal, are focused on our needs. Our goals are goals that interest us and us alone.

To embrace the God-questions allows our needs to take their shape and significance from something larger—from an enterprise that is no longer focused on ourselves alone, an undertaking that involves others and serves others. And because it is God's work, the significance of our efforts no longer rises or falls with ourselves alone. Freedom, release, and spiritual balance follow. It is an approach to spiritual wisdom that rests on two great truths: (1) There is a God. (2) You are not God.

Elizabeth White observed:

Have you anything more important to do? Ask yourself that question when interruptions threaten and you are tempted to set this hour aside. . . . It is not a futile task. Once the interrelation of all created things is even dimly sensed, one cannot be small. The mantle of magnitude is over the most humble part of the whole.[19]

When our vision of the created order is wrenched from its natural center in God and forced into an orbit around our lives, the "mantle of magnitude" is something that we can weave only for ourselves. We are forced to justify the energy that God and others focus on our lives. We are burdened with the need to defend and justify our every action. And if, temporarily, we are able to convince those around us that the narcissism controlling our lives is justified, then we easily fall prey to pride and vanity.

I once worked with a priest who, at an early age, was made a bishop. Fashioning his own mantle of magnitude, he lowered his voice two octaves, gained over a hundred pounds, and began talking about himself in the first-person plural. The loss of soul in this transformation was palpable, and the story of Faust's selling his soul to the devil acquired a tangible reality that I had never expected to witness.

When you start with God-questions, you begin with a sense of the way in which the whole of creation is interrelated and "one cannot be small." The mantle of magnitude will rest upon you everywhere you go. The obscurity of the good that you do will have no bearing on its significance, and the need for self-justification will evaporate. With the mantle of magnitude comes freedom. The voice and the visage that were given you at birth are enough. There is no need to inhabit someone else's body or use someone else's voice. There is no need to wrap yourself in office and position.

Saint Augustine speaks about the same dynamic using terms that have all but lost their significance for us. Comparing the city of man with the city of God, Augustine describes the blood-feud between Romulus and Remus, the mythic founders of ancient Rome. Human glory, Augustine observes, is a finite commodity. The gravity, the power, the significance that any human being can amass is limited and exhaustible. It can be divided and shared in only a limited number of ways. And so Romulus killed Remus, seizing as much glory as possible.

Where I-questions dominate, sisters and brothers are drawn irresistibly into conflict with one another. The question of what God is doing disappears from our conversation. The imperative to love others as the measure of what it means to find and do the will of God is eclipsed in the apparently well-meaning search for something more profound and mysterious that is neither profound nor mysterious.

By contrast, Augustine observes, the glory of God is boundless and shared with us. Like a flame spread from candle to candle, there is ever more light, but no less fire. Our lives acquire gravity and significance, but not at the expense of anyone else. In a city where the God-questions dominate, the boundless glory of God dominates as well.[20] Not a bad place to find sanctuary in a first-person-singular world.

Spiritual Exercises for Asking God-Questions

- Identify the three names or images that are most powerfully at work in shaping your understanding of God.

- What do these names reveal or conceal about the presence of God in the world?

- Evaluate why they are so significant for you.

- Should you nurture other names or images for God?

- Identify some specific areas where you see God at work in the world.

- How could you participate in what God is doing?

- Experiment for a day with limiting the number of times you draw people into a conversation about your own life.

- Try instead to ask as many people as possible about their lives and the challenges they face.

- In what ways does that kind of disciplined attention to the needs of others move your own conversation beyond a preoccupation with I-questions?

———— ◆ ————

Two

TRIAGE THEOLOGY

"Faith and Life Negotiate." How right they should, if life is to be faithful and faith is to be alive.

Kenneth Cragg[1]

Despite all of their effort, none of the philosophers before the coming of Christ was able to know as much about God, and about what is necessary for life, as one old woman knows by faith after Christ's coming. Hence it is said: "The earth is full of the knowledge of God."

Thomas Aquinas[2]

We are all triage theologians. We may not be card-carrying professionals, but step by step in conversation with life, we build an understanding of God and the way in which God is at work in the world and in our lives.

As happens with the on-call triage nurse in a hospital emergency room, crisis bursts through the front door of our lives and demands our immediate attention. With the clock ticking, the triage nurse responds quickly, making instant decisions about how to stop the bleeding long enough to allow for a more thorough analysis to come later.

Like the triage performed in an emergency room, triage theology is done "on the run." We do it with the kind of limited time that allows for only a cursory glance at life and faith. It is not the work of a monk with long hours for prayer and meditation. Nor is it the work of a scholar with long hours for research and reflection. It is the work of one who cares—but cares under pressure.

You hear triage theology in the ways people reflect on their lives, mostly in passing. "I guess this (or that) wasn't God's will." "God did (or did not) answer my prayer." "God led me to do this." You find people doing triage theology in the waiting room at a hospital, over coffee or lunch with a friend, in the wake of a major disappointment, and in anticipation of a momentous choice.

Like its medical analogy, triage theology is also accomplished with a minimum of resources. The ideas that most of us forge out of our experience with God, life, and the intersection of God and life usually come to us without the benefit of formal academic preparation. Instead, we draw on what little we have learned, and we weigh our convictions about God against the backdrop of that experience.

Like the triage done in an emergency room, theological triage is deeply enmeshed in the dailiness of our lives. Up to our elbows in it, we love and learn. We bind up our wounds, grieve our losses, celebrate our successes, and rehearse our failures. In the midst of those experiences, we draw conclusions about the way in which God has or has not been present in it all.

The reflection we do is rarely abstract. It is almost always imbedded in the messiness of our lives. The wisdom we seek in those moments is almost always sought as a means of making life work.

Finally, like nurses determining the amount of care to give to patients based on their condition, we perform theological triage by weighing which of the ideas about God that come to us in the midst of life are the most viable. We save and nurture the ones we deem likely to survive and to serve us well. We rely on those ideas and we build on them. They shape the way we talk about God. They shape the way we pray. They shape the way we describe our spiritual journeys.

In life's triage, we turn our attention next to new ideas. Like a patient whose chances of surviving are more difficult to assess, new ideas about the spiritual life may be laden with unproven potential. Over time we may come to depend on them and value the contribution they make. But it is only the rare chemistry of life and conviction that brings them more quickly than that to center stage in our lives.

By contrast, as with a physician attempting to decide where to spend precious time, the ideas that do not seem viable are the ones we abandon. They may be old and cherished convictions we have slowly surrendered. Their chances of survival may have been obscured by our love for them. They may be new ideas to which we have just been introduced but that lack obvious promise. Whatever their age and origin, as the dissonance grows between those ideas and the shape of our experience, we either quietly or more vocally set them aside.

It is in this sense that you and I are all theologians, even though most of us would protest—either in modesty or in horror—that we are not. And truth be told, *in this sense* the formally trained theologian and people who specialize in other kinds of knowledge and skill are on equal footing. The experience of life is the place where we all struggle to find and do the will of God—if we seek God's will at all. It is in the particularity of life—in its strife and moments of celebration—that we are first moved to look for God's will. And it is there that we fail or succeed in finding answers that nurture us.

In dialogue with the events of our lives, we make decisions about what we can and cannot expect from God. We decide what we can and cannot expect from life. And in our struggle to understand the will of God, we decide what we should and should not expect of ourselves and our communities.

At some points in history, spiritual leaders have attempted to restrict this kind of work to those specially prepared for the task, people who are educated and certified to "do" theology. It is an activity that large numbers of people still generally assume should be left to those who are specially trained to do it. But in fact all of us form a private triage theology—a quick resource theology tool kit—that shapes the way in which we live our lives. The problem is that the triage we do often goes unnamed and unexamined. So in this chapter I would like to

- Explain why our triage theology is part of our garden-variety lives as we seek the will of God

- Examine some inherited assumptions that inform our triage theology

- Offer alternative tools for doing better triage theology

- Talk a little bit about the challenges involved

Put another way, I want to give back to you the gift that is yours and invite you to take up the tools that will help you to use that gift.

Garden-Variety Lives

Triage theology is not the kind of effort that requires you to drop out of life, enroll in a divinity school, abandon your family and career, or move to a hermitage. Truth be told, doing those things would simply introduce you to a different world where it is equally difficult to find the time for the reflection we all need. When I first began teaching, one of my advisers wrote to say, "Dear Fred, I am delighted that you have found a teaching position. I hope you have time to read and re-flect." Years later it is clear to me that he had good reason to be concerned.

For all the hours of formal theological education I have enjoyed, my own triage theology continues to be done in fits and starts and between phone calls and appointments. I stay up late to find some quiet moments to write, I carry a tape recorder in my briefcase to capture ideas that come to me on the run, and I work in a world that rewards what it can see in the way of productivity.

Like me, you may find it enormously helpful to know that you are already practicing triage theology, and it is important to reflect on the way you go about doing it, even if much of that reflection is done on the run. For triage theology is the first step that most of us take in searching for the will of God.

In spite of this realization, more than one person I have met labors under the false impression that their life, made up of simple elements like relationships and work, cannot possibly merit a search for anything quite so grand as the will of God. Still others think they might be too young or too old to search for the will of God.

If such assumptions were simply theoretical in character, they might not merit attention. But they lead large numbers of people to then further assume that it is not important for them to find and do the will of God; such assumptions also have a way of narrowing and distorting our definitions of who should. The result is that many people are spiritually disenfranchised. Worse yet, perhaps, they adopt a view of God as one who cares most for those with special vocations, rarefied lives, and the advantages of age (however that might be defined!). So both issues deserve further attention.

Begin by remembering that the only life we can bring to a conversation with God is the one we are living. If your life—like the lives that most of us lead—is a garden-variety life, that does not mean you are spiritually inferior or any less deserving of God's attention. Teaching a class on spiritual disciplines twice a year at a monastery, I see this misgiving quite often. Students are at once repelled and attracted by what they see as the exotic, if not rarefied, life of the monastery.

On the one hand, they are sure that they have little interest in a life shaped by close-quarters communal living and the strictures of spiritual discipline and celibacy. Even a cycle of daily prayer often strikes them as impractical and restrictive. As a result, most of the students I interact with find it difficult to believe that they will discover patterns in monastic life that they can appropriate for themselves.

At the same time, however, they often struggle with the unspoken or unacknowledged assumption that monastic life is so different from their own that those who live a cloistered existence enjoy special access to the divine. For that reason, they also quickly conclude that monks understand the will of God more readily and more fully than they do. It is at this point that the garden-variety character of my students' lives weighs heavily on their minds. Apologies for the lives they lead and the work they do soon follow, and sentence after sentence begins with the words, "I'm just a . . ."

After spending a week in prayer and conversation with those same monks, the students learn that the monks' lives, no less than their own, are shaped by relationships and work and that the way forward is often no less clear to the monks than it is for them. They meet Brother David, who once worked as an ER nurse in New York and who loves to tease visitors to the monastery by suggesting at meals that they have inadvertently broken a monastic rule by eating ketchup. They meet Father Michael, who was trained as an engineer but has found his true vocation helping handicapped children regain some measure of motor control through equestrian therapy. And they spend time with Brother Joseph, who planted three hundred trees around the monastery (much to the frustration of one abbot who preferred not to obscure the architecture of the building). Brother Joseph also built a motorcycle twenty-seven years ago out of nonmotorcycle parts, dubbing it "Re-cycled Grace." My students hear the monks talk about awkward interpersonal relationships, express pride and disappointment in their day-to-day labor, and ask questions about their monastic vocation.

Slowly, it becomes clear that the distance between the monastery and "the world" is not as great as the students supposed. Reflecting on her experience at the end of the week, one student captured the experience in her journal in a day-by-day, staccato style:

> STRUCTURE. Stifling rules developed to eliminate unique-ness. Demands that silenced the soul. Inconsistencies that caused dilemma. A format not embraced by me.
>
> MONDAY. Service structure caused irritation. Religious icons became a distraction. Dictated psalms left the heart empty. Ritualistic motions anchored disbelief. Segregating barrier was constructed. Value of experience was questioned. No rest for the weary.
>
> TUESDAY. Deconstruction of Benedict's Rule began. Ap-plications to life issues surfaced. The heart started to hear music in services. The eyes started to appreciate natural gifts. Humanity of a Benedictine order chipped away at the bar-rier.
>
> WEDNESDAY. An abbey tour dispelled misconceptions. A brother's irreverence made the rule more palatable. A monk's genuine hospitality uncovered mechanical creativity. A priest's temptation raised tears and songs of thanksgiving. The heart sang all day. The mind allowed silence. The body rested in true peace.
>
> THURSDAY. Camaraderie released inhibitions. A medal became a step toward contemplative prayer. Time constantly checked in anticipation of holy ritual. A brother's hobbies and vocation brought true joy. Excitement about peace and silence. I must never forget.

STRUCTURE. A foundation that prepares me for learning. A practice that opens my heart. A ritual that waits for God. A rule that offers true freedom.[3]

The commonalities that this student shared with those living in the monastery had emerged. It became clear that she could not escape the garden-variety elements of her life—the relationships and the work—nor did she need to escape them. Monastic rules were in fact fashioned to address the ordinary character of life, nurturing places in life where one could find and do the will of God.

Ancient Gardens and Garden-Variety Lives

The reason, of course, that our struggles with both relationships and work figure as prominently as they do is that they both represent something far larger. Call it a quest for meaning, unity, purpose, harmony, or peace—for most if not all of us, the relationships we forge and the work we do are part of a piecemeal search, one conducted in fits and starts, for something far more profound and far more enduring.

It is no mistake perhaps that the story of the archetypal garden-variety lives, Adam's and Eve's, is one told around these two poles of human experience. The mythic and much larger truths of the story found in the early chapters of Genesis have been lost in misguided conversations about the historicity of the narrative. The story is not a blow-by-blow account of our primeval origins but rather an account about what it means to live as God's creatures in God's world in the creative space that God has crafted.[4] God creates a world for Adam and Eve, presents them to one another, and gives them work to do in the garden. As such, the relationships described in the story are archetypal. They are woven into our consciousness and define for us what it means both to be fully human and to be God's creation.

We can almost hear the original teller of the story elaborating on the theme with us, saying, "That's precisely why two such basic experiences as relationships and work lead you right back to questions about God! The world may have changed, but from the very beginning life has been shaped by the relationships and work that God has given us. The particularities of life remind us of who—and whose—we are." So don't hesitate to bring them along on this journey. The life you live is the life you have to contribute to the conversation.

The natural and good thing about triage theology is that it signals our willingness to engage God in that conversation. The difficulty is that because the spiritual logic of I-questions dominates our lives, most of the "discerning" we do revolves around our lives and the choices we make. We rarely assume responsibility for looking more broadly at life. Nor do we ask ourselves wider-ranging questions about how God is at work in the world. Like the household gods of the Greco-Roman world that served as the special protectors of ancient families, each of us tends to define the work of God in ways that are narrowly focused on our individual lives. But we do not readily or necessarily think of God as one who embraces the *whole* world.[5]

Yet, as *discerners*, that is precisely the vision we are meant to nurture. "Children of God," "prophets," "sages," and "disciples" are not terms used to describe mere beneficiaries of God's grace. They are terms used to describe people who understand themselves to be the keepers of a far larger and divine ecology. They represent a way of being that requires that we be able to see beyond our own interests and to probe more deeply into each situation than a first-person-singular world asks or requires.

So, having acquired some strategies for asking God-questions, how do we weigh and evaluate the answers we get as we bind up our wounds and celebrate our successes? There is no litmus test to apply, but I can suggest a few ways in which we can craft our triage theologies in a more reflective fashion.

Triage Theology: In Dialogue with a Tradition

One way to begin crafting a triage theology is to connect with a tradition and stay in dialogue with it. When I worked at Washington National Cathedral some years ago, there was considerable enthusiasm for new programs in spirituality that had no identifiable roots in a tradition. The coming of the new millennium had given impetus to this interest and inspired many to experiment with a variety of spiritual practices. It was not uncommon to have lengthy conversations about spirituality without mentioning a god of any kind. It was enough to find meaning, connection, or significance.

Now, on the one hand, an emphasis of this kind strikes most of us as inviting, and in one sense it is. Spiritual practice without roots in a specific tradition is endlessly pliable. It can be molded to fit the contours of our lives. It can be trimmed and cut in ways that avoid the seemingly abrasive, restrictive character of religious commitments, and it can be pursued without meeting the expectations of either creed or community.

The difficulty is that a spirituality of this kind is one that is shaped and informed—from start to finish—by I-questions. They not only define who we are and our relationship to the rest of the world but sift and filter the connections we forge with the world around us and anything that we may (or may not!) call divine.

There is no conclusive argument that can draw the logic of that way of living into question, and in the cathedral community hundreds of people were drawn to that kind of programming. People with intense, but finally I-centered spiritual needs would gather for a day, celebrate life, engage in a variety of largely unrelated and unintegrated spiritual practices, and then make their way home. What was striking about those events, however, was that the participants felt strongly drawn to "weave"—as they often put it—an ad hoc community. Music, celebration, visible images, makeshift liturgies, and an unacknowledged theology shaped their interaction—at least for a few hours. As important as that exercise appeared to be, however, one had the sense that this community largely evaporated with the event itself, except for the small band of workshop presenters who, given the nature of their work, found themselves, year after year, involved in much the same effort. In a very real sense, there was no reason for things to have been otherwise. I-questions so dominated the community created by the workshops that individual agendas finally prevailed.

Some argue that an experience of this kind is enough. But how can that possibly be true when, even if all we are looking for is meaning and purpose without any sign of the divine, we are finally forced to search in isolation? Such individual and private construals of what it means to be spiritual ultimately evaporate. Whether they disappear when changes happen in our own lives or simply perish with us—as so much of our private lives do—they do in fact disappear.

A religious tradition, on the other hand, offers something more enduring. It is difficult to say how long it will endure, of course. Some traditions have left no more than a few artifacts of their faith, and still others have disappeared completely. Nonetheless, to paraphrase Huston Smith, tradition is how spirituality gets traction in history, and I think it could be argued by extension that tradition is how spirituality gets traction in our lives.[6]

Only a religious tradition can call us, time and time again, to give our attention to something that lies outside the narrow interests of our first-person-singular worlds. And while we may be inclined to describe that call as restrictive, it actually offers far more freedom, connection, and enduring depth of meaning than can be woven in the course of several hours—or even in the course of a single lifetime.

As it applies to the triage theology that each of us fashions, a religious tradition draws us into a conversation with a millennia-old dialogue about the nature and the will of God. That river of words that runs through a tradition is not unchanging, and it inevitably cuts its way through virgin territory. But those who navigate its waters have the benefit of knowing when they are part of the same river of words. And because that dialogue is rooted in the shared understandings of a community, it is infinitely easier to hear the God-questions above the urgent shouts of our own I-questions. Attached as they are to creeds and practices, word and worship, God-questions acquire a reality that makes a claim on our lives and can re-present itself as something outside and independent of us.[7]

A life lived in lively dialogue with a tradition is better understood as a life lived out in the direction set by that tradition than it is as an endless march around it. We take our tradition very seriously when we let that dialogue speak to our lives in ways both profound and fully contemporary.

This does not mean that our triage theology needs to parrot the words of the tradition. But it does mean that it is worth asking whether our understanding of God's movement in the world is congruent with that stream of tradition. Judgments of this kind are difficult to make, of course. They cannot be scripted or prescribed, although some traditions attempt to provide that kind of guidance.

Living with tradition in this way is in some ways simply unavoidable, given the nature of human history and the change it brings. In the medieval world, for example, when the monastic rules I mentioned earlier were refined, relationships were shaped by a very different set of assumptions than they are today. Anthropologists describe the medieval world as a *positional* culture—one in which social positions and roles defined the way people related to one another. Birth was destiny, and the way to adulthood was clearly marked. You knew where you belonged before you arrived, and more often than not the will of God was identified in immediate ways with that destiny. One could argue that the will of God was wed to the social order in a way that made *finding* the will of God virtually unnecessary.

Today that way of life is all but gone. Ours is a *relational* culture in which, from the beginning, we are compelled to take our cues from the people around us for finding our place in the world. In the absence of structured roles, we are limited to the personal and the emotional. We intuitively position ourselves in order to build friendships and make our way in the world. We look for affirmation and reassurance that we are "on the way." With no other social clues, the process is inevitably difficult and marked by uncertainties.

In a social climate where choice dominates, the question of God's will presents itself in a way that is very different from other stages of the tradition. And for that reason, the wisdom of earlier generations cannot be flatly applied to the world in which we live. The willingness, for example, of an earlier generation to introduce the "law of love" into the institution of slavery will not suffice in the world in which we live. But deep listening to the tradition prompted another generation of Christians to see the movement of God in rising opposition to the institution of slavery. Their efforts constituted something new—the stream of tradition cut through virgin territory—and yet the characterization of God as love also kept the antislavery movement in dialogue with the same stream of tradition (Ephesians 6:5ff.).

Triage Theology: In Dialogue with Life

A dialogue with tradition is not enough, however. We also need to be in dialogue with life in all its richness and, sometimes, its frustrating complexity. It is often difficult for us to realize the importance of this movement between life and tradition.

In large part, that difficulty is rooted in our assumptions about tradition, experience, and the relationship between the two. Increasingly we describe our traditions and our lives in hard, sharp lines that pit them against one another, as if they were desperate enemies. We see it, for example, in national and global debates over social change as cultures and subcultures take radically different approaches to the complexity of contemporary life. You see it in the distinctions drawn between religion (with which tradition is closely associated) and experience (with which spirituality is closely associated), and you see it in the ever less tolerant conversations between people of faith.

In those polarized and polarizing debates, tradition is presented as hidebound and oppressive—a product of the past, utterly abstract, without connection to human need, a tool used by religious leaders to control and constrict life, the refuge of fundamentalists seeking certainty. Experience fares no better. Those who fear that the shape of our lives will drive out values of any other kind describe it as the canonizing of our desires and the elevation of what we *want* disguised as what we *need*. Experience is demonized as the one and only value of the self-indulgent. Tradition is demonized as the tool of controlling dinosaurs.

In fact, only a small number of people advocate positions that justify these caricatures. There is a vast difference between drawing on the richness of a tradition and traditionalism. There is an equally important difference between listening to experience and allowing experience to dictate the shape of our lives. But as our global culture wars become more shrill and sometimes violent, the excesses of a few are used as examples in ever more acrimonious debates over what will happen if either tradition or experience becomes the only measure of where and how God is at work in the world. Sadly, this pitched debate is possible because together its participants misrepresent both tradition and experience and, as a result, obscure the common origins they share.

In dialogue with our understanding of God, experience is—at its best and most valuable—life lived prayerfully and reflectively. It is the product of the struggle to live as if God matters. The ancient Hebrew prohibition against using the name of God in vain is not about using God's name in profanity, nor simply about frivolous vows. It is a caution against living as if God does not matter (Deuteronomy 5:11).[8]

Similarly, tradition, is the accumulated experience of a *community* committed to a life lived reflectively. Although Scripture, creeds, and councils give the impression of something fixed and finished, each is in fact the collective record of a community's struggle to do the same thing its members seek to do — to live life as if God matters.

In the face of shrill debate, it is difficult to remember that our lives, lived reflectively, are the only places we have for nurturing a deeper relationship with God. That relationship cannot be achieved once and for all, nor can it be given to us apart from experience. It is shaped and deepened in our prayers and in our tears, in our successes and our failures. Tradition, in a very real and important sense, is simply the product of a community's collective effort to do the same thing — enlightened, deepened, and broadened by an experience that is larger and richer than the experience of any one individual — but experience nonetheless.

As such, tradition and experience share the same fertile ground. It is only our need to tease apart the individual dimensions of our effort to find the will of God that makes it necessary to talk about them separately. It is an ill-conceived debate that characterizes tradition and experience as the enemies of one another and (depending on one's point of view) enemies of the quest to know God. To pit the one against the other is to cut us off from one half or the other of what it means to be human. Those who are humble desire to know God in ways that no individual life can ever adequately embrace. At the same time, no one community can claim to know all that might be known about God through even the deepest of traditions.

Triage Theology and Spiritual Humility

It is with this realization, however, that the significance of spiritual humility becomes apparent, and it is here that we are most in jeopardy as post-postmodern seekers. Years ago I asked a class what the word *meek* meant to them as it is found in the beatitudes: "Blessed are the meek, for they will inherit the earth" (Matthew 5:5). Aware of the way in which our culture and others worship power, I was not surprised by their answers: "weak," "self-effacing," "flaccid," "humble." One student even mentioned that he had heard the beatitude altered to read, "Blessed are the meek, for they will inherit the earth—just as soon as the strong are finished with it." Generally speaking, our cultural associations with the words "meek," "humble," and "humility" are all negative.

For that reason, it came as a surprise to them to discover that the Greek behind the English translation was used in the ancient world to describe a desirable warhorse! "Who," I asked them, "wants to ride a meek warhorse into battle?" The answer to the puzzle lies, of course, in the nuance that attached to the word in first-century Palestine. "Meek" did not mean "wimpy" or "humble"—it meant "obedient" or, even more appropriately, "instantly responsive." In other words, a good warhorse stops when you pull on the reins, moves left when urged to move left, and moves right when urged to move right. It is a horse that knows its role and responds to its master's expectations.[9]

The word *humility* captures all of this but is rooted in the unique character of its origin, which is the Latin *humus*, or "earth." The person who is humble is not the victim of false consciousness, nor does he or she indulge in self-effacing behavior. Humble people are those who understand their nature as one with the earth. They are God's creation, they are aware of it, and they live accordingly.

It is this realization and this realization alone that allows both tradition and experience to shape our lives as they should. Without spiritual humility, we are likely to manipulate one or both to our own benefit, and ultimately to our own spiritual detriment. To be humble is to know the limits of both our individual and collective experience. We are pilgrims of the Absolute, not its possessors.[10] As a result, what we fear might be lost—direction, because our experience trumps everything else, or freedom, because we are enslaved to tradition—is instead given back to us. Aware of our nature, we are open to the correctives and direction that God gives us through both.

Most of us find it difficult to acknowledge this. We vacillate between looking for direction in our lives by hedging in our world with understandings of tradition that are hard, fast, and prescriptive, on the one hand, and pushing away tradition in order to protect our freedom, on the other. But without humility of the kind I have described, the truth is that we are unable to have either direction or freedom.

Seen in this light, humility is an indispensable gift, a reminder that each of us has been granted a bit of the truth about God, but that we neither know all there is to know nor completely own that part of the truth entrusted to us. Far from being evidence of diffidence or weakness, humility is a source of strength.

Through humility, we learn to listen, we open our lives to the voice of God, and we begin to recognize the movement of God in the world around us. The story is told of a young monk who emerged from his meditations with a revelation. He was so surprised and elated that he had to tell his master. "Master!" he exclaimed, "I understand now!"

"Good," replied the old monk. "What do you understand?"

"What you have been teaching me," he said. "How I am one with God."

"I see, and how are you one with God?" asked the old monk.

The young monk held up his hand. "This is the hand of God," he said.

"Yes, it is," replied the old monk.

The young monk pointed to his ears. "These are the ears of God."

"Yes, they are," replied the old monk patiently.

"And these are the eyes of God!!" the young monk exclaimed.

"Yes, they are," replied the old monk without blinking. "What will you do with this newfound knowledge?" he asked.

"I must go out into the world and see the rest of God's creation," the young monk declared. With that, he stood up, made his good-byes to his master, and left the monastery. Just outside the gates he saw a tree. *That is the tree of God. I am one with that*, he thought to himself. He came across a turtle. *That is the turtle of God. I am one with that*, he continued his meditation. As he walked down the road he saw a house. *That is the house of God. I am one with that*. And so went his day, one spent marveling in God's creation. As he was walking down the road he came upon a man on an elephant riding toward him. "That is the elephant of God. I am one with that," he commented.

The man riding on the elephant's back called to him. "Get out of the way!" For the young monk was walking down the middle of the street.

"I am one with God. Why should God fear the elephant of God?" and the boy continued down the middle of the street.

"Move aside!" yelled the elephant driver, but the young monk kept walking.

Soon enough, the elephant was on top of the young monk. The great beast wrapped his trunk around him, picked him up, and threw him to the side of the road and into the mud. The young monk was shocked, dismayed, and shattered. He returned to the monastery and sat outside his master's domicile without saying a word.

"Why do you sit there?" asked the old monk.

"I am not worthy to ask your audience, my master," said the young monk.

"And why aren't you worthy?" asked the old monk.

"Because I am a fool," he replied.

"Why are you a fool?" asked the old monk.

"I do not know," he began. "This is the hand of God." And he raised his hand. The old monk nodded.

"These are the ears of God." And he pointed to his ears again. The old monk nodded again.

"And these are the eyes of God." He closed them in shame. The old monk just smiled and nodded again.

"Why did the elephant pick me up and throw me away?" pleaded the young monk.

"Because you weren't listening to the voice of God on the elephant's back telling you to get out of the way."[11]

Triage Theology: In Dialogue with Life's Larger Realities

Because the spiritual logic of I-questions dominates our thoughts and prayers, most of the discerning we do revolves around *our* lives and the choices *we* make as individuals. Time and again, people grapple deeply with the issues presented by their own lives, only to then generalize from that experience in ways that completely ignore the larger human experience.

The questions I asked my mother at age seven were evidence of an emerging interest in things divine and a natural part of my own development. The solid grounding of these first questions in my own life and questions was legitimate, and a sign of good things. But if those had been the only questions I ever asked, or if the questions I continued to ask remained solidly focused on a set of first-person-singular concerns, then the triage theology I took into adult life would have been severely constricted. Focused in that way, my ability to appreciate the movement of God's presence in the lives of those around me would have been narrowly defined and self-invested—and so it is with all of us.

But it is precisely that larger sensibility that we are meant to nurture as children of God. The prophets, sages, and disciples mentioned in Scripture were not religious functionaries with a unique responsibility to look beyond the shape of their own lives. They were people who understood themselves to be the keepers of a divine ecology that exceeded those boundaries. They represented a way of being that required a capacity to see more deeply into each situation than a first-person-singular world asks or requires.

Formed in the prophetic tradition, Jeremiah understood this. Repeatedly, he—like other prophets—appeals to the recognizable presence of God moving in the nation's history. He laments the failure of the people to look for God, and he clearly indicates that the spiritual world, no less than the natural world, abhors a vacuum. In failing to search the world around them for the presence of God, the people of Israel fall prey to things that are worthless:

> Thus says the Lord: I remember the devotion of your youth,
> your love as a bride,
> how you followed me in the wilderness,
> in a land not sown.
> Israel was holy to the Lord,
> the firstfruits of his harvest. . . .
> Hear the word of the Lord, O house of Jacob, and all the
>   families of the house of Israel. Thus says the Lord:
> What wrong did your ancestors find in me
> that they went far from me,
> and went after worthless things,
> and became worthless themselves?

They did not say, "Where is the Lord
who brought us up from the land of Egypt,
who led us in the wilderness,
in a land of deserts and pits,
in a land of drought and deep darkness,
in a land that no one passes through,
where no one lives?" (Jeremiah 2:2b–6)

The wisdom tradition combines a trust in God with the powers of observation, fashioning a spirituality that at its heart is shaped by the task of discernment. The daily conduct of life is characterized as one laden with choices that make for life or death. Here, as in the prophetic tradition, the moral and theological dimensions of the discernment are in the forefront. And wisdom herself is characterized as one who makes her appeal in the street:

Wisdom cries out in the street:
in the squares she raises her voice.
At the busiest corner she cries out;
at the entrance of the city gates she speaks:
"How long, O simple ones, will you love being simple?
How long will scoffers delight in their scoffing
and fools hate knowledge?
Give heed to my reproof." (Proverbs 1:20–23a)

As an heir to both the prophetic and the wisdom traditions, Jesus issues a similarly pointed challenge:

When you see a cloud rising in the west, you immediately say, 'It is going to rain'; and so it happens. And when you see the south wind blowing, you say, 'There will be scorching heat'; and it happens. You hypocrites! You know how to

interpret the appearance of earth and sky, but why do you not
know how to interpret the present time? (Luke 12:54–56)

Clearly, being spiritual means living in ever deeper connection
with the world around us and in ever greater tension with it at the
same time. We are urged to take our understanding of God—as well
as the light we gain from our traditions, creeds, and sacred literature—back into conversation with the world around us. To be sure,
the shape of our triage theology will be changed by that conversation. We will move beyond the questions we asked our mothers and
fathers and beyond the questions our own lives have raised for us. As
a result, we ourselves will no doubt be changed, but that is as it
should be.

Jeff and Joy discovered this with their work in the Dominican Republic. Deeply involved in the lives of the people there, they were focused on the construction of a dispensary and the creation of safe
water sources. Through their efforts, they met a number of native-
born physicians, including Eduardo. They were shocked when he
announced that he planned to move to Nigeria. "I need to be working with people who are poor," he announced.

From Jeff and Joy's point of view, Eduardo, his family, his
friends, and his community *were* "the poor." With a far different
sense of what the word *poor* means, however, Eduardo sensed the
movement of God in his life, and Jeff and Joy's sense of God's presence in the world was enlarged by their friendship with him.

Treasured and nurtured, these gifts come to us in the quest to
find and do the will of God. Forged in dialogue with tradition, experience, and the larger realities of life, the understanding we acquire is
not the accumulation of more information. It is an ever richer knowledge of where and how God is present. In turn, that knowledge allows the life of God to find an ever larger place in us.

The Passion to Understand

It is one kind of challenge, of course, to ask God-questions and embark on the work of a triage theologian. It is a completely different challenge to receive or to embrace the freedom needed to raise the necessary questions. I use the verbs *receive* and *embrace* intentionally. The freedom to ask God-questions is already ours, and we can learn how to ask them. But what we lack is something we cannot *achieve*. What we lack is the deep, inner knowledge that we already have permission to ask those questions.

The precedent for asking God-questions has long-standing roots in the Judeo-Christian tradition. If you have ever read the work of Habakkuk, you have undoubtedly wondered why it appears in the Bible at all. The book is filled with troubling, painful questions, most of which the prophet never effectively answers—or even attempts to—and it is difficult to know what kind of contribution it could possibly make. A few lines suffice to illustrate my point:

> O Lord, how long shall I cry for help,
> and you will not listen?
> Or cry to you "Violence!"
> and you will not save?
> Why do you make me see wrongdoing
> and look at trouble?
> Destruction and violence are before me;
> strife and contention arise.
> So the law becomes slack
> and justice never prevails.
> The wicked surround the righteous—
> therefore judgment comes forth perverted. (Habakkuk 1:2–4)

There are, of course, a number of good historical reasons for the character of Habakkuk. Prophetic pronouncements were originally oral in nature, and they were often preserved in writing only long after a prophet's life and ministry had ended. It is hard to be sure how many of those pronouncements survived and in what form they survived. Material may well have been added, subtracted, and lost in the process. In addition, the message of most prophets (Habakkuk included) was not welcome at first. For this reason, the process by which their writings gained sacred status was gradual and fragmentary, adding to the complex character of the material we read today. None of this explains, however, why the ancient Hebrews were at all willing to embrace this annoying book, whatever explanations might be given for its character.

The answer, I think, lies in the passion that gives Habakkuk the freedom to ask those questions. The prophet is driven by a longing to understand how and where God is at work in the lives of those around him. He strives to identify with God's way of being in the world and is obliged to live in a way that is in sympathy with God's longing for relationship with it. He discerns the difference between the presence of God and other forces at work in the world. He weighs what it means to cooperate with divine purpose. He pleads and protests when the voice of God goes unheeded. And in those desperate moments when he and his community fail to heed the voice of God, he scans the horizon for new indications of God's presence.

As Abraham Heschel, the great student of prophetic literature, puts it, God's passion is the prophet's passion:

It moves him. It breaks out in him like a storm in the soul, overwhelming his inner life, his thoughts, feelings, wishes, and hopes. . . . The unique feature of [his] religious sympathy is not self-conquest, but self-dedication; not the suppression of emotion, but its redirection; not silent subordination, but active co-operation with God; not love which aspires to the Being of God in Himself, but harmony of the soul with the concern of God.

> The prophet is *homo sympathetikos*—someone who is sympathetic with the purposes of God and anxious to understand them.[12]

For the prophet, in other words, questions come freely. In asking them, he may not always find an answer. But in raising them, he identifies with the divine purpose and so lives in ever closer proximity with that purpose. His longing echoes the longing of God as he listens for the gentle nudging and persuasion through which God speaks to the world. This is the context in which the prophet raises even the most pointed of questions. Because the prophet is passionate about understanding and confident that God is gracious, his search for answers is safeguarded by the very God whose behavior, at times, is in question.

That is also why the life of those who trust in God is marked by the greatest degree of candor. As a result, the Bible is replete with lament and complaint. In vivid and even painfully raw language, writers of song and poetry describe the dissonance they experience when they witness the suffering of innocents and the unchecked cruelty of others. Habakkuk is not a spiritual Eeyore who lacks the kind of blind optimism supposedly required to be a person of faith. He and his annoying questions are representative of spirituality's deepest passion—to see God.

Misunderstanding the Freedom

Most of us respond to this kind of freedom to ask Habakkuk-like questions in one of two ways. For some of us that freedom is easy to embrace, but we are likely to misunderstand the invitation we have been given. Asking difficult questions about God in many parts of the Western world is not a matter of asking Habakkuk-like questions. Tinged with cynicism or skepticism, they often have a much more banal character. In its most exaggerated form, this kind of question-asking is a matter of asking questions for the questions' own sake, or with a view to subverting the trust we place in God. C. S. Lewis once told the story of a man so in love with the task of asking questions that when he found himself offered the truth, he resisted it, protesting, "Will it leave me the free play of Mind?"[13]

I am not convinced that Lewis's illustration is entirely fair to those of us in the Western world. The capacity to ask questions has served our culture well and opened the way for discovery of every kind; our questions can serve a more subtle purpose than promoting skepticism or a sophomoric relativism. But what Lewis rightly parodies, and what some people too quickly identify as the freedom to ask questions, is often born of a bald, cold cynicism or a lack of spiritual, intellectual, and moral rigor. The maxim "It's not about the answers, it's all about the questions," is sometimes born of humility. But it can also reflect an absence of the courage and maturity required to make the commitments that every adult needs to make—albeit, from time to time, in the absence of complete information.

Even the best of our Western questions, however, do not represent what Habakkuk is trying to do. The freedom he exercises is, at once, both more radical and more profound. The *homo sympathetikos* wants answers to his questions, but getting the answers is not a precondition for trusting God. Trusting God is never predicated on God's giving satisfactory answers to our questions, but on God's steadfast faithfulness and tireless desire for us.

The story is told of a rabbi who gave a lecture, declaring that in the wake of the Holocaust one could no longer believe in God. Protesting, a man in the audience rose to his feet and shouted, "But, Rabbi, if there is another Holocaust, then what will you do?" The rabbi responded, "I will pray to God."[14] The passion to understand was there in all its fullness—even to the point of expressing skepticism—but never in a way that finally overwhelmed the rabbi's capacity to trust.

Fear, Faith, and Asking Questions

For others of us, however, asking questions can seem pointless or worse. Why ask them if we're forced to leave them lying around without a complete or final answer? What possible reason could there be for raising questions for which there are no clear, complete, readily available answers? Are we trying to put God on the spot? Why burden the faithful with questions that might create doubt? Some people even respond to the dilemma by intoning, "You shall not put the Lord, your God, to the test."

There are any number of reasons for these reactions, some of them buried so deeply—emotionally, culturally, and intellectually— that we are scarcely aware of them. Some of those reasons can be traced to the philosophical inheritance of the West (or more accurately, to our misappropriation of it): the Enlightenment bogeyman to which we all hear so many references. The seventeenth-century philosopher René Descartes (to whom the Enlightenment owes a great deal) argues, "I think, therefore I am." In so doing, he distinguishes sharply between "you" and "I" as "knowers" and other things as objects. In a world of knowers (you and I) and things known (name a thing, anything), analysis is the gold standard for finding the truth. Take it apart, Descartes recommends, piece by piece—that's always easier. Ask questions, look for answers, build on them as you go. Once you've finished taking apart the thing you are studying, then you can put it back together the way you found it.

For Descartes (who was a Christian), this method was not only a way of knowing about things in the world around us but also a way of proving that God exists. Using this method to prove God's existence is probably not possible, but by suggesting that it could be done, Descartes opened the way for people to try. Of course, it wasn't long before others used his method to make the opposite case. "I think, therefore I am," became "I doubt, therefore I am."[15]

Combine this misadventure with our culture's tendency toward anti-intellectualism, and it is not difficult to imagine why the practice of asking questions has fallen on hard times. The mind is suspect. In some circles it is treated as distinct from the soul, and therefore from the spiritual dimension of life. And even more negatively, still others consider the intellect an obstacle to the spiritual life.

Our ability to embrace questions has been further compromised on the North American continent (and to a lesser extent in other parts of the West) by the conviction that the only real truths are facts.[16] Trust *in* God is reduced to faith in a series of propositions *about* God. Our relationship to God hinges on getting the details of those propositions right, and as a result, any outstanding issue becomes an occasion for anxiety and turmoil. That's why, I suppose, one church signboard I often pass driving to and from work proudly declares, "Don't put a question mark where God puts a period."

However, behind this reluctance to ask questions is something far deeper and far more visceral. A story that Henri Nouwen told some years ago names that something well. Recalling the early days of his move from the academic world into life in community with the handicapped, Nouwen writes:

[I was invited to tea with] John Fraser, the European correspondent of the *Globe and Mail,* one of Canada's national newspapers. . . . We talked about the people of China and North Korea, and the Pope's recent visit to Holland. John . . . is a well-traveled, very knowledgeable journalist who is both a keen observer of world events and a man with a deep interest in the religious life.

Among all his stories about world events, [he] told us a [short] story about his daughter Jessie. It is this story I will remember most:

One morning when Jessie was four years old, she found a dead sparrow in front of the living room window. The little bird had killed itself by flying into the glass. When Jessie saw the dead bird she was both deeply disturbed and very intrigued. She asked her father, "Where is the bird now?" John said he didn't know. "Why did it die?" she asked again. "Well," John said hesitantly, "because all birds return to the earth." "Oh," said Jessie, "then we have to bury it." A box was found, the little bird was laid in the box, a paper napkin was added as a shroud, and a few minutes later a little procession was formed with Daddy, Mama, Jessie, and her little sister. Daddy carried the box, Jessie the homemade cross. After a grave was dug and the little sparrow was buried, John put a piece of moss over the grave and Jessie planted the cross upon it. Then John asked Jessie, "Do you want to say a prayer?" "Yes," replied Jessie firmly, and after having told her baby sister in no uncertain terms to fold her hands, she prayed, "Dear God, we have buried this little sparrow. Now you be good to her or I will kill you. Amen." As they walked home, John said to Jessie, "You didn't have to threaten God." Jessie answered, "I just wanted to be sure."[17]

Apart from its charm, this story is also memorable, Nouwen notes, because it underlines a basic truth about our lives: fear shapes the way we live. I would go further and argue not only that fear is a powerful force in our lives, but that it is fear—not questions, not doubt—that is the opposite of faith.

I learned this a long time ago through teaching an introductory class in biblical studies. Very early in the semester the students would often begin to balk at the things I tried to teach them. As a young professor, I found this almost incomprehensible. Weren't they here to learn? Did they really think that they knew everything there was to know at the ripe old age of eighteen? And they were not just resistant to the work—they also seemed deeply angry about the content of the course. If I tried to teach them that something should be taken poetically instead of literally, for example, some of them would explode in class—or run to the dean.

At first I assumed that the problem lay with my illustrations. They were probably just too debatable, I concluded, or too hard to explain. So I found simple, undeniable examples of some of the things I was trying to teach them. These illustrations, of course, generated even more resistance.

Then it dawned on me. Their faith in God as an *ultimate* authority in their lives was mediated through their faith in *proximate* authorities—including the understandings of the Bible that they brought with them to college. In other words, they believed in God *because* they believed that certain things were true about Scripture. And when I tried to teach them something else, or when my views seemed to contradict their views, the students saw this not as "new information" but as a threat to their ability to go on believing in God. So instead of seeing the classroom experience as an invitation to a deeper and more immediate dependence on God—as well as a more sophisticated understanding of Scripture—they saw the course material as a threat to their faith, and then, *out of fear*, they struck out in anger and frustration.

With a little more humor about it all than I used to be able to muster, I can still remember one class in which, midway through the course, I used a feminine pronoun to refer to God. Brian's hand shot up as if he had been poked in the ribs. Thinking, *You know, Fred, this isn't a teachable moment*, I suggested that we come back to his question right after a break. A few minutes later, with coffee in hand, we settled back in, and turning to Brian, I said, "Brian, I'm assuming that you take exception to my using a feminine pronoun to refer to God." And Brian responded, "No . . . I take exception to . . . pretty much everything you've said up to this point!"

Fear has a way of making college freshmen out of all of us from time to time. We deepen in our acquaintance with God, in part, thanks to proximate authorities. Like training wheels on a bicycle, they start us on the pilgrimage of life. But it would be a mistake to confuse the best of those authorities with the authority of God, and it would be an even greater mistake to confuse our provisional and imperfect understandings of God with God herself (sorry, Brian). As Thomas Merton once observed, there are times when, in mercy, God must shatter our most cherished assumptions.[18] But we should not mistake the shattering of our assumptions with the shattering of God. Freed of our fears, we should instead see the task of asking questions as a means of moving, ever more freely, in the presence of God.

Spiritual Exercises for Changing How We Do Triage Theology

- What core beliefs or assumptions about God and life do you rely on in times of crisis?

- What are the experiences that have informed your own triage theology?

- To what extent is your triage theology shaped by a dialogue with tradition?

- To what extent is your triage theology shaped by a dialogue with life and its larger realities (such as the experience of others)?

- Do you enjoy the necessary freedom to ask God-questions?

- Does fear (or something else) keep you from asking God-questions?

- If so, name those obstacles.

- Has God been replaced by proximate authorities in your life?

- If so, name the proximate authorities in your life.

Three

SIGNS AND WONDERS

You speak of signs and wonders
I need something other
I would believe if I was able
But I'm waiting on the crumbs from your table.

Bono[1]

It helps, now and then, to step back and take the long view. The kingdom is not only beyond our efforts, it is beyond our vision. We accomplish in our lifetime only a tiny fraction of the magnificent enterprise that is God's work. Nothing we do is complete . . . but it is a beginning, a step along the way, an opportunity for God's grace to enter and do the rest. We may never see the end results, but that is the difference between the master builder and the worker. We are workers, not master builders, ministers, not messiahs. We are prophets of a future not our own.

Oscar Romero[2]

Near the end of the first century of the Common Era, signs and wonders were all the rage. Between 64 and 68 C.E., both Peter and Paul had been executed in a brief but intense period of persecution. Two years later the Romans destroyed the Temple in Jerusalem. The suffering that some Christians had experienced, combined with the widespread anxiety that reverberated throughout the church, convinced many believers that the end of all things was at hand. A wave of apocalyptic enthusiasm swept the fledgling church, and more than a few of its members began to entertain the thought that the demands of discipleship were finally unnecessary. Today we might call it "irrational exuberance" or a serious case of "millennial madness."[3]

Disturbed by this trend, one leader of the church (the tradition refers to him as Mark) retold the story of Jesus, focusing on what he perceived to be the irrational exuberance of Jesus's own day. Thinking the story would be instructive, Mark pointed out that then, as now, people were drawn to signs and wonders—healings and miracles.

There are considerable differences between our day and Mark's. There are differences in culture, differences in our perceptions of the world around us, and differences in what we count as a sign or wonder. The nature of our religious expectations has changed as well. But for many of us, when we turn to the God-questions that we need to ask, finding and doing the will of God is still driven by the same preoccupation with signs and wonders. So in this chapter, Mark and his readers are going to be our conversation partners. We will listen in on their struggles and give some thought to ours.

Years ago I became friends with an air force pilot. He was bright and capable, a caring father, a devoted husband, and a Christian. Flying one of the military's more formidable tactical fighters, his work could be dangerous, and the plane he flew placed enormous destructive potential at his fingertips. While I didn't assume for one moment that he could not justify his work, I was curious. How did he reconcile his responsibilities as a pilot with his faith? What led him to believe that he was doing the will of God?

In response to my questions, I expected him to describe the reasoning and reflection he had done. I expected him to talk a little bit about the ethical questions he had faced and his understanding of war. Even the way in which I framed the questions presupposed that kind of answer. What he gave me was a description of signs and wonders. Chuck had applied to the Air Force Academy and successfully navigated its rigorous application process. After being accepted for admission, he pursued a demanding course of study with similar success, which led to still other training opportunities. He competed for a coveted pilot's wings and was rewarded for his efforts. "God just opened the doors," he concluded.

At first I was surprised, but in fact Chuck's story is not very different from that of many others. For a large number of people, their reflections on the answers they have given to life's I-questions are all but secondary. It is much more common to hear people of faith talk about open doors, unexpected opportunities, an extraordinary sequence of events, a providential conversation, and even the chance juxtaposition of a word or two. I have known adults of every age and description who have made momentous decisions—choosing houses, jobs, and lifelong partners—on the basis of just this kind of experience, or justifying their choices in retrospect with much the same justification.[4]

For that reason alone, the subject of signs and wonders merits discussion. In what follows, it will become clear that I have serious reservations about this practice. So the questions asked here might appear to be raised by way of criticism. In fact, I want to invite you to reexamine the deeper logic behind the search for signs and wonders, even if you have relied on them deeply or still do. Ask yourself three questions:

1. What drives us to look for signs and wonders?

2. How does a dependence on signs and wonders shape our spiritual lives?

3. If we don't rely on signs and wonders, what do we depend on?

What Drives Us to Look for Signs and Wonders?

To answer the first question, let's go back to Mark and his church for a moment. Mark doesn't tell us why the people in his church were predisposed to see the events of the late sixties C.E. as a sign that God's will was unfolding in history.[5] We are forced to read between the lines. But it isn't difficult to imagine at least some of the factors that would have prompted Mark's community to believe that "God's hand" was in the events of the day.

No doubt one factor that drove them to this conclusion was the persecution that the church had already faced. Life in Rome, where the fledgling community was probably situated, had not been easy. Nor was the message of the church well received everywhere. Even though its roots were dominantly Jewish, few from within the Jewish community had converted to the new faith. To make matters worse, by 70 C.E. many in the first circle of believers had died without witnessing the return of Christ. There is evidence that at least some people were deeply disturbed by this development because they had not expected anyone in the first generation of believers to die.[6]

Finally, the destruction of the Temple itself loomed large in their lives. Many in Mark's community had never been to Jerusalem, and most if not all of them were probably Gentiles. But the city's destruction had an impact that reverberated throughout the Mediterranean world. Anyone who remotely identified with Judaism experienced the loss as cataclysmic: it had swept away visible reminders of not only their national identity but their religious identity as well.[7] The disappearance of both could only mean that their faith had been misplaced or that God was about to do something entirely new.

Against this backdrop, signs and wonders offered reassurance, certainty, and a sense of God's presence in the midst of seemingly meaningless and painful events. In fact, the church's preoccupation with some visible confirmation of its faith led people to construe the tragedy as evidence of God's presence. So when the Temple was destroyed, they took it as a sign of divine judgment. This was a sign that could be witnessed, that required no defense or explanation, and that vindicated the church's faith.

It Will Be All Right

There were several threads of need in Mark's church, then, just as there are several reasons we look for signs and wonders today of a different kind. One reason his followers were looking for signs and wonders can be traced to a need for reassurance. They needed to hear at some profound level, "It will be all right," and so do we.

Life in the ancient Mediterranean world was not easy for Mark's community. A sect within a sect—a minority movement within a minority movement—Christians constituted a subset of Judaism. In turn, Judaism was itself a marginal religion in the ancient Greco-Roman world.

As a result, Mark's first readers lived in considerable tension with the world around them. Those outside the Jewish faith had little or no sympathy for them. The exclusivistic nature of their faith helped to create considerable tension between the fledgling church and the vast majority of Roman citizens. Thus, most of Mark's readers were uncomfortable with their surroundings, and their countrymen were not particularly comfortable with them.

In some ways the tensions between the Christian sect and Judaism were even greater. It would be a mistake to characterize the attitude of Mark's community as anti-Semitic. To the contrary, the tensions were heightened by the significant role that Judaism played in shaping the community's own self-understanding. Large numbers of Gentiles probably belonged to Mark's church, but they were keenly aware of the Jewish roots of their faith. Even as ever larger number of Gentiles embraced the faith, its Jewish roots introduced still more dissonance into their lives.

For that reason, the fate of the Temple and the fate of Jerusalem played powerful, symbolic roles even in the lives of those who had never visited the city. For people who needed to know that everything would be all right, Jerusalem represented the ongoing goodwill of God. With its destruction, the question of God's goodwill became more problematic. Had they risked all by adhering to this new faith, or would God do something new? By abandoning the normative religious practices of the world and adhering to an isolated strand of the Jewish faith, Mark's readers found themselves in crisis, and they needed reassurance.

Today we may not look for signs that are quite so dramatic, and we may not associate signs with issues that are quite so basic to our spirituality. But most of us still long from time to time for some kind of reassurance and the sense of security it brings.[8] How quickly we need it and how we go about finding it varies from person to person.

Depending on the nature of our own personality, some of us need that reassurance almost immediately. In asking questions designed to help people who are seeking spiritual direction over the years, I have known some who grasped what they needed to do right away, but then they revisited the decision over and over again.

Jenny, for example, had inherited the family business, and she had stepped into a role that her in-laws had defined in building the enterprise they managed. Like many entrepreneurs, Sam and Margot had very specific ideas about how the business ought to be run. And they stayed around to ensure that Jenny performed her duties in accord with their expectations. Try as they might, Sam and Margot were never able to let go.

To make matters worse, Jenny discovered that her deepest passions found no real fulfillment in the work she was doing. When we first talked, it was clear to her from the beginning that she needed a change. She was even able to name the kind of work that she would find instantly fulfilling and that would represent what she considered the will of God for her life. But for months she returned to ask the same questions over and over again. It was a year later that she finally spoke to her in-laws and began doing the work that she had identified from the beginning in our conversations. There were many questions she revisited time and again, including the fear that she would offend Sam and Margot, but at an even deeper level she needed to know that it would be all right.

Others conduct much longer postmortems on the decisions they make. That is certainly my weakness. I can review and re-review a decision, examine and re-examine the rationale, for weeks on end. My wife has even threatened to bury me under the epitaph "It didn't live up to his expectations."

This tendency is partly rooted in my personality. By nature I am a perfectionist, and by preparation I am an academic. So I am both tempted and trained to sift every decision I make through a very fine sieve. I owe the adaptive behaviors I possess today for making decisions to a man who supervised my dissertation and shared deep wisdom with me: "Fred, just finish the damn thing!"

In my own defense, however, my tendency to conduct postmortems is also rooted in the apples-and-oranges decisions that I have had to make and that life forces on all of us. Moving to Texas after having lived in the eastern United States and overseas all my life was a huge cultural shift. I am still on a "green card," in fact, and native-born Texans probably think that is as it should be! The decision to move was largely driven by a sense of vocation (apples), not by geography (oranges). For that reason, when we moved to Dallas, the geography and the cultural differences drove a great deal of my anxiety about a decision that I knew was a good one in vocational terms. The postmortem lasted until I dreamed that I had gone back to a previous job. When my unconscious mind sat down at the same desk and assumed those old responsibilities, it became clear to me that the choice I had made was even more profoundly necessary than I had been able to articulate.

Still others of us vacillate back and forth. William James, physician, philosopher, and psychologist, began to contemplate retirement in 1903. Beginning in 1905, he wrote in his diary: "October 26, 'Resign!'; October 28, 'Resign!!!'; November 4, 'Resign?'; November 7, 'Resign!'; November 8, 'Don't resign'; November 9, 'Resign!'; November 16, 'Don't resign!'; November 23, 'Resign'; December 7, 'Don't resign'; December 9, 'Teach here next year.'" He finally retired in 1907![9]

You may struggle with decisionmaking in a way that I have not mentioned, but the same need for reassurance drives us all. A family moves to another part of the world, or even to another part of the same country, and the challenges of acclimating to a new home set in motion the need for reassurance. Spouses look for jobs, children adjust to new schools, and everyone searches for new friends. The uncertainties of a new situation, matched against the uncertainties of an old one, multiply and loom large in our lives.

We are finally forced to choose—choose a course of study, choose a profession, choose to marry, choose not to be married. Each moment is freighted with anxiety. Did I make the wrong choice? How long will it take to adjust? What have I lost or gained? How will those whose lives are intertwined with mine be shaped for good or for ill? The need for reassurance is there, imbedded in the phrase we all want to hear, "It will be all right."

The Right Choice

Of course, the need for reassurance can easily give way to a need for certainty. For some of us, in other words, it is not enough to hear the words, "It will be all right." Instead, we need to hear that we have made the *right* choice. For a variety of reasons, the one need is intimately connected with the other for many of us.

Some of us need to hear those words because we identify a sense of certainty with loyalty to God or to our faith. Anything less strikes us as evidence of a weakness in the spiritual fiber of our lives. Only those who are certain and who project that certainty are, so we think, genuinely faithful.

The realization that some people need this kind of certainty came home to me some years ago. In a fit of pedagogical idealism (mixed with a fair amount of political naïveté), those of us on a faculty team decided to use the now notorious film directed by Martin Scorsese, *The Last Temptation of Christ* (1989). Based on the book of the same name by Nikos Kazantzakis, the film, we thought, might be a vivid means of exploring early church history and the theological debates that dominated its life.[10]

It is not an easy film. Long and poorly edited, it is also filled with imagery from the author's Greek Orthodox heritage that is familiar to only a small number of people, never mind a random sampling of undergraduates. But neither the film nor the book attempts, as some have supposed, to undermine anyone's faith, and the book is not a piece of heresy written to suggest that Jesus was undone by sexual temptation. In fact, in his introduction to the book Kazantzakis makes it clear that the story is an exploration of the question of whether or not one can lead a conventional domestic life and follow God. And the "last temptation" is one that Jesus successfully resists, as those who are patient or thoughtful enough to finish the book or sit through the whole movie can discover.

Be that as it may, some of our students were deeply incensed that we even used the movie. And they let more than a few people know how deeply incensed they were. What was particularly interesting to me, however, was their response to the characters in the film. They loathed the portrayal of Jesus, which explored his humanity and with it his uncertainty. But they loved Judas, who was certain and assertive from the very beginning of the film (often wrong, but never in doubt).

The reason for their reaction, I think, had to do with their view of the spiritual life. Spirituality, for some, is a fix for the uncertainty that goes with being human. Answers are given where there are questions, courage where there is fear, serenity where there is struggle, and direction where there is confusion. If you are faithful, the one right answer surfaces where there appears to be more than one choice. For some of my students, there was little reason to have a spiritual life unless it addressed those challenges. So, to portray Jesus in ways that were at odds with those expectations was to portray the central figure of their faith in terms that were completely foreign to the lives they expected to live. (It only made matters worse that the film portrays the quintessential traitor in a more flattering light.)

Others of us long for the one right answer because from time to time the complexity of modern life and the burden of choice overwhelm us. A spiritual primitivism sets in, and we long for divine directives instead of the struggle associated with the task of discernment. Aware that the choices we make may have unintended or even negative consequences, we want a God who will point us to the right decision with the bright, white light of signs and wonders.

It is not difficult to imagine either the anxiety that accompanies those choices or the overwhelming sense that there ought to be one right answer. Deeply troubling dilemmas can put us on our knees, looking for signs and wonders. Should I put my aging mother in an assisted living facility? Will she really be better off? Or am I captive to my fatigue? Or worse yet, am I motivated by selfishness?

Should I stay married or file for divorce? Have I really done everything I might to save my marriage? Am I rationalizing when I tell my friends that the children will be happier than they are now? Are the growing tensions in our relationship as real as I suppose?

Should I abandon a job that is filled with frustrations, knowing that if I take a different job I will force my spouse to look for new employment? What about my teenage children? Will they thrive if they have to forge new friendships and make adjustments to a new environment at one of the most volatile times in their lives?

We look for the one right answer in spite of the fact that—as we will see in the next chapter—questions of this kind rarely have only one right answer. Only when the variables of a decision point overwhelmingly in a single direction, or when the moral demands of a choice dictate a specific course of action, are we justified in arguing that we have no other choice. In fact, the search for certainty can keep us from taking action at all, obscure our role in making choices, and lead us to place a premium on the kind of predictability that may keep us from doing something that is genuinely creative.

The Quest to Re-sacralize Life

I am also convinced that for many of us the search for signs and wonders is a quest to "re-sacralize" our lives—to infuse them with the sanctity and significance that (rightly) we sense only God's presence can give.[11] You see this tendency in the lives of those of us who search for yet another spiritual high to confirm that God is there. You see it in the lives of those who quietly despair of ever having an experience of that kind again. You can hear it, too, in the conversation of those who anxiously examine the commonplace details of their lives for some evidence of God's presence.

We may find it difficult to address the philosophical and sociological trends that have landed us in a world that possesses all the feeling of stainless steel. We may be embarrassed to own spiritual

commitments that oblige us to live this way or that. But we intuitively realize that we can recapture some sense of God's presence by
naming this event or that as the work of God. After all, who can say
but us? That, however, is a fragile place to live. With every failure to
find a sign or a wonder, we risk a loss of the divine and any confidence that we live in God's presence.

Perhaps even more seriously, it is also an impoverished and thin
place to live. Restless people who seek signs and wonders are often
unable to accept the commonplace as a gift that is not so commonplace. The genuinely miraculous character of life itself, the web of
loving relationships that are a part of that life, and the gift of human
creativity are all eclipsed by the need to find the spectacular. This
may be in part why Mark tells the story of Jesus's transfiguration:

> Jesus took with him Peter and James and John, and led them
> up a high mountain apart, by themselves. And he was trans-
> figured before them, and his clothes became dazzling white,
> such as no one on earth could bleach them. And there ap-
> peared to them Elijah with Moses, who were talking with
> Jesus. Then Peter said to Jesus, "Rabbi, it is good for us to
> be here; let us make three dwellings, one for you, one for
> Moses, and one for Elijah." He did not know what to say, for
> they were terrified. Then a cloud overshadowed them, and
> from the cloud there came a voice, "This is my Son, the
> Beloved; listen to him!" Suddenly when they looked around,
> they saw no one with them any more, but only Jesus. (Mark
> 9:2–8)

Overcome with millennial madness, those who first heard Mark's
gospel are like Peter. They want to build a tabernacle that will house
Jesus, Elijah, and Moses on the mountaintop. They want to live
there and they can't. Aware of this, Mark places the brief vision of

God's glory just ahead of a daunting description of discipleship, emphasizing where we must live.

We, like Mark's church, want to take up permanent residence anywhere but in the world in which we live. Widespread evidence of this misconceived quest was on display everywhere at the turn of the millennium. While working at Washington National Cathedral, I had the opportunity to witness the variety of ways in which our desire to stay on the mountain manifested itself. An apocalyptic, *fundagelical* expectation of the end of all things was one version. Everywhere you turned there were those who pointed to signs and wonders built into the calendar and the politics of the day. (Although some people had difficulty deciding in which year the new millennium began!) Yet another version was a loosely New Age expectation that an updated "Age of Aquarius" for baby boomers was imminent. Some of what was said, planned, and anticipated for the arrival of the new millennium was dangerous, mean-spirited, and exclusivistic. Some of it was naïve and dangerous in another way, predicated on the belief that a new world order was dawning that was anything but new. And candidly, some of the hopes for a new millennium were just silly.

Taken as a whole, these millennial expectations reflected the kind of speculative search for evidence of the divine that was possible only in a culture that was enjoying record-setting prosperity. The first few years of the new millennium, however, quickly underlined the need to look for more than spiritual fireworks, and the truth of the old adage, "Wherever we go, there we are," became painfully relevant.

None of this is meant to suggest that there are no good reasons to search for signs and wonders. We live in a world in which it is increasingly difficult to detect the presence of the sacred—to discern God working in the world. People who are attuned to their spiritual needs undoubtedly find this world an alien and empty place.[12] But in relying as we do on signs and wonders as a means of re-sacralizing life, we have resorted to magical categories and overlook God's gift of sacred significance in the commonplace events of our lives.

As a result, we may choose to take a particular job because of what we describe as God's leading, but then do the job with little or no sense of the sacredness of the work. We may claim to have God's leading in our relationships, but then completely ignore the ways in which our words and behavior toward one another diminish a shared sense of God's presence. What we need, in other words, are not signs and wonders but a deeper determination to nurture the presence of God in the midst of the commonplace—what Brother Lawrence, a seventeenth-century monk, describes as "practicing the presence of God."[13]

One woman's story illustrates what I have in mind. "I am a mother of three (ages fourteen, twelve, and three) and have recently completed my college degree. The last class I had to take was sociology. The teacher was absolutely inspiring and had the qualities that I wish every human being had been graced with. Her last project of the term was called 'Smile.' The class was asked to go out and smile at three people and document their reactions. I am a very friendly person and always smile at everyone and say hello anyway, so I thought this would be a piece of cake, literally.

"Soon after we were assigned the project, my husband, youngest son, and I went out to McDonald's one crisp March morning. It was just our way of sharing special playtime with our son. We were standing in line, waiting to be served, when all of a sudden everyone around us began to back away, and then even my husband did. I did not move an inch . . . an overwhelming feeling of panic welled up inside of me as I turned to see why they had moved.

"As I turned around I smelled a horrible 'dirty body' smell, and there standing behind me were two poor homeless men. As I looked down at the short gentleman, close to me, he was 'smiling.' His beautiful sky-blue eyes were full of God's light as he searched for acceptance. He said, 'Good day,' as he counted the few coins he had been clutching. The second man fumbled with his hands as he stood behind his friend. I realized that the second man was mentally challenged and the blue-eyed gentleman was his salvation.

"I held my tears as I stood there with them. The young lady at the counter asked him what they wanted. He said, 'Coffee is all, miss,' because that was all they could afford. (If they wanted to sit in the restaurant and warm up, they had to buy something. He just wanted to be warm.)

"Then I really felt it—the compulsion was so great that I almost reached out and embraced the little man with the blue eyes. That is when I noticed that all eyes in the restaurant were set on me, judging my every action. I smiled and asked the young lady behind the counter to give me two more breakfast meals on a separate tray. I then walked around the corner to the table that the men had chosen as a resting spot. I put the tray on the table and laid my hand on the blue-eyed gentleman's cold hand. He looked up at me, with tears in his eyes, and said, 'Thank you.'

"I leaned over, began to pat his hand, and said, 'I did not do this for you. God is here working through me to give you hope.' I started to cry as I walked away to join my husband and son. When I sat down, my husband smiled at me and said, 'That is why God gave you to me, honey. To give me hope.' We held hands for a moment, and at that time we knew that only because of the grace that we had been given were we able to give.

"We are not churchgoers, but we are believers. That day showed me the pure light of God's sweet love. I returned to college, on the last evening of class, with this story in hand. I turned in my 'project,' and the instructor read it. Then she looked up at me and said, 'Can I share this?' I slowly nodded as she got the attention of the class. She began to read, and that is when I knew that we as human beings, being part of God, share this need to heal people and to be healed."[14]

How Does a Dependence on Signs and Wonders Shape Our Spiritual Lives?

Some of what we seek, then, when we look for signs and wonders is understandable, if not laudable. At some point in our lives, all of us need reassurance, certainty, and a sense of the sacred. As will become clear in the next chapter, there is a particular kind of reassurance and a particular sense of the sacred that I think are available to us. I am not convinced, however, that the kind of certainty I have described is ever possible, and I discuss that in the next chapter as well.

Here, it is more important to note that if we listen long enough to the language we use, it becomes clear that even if our needs could be satisfied, a dependence on the bright, white light of signs and wonders can be profoundly misleading. In what follows, I try to explain just how misleading that dependence can be.

My portrayal of those difficulties may seem overdrawn, simply because most of us never so completely depend on a single approach to finding and doing the will of God that it shapes the whole of our lives. So you will want to bear in mind that I am talking about the *direction* in which signs and wonders can take us. Just how far a dependence on signs and wonders can mislead us depends on the extent to which we use them as a means of discernment. I have tried to outline the difficulties of this dependence by dealing first with the basic problem (a dependence on success, closure, and expediency), then discussing the specific implications for the way in which we live and the triage theology that emerges from it.

Success, Closure, and Expediency

The basic problem is that when we begin to focus on the fireworks of faith, then the values of success, closure, and expediency dominate. The language of open doors and opportunities—even the spiritualized language of serendipity and providence—can and often does place a premium on those values.

This approach to finding and doing the will of God inevitably shapes the way we live our lives, because the language of signs and wonders tempts us to look for efforts that will succeed. Success—so we think—is the evidence that God is present, because we have been taught to assume that success characterizes any manifestation of the divine. The things we do in the name of God are, by definition, activities that succeed.

The pattern becomes a self-fulfilling prophecy and a governing principle: "Where God guides, God provides," so the phrase goes. I have never heard anyone offer the reassurance, "Where God guides, God goes along for the ride, no matter how rough the ride proves to be." Nor do you hear people say with enthusiasm, "Where God guides, it's important to follow—even if God doesn't provide." The net result of seeing the presence of God manifested only in successful endeavors is a spirituality that emphasizes the near-magical. This emphasis is widely characteristic of contemporary spirituality at every point along the theological spectrum in the United States.

This expectation has shaped how we pray, reducing much of our prayer life to petition and intercession. It has also driven elements of the practice of prayer to the margins of our lives that were once thought to be of equal, if not greater, importance, including communion with God and the act of placing ourselves at God's disposal. It has prompted us to comb Scripture for promises from God that we can "name and claim." The result is an approach to the life of faith that is completely captured by I-questions; one writer has even suggested, without blinking, that spiritual transformation begins with the prayer, "Father, oh, Father! Please bless me! And what I really mean is . . . bless me a lot!"[15]

The tendency to look for success, closure, and expediency is not uniquely American, nor is it purely contemporary. In ancient Israel, it was the guiding principle in a great deal of Hebrew theology. Good things happen to good people. Bad things happen to bad people. Referred to as the Deuteronomic principle by students of that literature, it is so named because the logic is asserted over and over again in the fifth book of the Pentateuch.[16] But the biblical pedigree and popularity of this principle is no evidence of its theological or spiritual value. Indeed, its continued hold on the hearts and minds of many is possible only because those of us who cling to it look at life selectively. Later writers in the Old Testament, such as the author of Job, knew this and told stories about bad things happening to good people for a reason. That is why the writer introduces us to a clearly righteous man at the very beginning of the book of Job and then has his "comforters" mouth the Deuteronomic principle. Eliphaz tells Job:

> Think now, who that was innocent ever perished?
> Or where were the upright cut off?
> As I have seen, those who plow iniquity
> and sow trouble reap the same.
> By the breath of God they perish,
> and by the blast of his anger they are consumed. (Job 4:7–9)

Mark, too, was acutely aware of how misleading this perspective could be. Knowing that the demands of discipleship were not a thing of the past, he contrasts the crowd's enthusiasm for the miracles worked by Jesus with the disinterest for those miracles that Jesus himself displays:

> That evening, at sundown, they brought to him all who were sick or possessed with demons. And the whole city was gathered around the door. And he cured many who were sick with various diseases, and cast out many demons; and he

would not permit the demons to speak, because they knew him. In the morning, while it was still very dark, he got up and went out to a deserted place, and there he prayed. And Simon and his companions hunted for him. When they found him, they said to him, "Everyone is searching for you." He answered, "Let us go on to the neighboring towns, so that I may proclaim the message there also; for that is what I came out to do." And he went throughout Galilee, proclaiming the message in their synagogues and casting out demons. (Mark 1:32–39)

Then, in a pivotal vignette, Mark underlines the nature of the lives to which the disciples are called:

[Jesus] called the crowd with his disciples, and said to them, "If any want to become my followers, let them deny themselves and take up their cross and follow me. For those who want to save their life will lose it, and those who lose their life for my sake, and for the sake of the gospel, will save it. For what will it profit them to gain the whole world and forfeit their life? Indeed, what can they give in return for their life? Those who are ashamed of me and of my words in this adulterous and sinful generation, of them the Son of Man will also be ashamed when he comes in the glory of his Father with the holy angels." (Mark 8:34–38)

"Get ready to suffer if you are going to follow me" hardly fits neatly under the headings of success, closure, and expediency. But Mark clearly believes that a preoccupation with signs and wonders carries with it certain implications for the triage theology of his community and the shape of their lives. Because he uses a story to underline those dangers, Mark never explicitly defines them. But the problems posed by a perennial search for signs and wonders, whether then or now, are still clear.

To be preoccupied with signs and wonders is to misread the purposes of God at work in the world. This preoccupation severs the moral nerve that gives us the strength to act in the face of adversity. It fixes our attention on dimensions of life that are often all but secondary in nature. And as Mark well knew, frequently we are not being honest with ourselves when we claim that we would follow God *if* he just gave us a sign. As Mark's own reading of Jesus's life makes clear, those who sought the signs abandoned him at the end. Peter, who was a witness to it all, found it easy to say, more than once, "I do not know this man you are talking about" (Mark 14:71).

A Life Without Self-Giving

The preoccupation with signs and wonders can also lead to a spiritual life that precludes the possibility of self-giving, sacrifice, or loss. It is perilously easy to assume that if God rewards the faithful with open doors, then others experience loss thanks to their own spiritual poverty. Indeed, some fairly influential writers all but say as much.[17] But a triage theology of this kind sounds more like the crowds in Mark's gospel than the message of his Jesus. Moreover, history is replete with stories that witness to loss not as a sign of spiritual poverty but of spiritual depth and courage.

One example is the life and ministry of Martin Luther King, Jr. Years ago I accompanied my wife to Atlanta, Georgia, where she was attending a conference. With a good deal of time to spare, I visited the Martin Luther King Center and purchased a children's biography of King for my six-year-old daughter. This was the first in a growing collection of King biographies that over the years have grown in sophistication. When she was nine, my daughter often played with a large group of children in the cathedral close, or compound, in Jerusalem. Among her friends was Jamie, a younger Canadian boy, and Alex, an American who had a reputation for being something of a bully. One day Jamie noticed Alex treating one of the other children pretty roughly, and at first he was inclined to confront Alex. But having done a quick body-mass comparison, Jamie concluded it was better to remain silent. Lindsay, with her well-honed sense of justice, said to her Canadian friend, "Jamie, go ahead and tell him what he did was wrong. Martin Luther King did. They killed him, of course, but he did it anyway."

You have to admire her values, although she could have learned something about the art of persuasion. It is probably not a particularly good approach to lead with martyrdom! And yet, that is in fact the point. King's efforts to address the social ills of racism were met with massive resistance and ended in assassination, and the struggle that he began is one that is necessarily renewed with each generation. None of this, however, diminished King's resolve to do what he plainly believed to be God's will.

A Life Without Adventure

More broadly, of course, a preoccupation with success, closure, and expediency makes it unlikely that we will risk an undertaking that might meet with failure, end without closure, or prove to be difficult. Our capacity for risk under those circumstances—or even adventure—all but disappears.[18]

The image that immediately comes to my mind is that of a photograph I saw years ago in a college textbook I was using. On one page was a picture of the small wayside chapel that Saint Francis of Assisi prayed in and repaired. The humble nature of the Chapel of San Damiano is reflective of Francis's life—his capacity for sacrifice and his awareness of the world around him, both wed to a keen sense of God's presence. But any picture of it taken today, like the one in the textbook, includes the mammoth gilded dome and frescoes of the Basilica of Santa Chiara that now stands over the little chapel.

The photograph is an apt image of the dangers inherent in a preoccupation with success. Surrounded and muffled by centuries of institutional aggrandizement, Francis's life and the little chapel that he repaired together represent a stark counterpoint to the lumbering self-preservation of today's institutional church. In a world in which the spiritual life has become just another furnishing in our comfortable existence, it needs to be said that to find and do God's will may just as easily lead to failure as to success.[19]

A Life Without Reflection

A dependence on signs and wonders also short-circuits any serious reflection when something successful happens. That is one reason why my friend Chuck, the air force pilot, never weighed his choices in consciously moral or theological terms. The doors opened and that was enough.

Couched in a conversation about faith, an attitude of this kind seems harmless enough. In fact, the willingness to walk through those open doors bespeaks an unqualified faith. But discernment requires reflection, and that kind of reflection is in evidence throughout the Old and New Testaments. Prophets weigh easy dependence on the power of ancient Israel's allies and the policies of kings toward the poor (Isaiah 30:12ff; 3:14–15). Poets and sages assess the natural order of things as a window into the divine order (Psalm 8; Ecclesiastes 3:1ff.). And our conversation partner Mark questions the events that others take to be obvious signs of God's intervention (Mark 13:5ff.).

In fact, in other settings we would be inclined to label this kind of unreflective approach to life as pathological. I still remember the

example offered by another of my college textbooks years ago. Re-
counting a series of interviews conducted with repeat offenders, one
researcher asked a man imprisoned for armed robbery, "Why do you
persist in robbing banks?" Obviously mystified by the question, the
man responded, "Because that's where the money is."

It may be a bit unfair to draw a comparison of this kind. Chuck's
intentions were hardly criminal, and no one would have labeled him
"pathological." But what should concern us is the extent to which
faith in God or following God is sometimes described in terms so devoid of reflection as to be anti-intellectual.

The roots of this tendency run deep in our culture. Some of it
can be traced to the fear of "reductionism," the conviction that what
we learn may render the concept of God unnecessary. The historical
roots of that fear run deep in religious life, and they have surfaced repeatedly over time. They first emerged in connection with the earliest discoveries made by Copernicus and Galileo. The realizations
that the sun is at the heart of our solar system and that our solar system is only one of many threatened to diminish the significance of
humankind by rendering God's interest in us a seeming impossibility
in so expanded a universe. It wasn't long before questions about that
assumption gave way to questions about the viability of our assumptions about God. After we first resisted and then painfully navigated
that discovery, the specter of reductionism reemerged with Sigmund
Freud's work in psychiatry, Charles Darwin's work in evolution, and
Max Weber's work in sociology. More recently, the same fear has surfaced with brain research.

None of this would seem to apply in any immediate fashion to
finding and doing the will of God. But if you decide that thinking
about your faith might threaten it, then thinking about any dimension of it becomes more difficult. Soon the ability to simply respond
without reflection begins to look like a virtue, and the practice of critical reflection begins to look like the devil's work.

This is why, paradoxically, the history of the church's struggle with various kinds of discoveries can feed an unreflective faith. The lesson of that history is not that reflection is a dangerous thing, but that a capacity for thoughtful listening has been worth practicing from the very beginning. The failure to embrace the truths yielded by legitimate discovery simply discredited the spiritual quest and slowed the process of coming to terms with those discoveries. And the fearful resistance and hostility that people sometimes embraced actually drove gentle, thoughtful souls from a faith they might have otherwise embraced.

A Life Without Love

Of course, these are not the only prices we pay for relying on signs and wonders. The difference between having made the right choice and being the *one who* made the right choice is a fine distinction, and one that we as human beings find it difficult to sustain. I have watched conversations about *what* is right turn into conflicts about *who* is right with breathtaking speed and ferocity. We are people who define ourselves in conversation with others, so comparisons are perhaps inevitable. We look to our parents early in life for models. We "compare notes" with our contemporaries to get some sense of how they are processing the challenges we all face. And if we are lucky, there are those in our lives who—advanced beyond our years—are prepared or willing to share with us out of the accumulated wisdom of their experience.

But when we rely on those comparisons, we are in serious spiritual peril and we are moved by all the wrong motives. Over and over again in human history, zero-sum spirituality—the conviction that I can't go to heaven unless you go to hell—has left its scars on the face of human history. The divisions in churches, the vicious epithets, the questionable motives we attribute to one another without engaging one another in conversation—all are examples of its impact. And far uglier chapters in history illustrate just how seriously compassion and understanding can erode. Zero-sum spirituality is not, I hasten to note, a disease or preoccupation that is unique to a particular point of view. It is the behavior that regularly and predictably shapes the face of fundamentalism, whether it be theological, political, or social.

This is why, when we make such comparisons, observable behavior, declarations of allegiance, and statements of faith loom so large in times of conflict. We are thus relieved of the responsibility to engage one another in conversation and allowed to assume that we know everything about another person because (we think) we know one thing about that person. And most significantly of all, we can leave large parts of our own lives unscrutinized since, having established that we are superior to that person in one way, we assume that we are superior in every other way—or at least in all the ways that count.

The problem, of course, is that the people who serve as the basis for such comparisons cease to be people and serve instead as ciphers—empty symbols of that with which we can be favorably compared. They can no longer speak to us as people whose life in God may illuminate or enlarge our understanding of God's will, and we become increasingly sure that we are right about the will of God. In time we learn nothing at all from the comparison. Instead, it simply deepens our own spiritual arrogance.

More frightening yet, of course, is that those with whom we compare ourselves are robbed of their humanity and become the targets of prejudice and abuse. This, tragically, is why many gentle and loving people instinctively fear the quest to find and do the will of God. Far too often, strength of conviction and spiritual passion have been identified with intolerance. Although the connection between the two is not at all necessary, they are increasingly identified with one another.[20] One can hear the echo of a similar debate in the words of

Thomas à Kempis, whose reflections were shaped by life in a monastic community:

> Above all things, keep peace within yourself, then you will be able to create peace among others. It is better to be peaceful than learned. The passionate person often thinks evil of a good person and easily believes the worst; a good and peaceful person turns all things to good. One who lives at peace suspects no one. But one who is tense and agitated by evil is troubled with all kinds of suspicions; such a person is never at peace within, nor does such a one permit others to be at peace. Such a person often speaks when one should be silent, and fails to say what would be truly useful. Such people are well aware of the obligations of others but neglect their own. So be zealous first of all with yourself, and then you will be more justified in expressing zeal for your neighbor. You are good at excusing and justifying your own deeds, and yet you will not listen to the excuses of others. It would be more just to accuse yourself and to excuse your neighbor.[21]

A God Without Grace

The difficulty, of course, is that a passion for signs and wonders tends to distort not just the shape of our spiritual lives but our understanding of God as well. You cannot have a cosmic Santa without a cosmic monster.[22] If we credit God with signs and wonders in the kind of flat way that many of us do, we are forced to give God credit for murder and mayhem as well. Tie the presence of God to prayers answered, and the presence of the divine will evaporate with the cold harsh light of day.[23]

One of the most poignant examples of just how quickly that can happen can be traced back to the experience of September 11, 2001.

In the wake of that tragic day, some who escaped the World Trade Center towers in Manhattan declared that they had escaped because "God takes care of God's own." It was an understandable word of gratitude for their lives, a combination of prayer, witness, and relief.

But what kind of inference can we draw from a sign and wonder of that kind? Where was God when so many others died? Why were the thousands who perished in the towers any less deserving of God's attention than those who emerged from the buildings shortly before they collapsed? And why are tens of thousands of children who die every day around the world neglected by God? This is the problem with a triage theology that assumes God is either the author of deliverance by signs and wonders or, event by event, the architect of everything that happens. The cosmic Santa and the cosmic monster are joined at the hip.

If Not Signs and Wonders, What Do We Depend On?

Are there any clues in life, then, that will guide us? Yes, there are. But the important clues do not lie in the brute events of life itself. As when an ER physician hastily misreads the symptoms presented by a patient, an unreflective triage theology can lead to a similar error in interpreting life's events.

I am not suggesting that God is not active in the world—far from it. But I am trying to preserve that space in which the presence of God is visible to the eyes of faith, whatever life's circumstances may bring. I am interested in helping you to apprehend a God who is passionate for communion with us and who, like the God of Genesis 1, broods over the waters of chaos, longing for us, ever present in moments both good and bad. I am also trying to describe that ability to see God at work in the world in a way that reduces God to neither an impersonal force nor to the likes of ancient Canaan's god Molech, who dispenses favor and spite with despotic caprice.

When we take the miraculous and the exceptional to be the measure of God's presence, rather than think of God as an enlivening presence throughout creation, we do not re-sacralize the world. Instead, we confine God to its margins and gaps. The key to seeing God at work in our world lies not in defining the events that reflect the movement of God but in what Paul describes as the renewing of our minds (Romans 12:1–2).[24]

The Power of Perception

In other words, the guidance we seek lies in our perception of the choices and events presented to us by life. It lies in the faithful and hopeful exercise of our imaginations. "Wait, watch," Mark would have said (see Mark 13:32–37). In one respect, this is simply "the way things are." There is no choice we make that is not profoundly shaped by the perceptions and assumptions we bring to it.

If our choices are governed by ambition, then we are likely to use even our noblest choices in ways that lack spiritual depth and character. It will be clear that even if we are engaged in a sacrificial way of life, at some level we are really satisfying personal ambitions of one kind or another. I once heard a religious leader concede, for example, that the position he had achieved was one he accepted for the sake of self-actualization. The motive that drove him to accept the post also shaped his work. He managed people's perceptions of him to the point of neglecting the tasks that were implicit in the position. The same could also be said of many other motives: fear, insecurity, avarice, and a desire for power are motives that turn the best of choices into instruments of destruction. The choice itself and the events surrounding it are largely secondary to the impulses that motivate us.

The same could be said of what we are able to see in events. If success and closure deeply shape your view of the hand of God, then you are less likely to see the divine in the eyes of a child, in the life of someone who is struggling for freedom from an addiction, or in the grateful tears of a homeless man at a McDonald's. Embrace one view of God and you will see yourself as an agent of divine judgment. Own your own frailty deeply enough and you will see yourself as an agent of divine mercy. Embrace a spirituality that includes the risk of failure and you will be open to a life that others might call into question.

Singing a Lasting Song

That certainly could be said of Mother Teresa. The educator Mary Poplin traveled to India in 1996 to work with Mother Teresa and the Sisters of Charity. Reflecting on her experience, Poplin writes:

> Many people complained that given her fame Mother Teresa should have gotten more politically involved in the economics of poverty. Others complained that she should not have simply fed the people but "taught them to fish." But Mother Teresa was not moved by these criticisms. She simply replied that God called others to do these things, he only called her to feed and care for the poorest of the poor. One of the most difficult things for a secular world to understand about her is that Mother Teresa did not do her work for humanity, she did not simply feel sorry for the poor. She was called by God to do what she did.[25]

Mother Teresa was not a sweet little old lady. She was motivated by neither sentiment nor calculation. She was not governed by the need to claim success or closure, and her work with others was not governed by expediency. She had a clear sense of what God was doing and how her life fit into that activity. As with Martin Luther King Jr., her capacity to respond included the freedom to take risks.

It would be a mistake to think that lives of this kind are lived by only a handful of well-known people. Mitchell Sviridoff died not long ago at the age of eighty-one, having spent his life taking risks and working without closure. For over three decades he worked in the area of social policy and philanthropy in New York. He focused on strategies for lifting people out of poverty and rebuilding neighborhoods. In 1985, at a party held to celebrate his life's work, he recited these lines from a poem by William Butler Yeats:

> God guard from those thoughts men think
> In the mind alone;
> He that sings a lasting song
> Thinks in a marrow bone.[26]

Asked why he quoted this passage from Yeats, Sviridoff responded: "That is the way I function. I do things that do not seem logical at the beginning and sometimes fail. But when they succeed, they tend to be lasting songs."[27]

The risks we run, the potential for failure, the endless attention demanded by problems that never quite go away—none of these realities should keep us from acting when we are convinced that we are doing God's will. The songs we sing under such circumstances may be the only witness to the presence of God that anyone hears.

The Mystic's Way

That is why, according to the great mystics of history, the prerequisite for finding and doing the will of God has less to do with identifying an event that has all the earmarks of "God's will" than it does with the transformation of the one who hopes to find the will of God. Purity of life, clarity of conscience, and an ever deepening familiarity with God are keys to the transformation of the one who hopes to sing "a lasting song."[28]

To contemporary ears, this may sound like a daunting task and far more like an achievement than anything else. To be sure, there have been chapters in history during which some have pursued the recommendations of the mystical tradition with just that kind of intention. The difference between a spiritual discipline that creates a space in which God can be heard and an asceticism of achievement can be difficult to distinguish at times.[29] But a deepening relationship with God that shapes how we see the world is what the mystics have in mind.

In that sense, it could be said that our perceptions are shaped by love and romance: love understood as a deep, abiding, unconditional desire to know God, and romance understood as the passion and palpable sense of emotional attachment that accompanies that commitment—what the Orthodox describe as praying with the mind in the heart. This is in fact the language often used by the mystical tradition to describe the nature of the relationship with God that shapes our perceptions of the world around us. And there is a good deal that commends the imagery of love and romance.[30]

One reason is that it is *intelligible* to us. We recognize love and romance as a part of our world. It is a dynamic that, if we have been fortunate, shaped the homes in which we were reared and has shaped the lives that we live. It is something we dream of and celebrate. We know that a good relationship is something that you need to "work at," but we also know that a good relationship has less to do with "doing" than with becoming.

The *intimacy* of love and romance is also something that transposes easily to a love for God and in fact flows from it.[31] At its best, an intimate relationship has a hand-in-glove character that lends a sense of oneness and belonging to our lives. A unity of purpose, understanding, and movement often marks a relationship blessed with intimacy. We also know the pain of isolation and the loneliness that can fill us when that intimacy is lost, disrupted, or distorted.

We know the *formative* character of love and romance as well. We joke about looking more and more like the one we love over time—and perhaps we always did. We come to the point at which we are able to complete one another's sentences, and we can also acknowledge that sometimes we are unable to complete a thought without the contribution of the one we love.

The image of love and romance also captures the closely related but distinct elements of an intimate and formative relationship. It stresses the *unconditional commitment* that is necessary to an enduring relationship—the resilience that is rooted not in our own needs but in our unqualified allegiance to the other. But it also allows for the *emotional depths* that accompany, enliven, and fill that kind of commitment with passion.

At the same time, the images of love and romance allow us to grasp that the emotional depth of love we feel for God *can be compromised by circumstances* both benign and malevolent. But the comparison is also predicated on a truth that shapes both our relationships with others and our relationship with God: *you cannot love what you do not know, and you cannot know what you do not love.*[32]

As that principle applies to finding and doing the will of God, we might add that we cannot see what we neither know nor love. And therein lies the alternative to a futile search for signs and wonders. Absent a lover's relationship with God, looking for indications of God's presence in the world is a good deal like trying to explain the sense of recognition that accompanies that look in her eyes. It cannot be quantified or analyzed. It has nothing to do with the fact that her eyes are brown. But it is instantly apparent to the one who knows and loves.

I carry a picture of my wife that is now over twenty-five years old. On the back of it my wife wrote that I was "perfect," and for that reason I have been careful to preserve the picture! When I once teased her by observing, "But you said I was perfect," she responded, "I meant that you are perfect *for me*." Presumably Elaine would not add the same qualifiers to her description of God, but the knowledge of and love for me implicit in her comment is what I have in mind. She knows me well enough and loves me deeply enough that she instantly recognizes the kind of thing that I do and say. Similarly, a love of God and a romance with God nurtures in us a capacity to see God where God is present.

Heart and Mind

Now, all of this may sound to you like the advice that our parents once gave us when we asked how we would know that we had found the "right" woman or man. "Oh, you'll know," they said. At one level, it is indeed like that. But at another level, it is not like that at all. It would be dangerous—or useless—to read this chapter without keeping in mind what I had to say in the last chapter about triage theology.

The knowledge I am talking about can be intuitive, and our emotions can even provide solid clues about where God is at work in the world. But that knowledge is not purely intuitive, and our emotions are not the only window into the activity of God in our world. My love for my wife is something I cannot completely explain without being specific about who she is or how she behaves. Similarly, our knowledge of God is grounded in the particular, and for that reason we need to be in dialogue with a tradition. Without that tradition, you cannot possibly say who it is you love, or where you are able to see the hand of the one you love at work in the world. You will look, instead, for a feeling—or perhaps even more accurately, you will be preoccupied with your feelings and with not much more.

Separated from what our traditions tell us about God, it is hard to know what discerning the presence of God might mean.[33] As I tell my students when we talk about the importance of spiritual formation and its relationship to the theological education they are pursuing, the two should complement one another. They are not in competition. Spirituality may keep theology from being dry, arid speculation, but theology keeps spirituality from being dangerous, errant nonsense.[34]

It is difficult for us to grasp this fact because we live in a society that has inherited a preoccupation with our emotional lives, and as a result our interior lives have assumed pride of place as the most important dimension of spirituality. But contrary to this development, centuries of spiritual practice held that love and knowledge complement one another.[35]

This is not to say that our feelings are without importance. In fact, it could be argued that emotions are suffused with intimations of where the divine is and is not present in our world. In that sense, emotions are potential bearers of things we "know" but cannot articulate.[36] But if our minds are subject to error, so are our feelings. Indeed, our emotions are probably more susceptible to distortion, shaped as they are not just by the circumstances around us but also by our sense of physical safety and well-being. As a teacher of mine once observed, "The mind travels by express, the emotions by slow freight."[37] As significant as they may be, emotions also fluctuate with the amount of sleep we have had, the state of our relationships with one another, the anxiety we may or may not feel, and an endless list of other variables. That is why a dialogue between heart and mind is so important. The two not only enliven and complement one another but together provide a wider window into the work of God in the world.[38]

Near the end of the first century of the Common Era, the signs and wonders in Jerusalem were a part of that complex mix. The destruction of the city and the Temple tapped into cultural and religious associations that were as deeply significant for the church in Mark's day as anything that might surface in our own lives today. And Mark's readers scrambled to understand their significance, fixed not on a dialogue between heart and mind but on signs and wonders, assuming that they were one and the same as the presence of God. In response, Mark brings them back into conversation with the story of Jesus and the tradition that had shaped their lives. With them, as with us, it was that dialogue that gave them the ability to wait and watch.

Spiritual Exercises for Identifying Our Dependence on Signs and Wonders

- Identify specific instances in your life when you looked for signs from God to help you with a problem or to make a choice.

- What motivated you to look for those signs?

- What needs of yours were met if you concluded that you had actually received a sign from God?

- What happened to you when there was no sign to be found?

- To what extent is your practice of discernment dependent on signs today?

- To what extent is your practice dependent on success, closure, and expediency?

- What would it mean for you to live without depending on signs and wonders?

- What would it look like for God to replace that dependence?

Four

PROVING THE WILL
OF GOD

There is nothing in life less susceptible to stereotype than a
Christian who follows Jesus on "the Way." Every Christian is an
original; the Holy Spirit doesn't go in for copying old masters;
every soul is a new creation. Sins after awhile all begin to look
and sound alike (the devil never seems able to inspire anything
beyond cheap reproductions). But every virtue, every act of
faith, every venture into obedience is one-of-kind. The Christian life, except in the overall sense that it derives from Jesus'
life and is composed on the plot of Holy Scripture, is unpre-
dictable in its free fall through the atmosphere of grace.

Eugene H. Peterson[1]

For many of us, the will of God is like a page from the Franklin
Planner I once used before changing to a Palm Pilot. Complete
with a page for each day, my Franklin Planner included space for
a to-do list. Alongside the list was a column for the letters A, B, and
C, indicating the urgency of the task: A was for urgent tasks, B stood
for tasks to be done in the immediate future, and tasks to be completed over a longer period of time were marked with a C. A second column gave me an opportunity to record the amount of
progress made. A check indicated that the job had been completed,

and an X was to be used on those rare occasions when a task was canceled. More frequently, an arrow indicated that a task was to be taken forward to the next day (and the next!) for future attention. For the obsessive-compulsive, a dot could be used to indicate that the task had begun. All of us keep to-do lists, if not always ones as complex as the Franklin Planner kind. What most of us don't want to admit is that we often write in tasks that we've already completed but forgot to list and then check them off in order to give ourselves a sense of accomplishment.

In a similar fashion, many of us are haunted by the notion that the will of God is a list of things to be done. The list is longer for some, shorter for others. There are those whose list focuses on a handful of life's decisions—choices related to crises, crossroads, and questions of vocation. For those of us who think in those terms, a great deal of life is lived out on our own recognizance. But at a few points along the way—because we find the choices either difficult or potentially life-changing—we turn to God for direction.

The challenge, of course, is in knowing when and why God might care about the choices we make. A further complication arises when we realize that some of life's apparently less significant decisions can have a profound impact on the ones that seem more important. Choosing the location of a new home, for example, might not seem particularly significant. A hundred and one choices associated with that task involve your aesthetic senses. Do you like homes that are modern or traditional? Do you like living in an established community or in a relatively new one? These are choices that have no wrong or right answer. They are a matter of preference. But the choices you make may shape your friendships and determine the kind of school your children attend. And that complex mix of choices may have an unanticipated impact on whatever you and your children decide to do with your lives—*including* a choice of vocation, for example.

For others, the list of choices for which they look to God for guidance is a good deal longer and even more detailed. That list often involves not just crises, crossroads, and vocations but the shape of their day-to-day lives. I went to college with someone, for example, who was convinced that God dictates every moment of our day, right down to the breakfast food we choose. It wasn't that he felt breakfast per se was that important. But the line in the cafeteria that served bagels and the line that served cereal were far enough apart that choosing one or the other put you in contact with a different group of people and thus could change your sphere of influence.

On this reading, the task of making choices is fairly frightening, of course. Life holds a huge number of choices. Ordering coffee today, for example, is not just a matter of choosing a "tall," "grande," or "venti" size cup. Nor does it involve only a simple choice of decaf or regular. You can now choose to have an extra shot of espresso, or two, or three. You can have a latte, but then you need to decide whether you want a full-fat, nonfat, or blended latte. And so on and on it goes. One store has now created a small book to guide you in making those choices, and it even includes a detachable card on which you can record the results of your quest for the perfect cup of coffee.

And then there's the issue of consequences. If in fact what seems to be a completely inconsequential choice is fraught with questions of God's will, how often can you go wrong in the course of a day as you weigh choices that seem to be of little or no significance? If you were meant to have cereal and you order a bagel instead, will you suddenly be out of touch with God's will for the remainder of your life? Or will God be forced to devote extra time and energy to correcting for the venti, low-fat, caramel macchiato with an extra shot of espresso that you decided to have yesterday afternoon?

Probably the vast majority of us take a view somewhere in between these two extremes. We look to God for guidance from time to time, especially when making decisions associated with life's crossroads, crises, and vocational choices. But we labor under the nagging, well-buried conviction that somehow our lives should be shaped in deeper ways by the will of God. We are at a loss, though, to know what that would look like.[2]

Is there something between the short list of crossroads, crises, and vocational choices, on the one hand, and the comprehensive moment-to-moment list of choices, on the other? If there is, does it represent a more balanced approach to life?

The answer is yes—there is an alternative. But strictly speaking, it does not lie on a spectrum between longer and shorter lists. In fact, as common as they are, all three positions I have sketched here are based on serious misunderstandings of what it means to "prove" the will of God.

So, in what follows, I hope to free us all from some of the Franklin Planner thinking that we do by describing:

- Why we *want* the certainty of a list

- Why we think we *need* the certainty of a list

- Why we can't have that kind of certainty

Then I would like to describe:

- The kind of certainty we *can* have

- Why it's enough

- What it means to "prove" the will of God without a to-do list

Why We Want the Certainty of a List

The notion that God has a to-do list for each of us is widespread. It is the product of both a desire to have that list and the conviction that God has one. At first blush, those might seem to be the same thing. But even though our desire to have a list tends to reinforce our conviction that God has a list, in fact they are very different.

As with signs and wonders, the desire to have a list stems from a desire for the reassurance that it offers us. If you manage to determine the will of God step by step, choice by choice, you also enjoy the confidence that you are right where you should be, step by step, choice by choice. And that confidence is no small thing. Given the ambiguity of the decisions we are forced to make, all of us crave the kind of confidence that a list could give us from time to time. Who would not love to know that this relationship, not that one, will be enduring or fulfilling? Who would not like to know that this job will work out well and that one will be a disaster? Who would not like to know where our choices will lead us—which doors to the future they will close or open?

Believing that there is a list also tends to diminish the anxiety, and subsequently the guilt, that we associate with making choices. The freedom to choose this course of action or that one carries with it, by definition, the potential for error. The potential for error also carries with it anxiety and, if things go badly, guilt.

Neither our anxiety about making choices nor our desire for a list is likely to diminish in the near future. To the contrary, observers are fast concluding that paralysis associated with choosing is actually on the rise—as is the depression and declining satisfaction with life that accompany that paralysis. Affluence has brought with it a burgeoning number of choices everywhere we turn. Factor in unrealistic expectations and the kind of talent or energy that makes many things possible and you have a complex mix that threatens to overwhelm us. One writer observes:

> This is the paradox: Here we are, living at the pinnacle of human possibility, awash in material abundance. We get what we say we want, only to discover that it doesn't satisfy us. The success of 21st-century life turns out to be bittersweet. And . . . a significant contributing factor is the overabundance of choice.[3]

I am convinced that the desire for God's to-do list is deeply imbedded in an effort to evade the choosing itself, the fear of getting it wrong, and the potential for subsequent guilt. We look for a way to drop out, reduce the complexity of the decisions we make, or shift the responsibility for deciding to someone else. Parents and authority figures, institutions and psychic forces all play a role in the choices we did not make.[4]

It is little wonder, then, that as people of faith we often address far deeper issues in our lives by shifting the responsibility for choosing to God. In a spiritual sleight of hand, we absolve ourselves of responsibility for our choices and their impact on our lives and on others. We see it in the language of those who insist, "I had no choice," and those who more directly attribute their behavior to God. Even those who do not believe in God are inclined to attribute responsibility for the decisions they make to a generalized notion of fate or destiny, no doubt often in an effort to find the same kind of absolution.[5] Put another way: we want the certainty of a list because we don't want the responsibility that comes with making a choice.

Why We Think We Need the Certainty of a List

Of course, many of us insist that God has a list because we have been taught to believe that he does. Our traditions, spiritual mentors, and parents have taught us that "God has a plan for our lives." For those who feel this way—including a few who are tormented by the logic of their own position—this expectation is simply what you would expect from a God who cares about every hair on our heads and every detail of our lives.[6]

It is a deeply held conviction imbedded in more than one religious, social, and intellectual dynamic. A simple sketch of the way in which many of us arrived at this conclusion would hardly satisfy historians, and rightly so. But at the risk of oversimplification, I am interested in describing—without getting lost in the details—how this conviction became such an influential part of our triage theologies.

For many, the certainty that there is a list appears to be rooted entirely in convictions about Scripture. The Old and New Testaments, the prophets, and Jesus all assert that God cares for us. God's care for the lilies of the field and the sparrows that fill the air is, according to Jesus, proof enough (Matthew 6:25–34; Luke 12:22–32). The argument he uses is an ancient bit of *qal vaḥomer*, "how much more" or "light and heavy." The logic goes this way: if in the less significant (the lighter) case of birds God cares, then *how much more* likely is it in the significant (the heavier) case of you and me that God cares? Factor in the stories of patriarchs, prophets, and apostles who respond to God's call, add to that the conviction that God is sovereign over all, and you have what many consider the biblical warrant for thinking that God has a list. If people get assignments and God is handing them out, then it stands to reason that there has to be a list!

This is fine as far as it goes. But this fairly flat reading is based on assumptions that make sense to you and me but are not necessarily the ones made by the biblical authors. In between us and them are more than two millennia of history. Notwithstanding what we have in common as human beings, a lot has changed—in degree, even if not in kind.

Their language and speech were more heavily shaped by story, metaphor, myth, and image. Ours are shaped more heavily by conceptual and factual categories. Their world was tribal, and they thought in terms of the collective experience. Our world is radically individualistic, and we think readily in terms of you and me, not us. They freely asserted views that at times spoke to the moment or only to a part of the human experience of the divine. We tend to think in terms of propositions that are once and for all. They lived easily with conflict and contradiction. We take the presence of conflict and contradiction as evidence of a defective argument.

Add to this the realization that the Bible is not one book but a library of books—written by many people over thousands of years, under a variety of circumstances, addressing specific and very different problems—and it is difficult to talk easily about "the plain meaning" of Scripture. This is not to say that it isn't worthwhile trying to understand it or that the biblical writers are wrong and we are right. Neither is the reverse true.[7]

It is to say, however, that the distance between the horizons of their world and the horizons of ours requires that we read Scripture imaginatively, knowing that it will not answer directly every question we need to have answered. So, for example, when we assume that the God behind those biblical stories is the God who directs our lives, list in hand, that is at best only one way of answering a question that the writers themselves have little or no interest in answering.[8]

This is why the dialogue with tradition that I mentioned in chapter 2 is so important. Tradition—even the part of it to which Scripture contributes—cannot dictate in detail how we ought to think about our lives in God. It can only shape and gently channel the "stream of meaning" that we share with the writers whose work is preserved in Scripture. Out of that dialogue, some views will emerge that bear a striking resemblance to Scripture. But new views may emerge as well, and almost any twenty-first-century attempt to explain what it means to find and do the will of God is sure to be cast in terms that differ to some extent from those used in Scripture. But the "shared meaning" that arises out of that conversation is the "glue" or "cement" that holds the participants in that tradition together.[9]

Why We Can't Have That Kind of Certainty

So, in dialogue with tradition, we are all forced to fill in the gaps. In my own quest to fill in those gaps, I have come to the conclusion that we cannot have a to-do-list-type certainty. Scripture makes a great deal of the sovereignty of God, but it also asserts over and over again that we have a responsibility to make decisions and choices. How that sovereignty and that responsibility go together is not something that the Hebrew or early Christian mind ever found it necessary to resolve. But for you and me the question is more acute.

The resolution, it seems to me, lies in recognizing that if there is such a thing as authentic choice, then divine sovereignty cannot be construed as the power to dictate how we behave, either in general or in particular. In fact, I think it could well be argued that at the heart of God's creative act is a self-emptying of power in which God willingly risks creating a world in which we are just as capable (or more) of turning against God as we are of turning toward God.[10] In turn, that risk is rooted in God's passion for a relationship with us—or to put it another way, it is rooted in God's love for us. This means that we have the freedom to choose and that there is a very real and as yet undefined future that, with God, we shape through the choices we make.

This picture of the world in which we live receives expression time and again in both the Old and New Testaments. For example, it is probably the original point of the Adam and Eve story (Genesis 3). Created for intimacy with one another and God, Adam and Eve are representative of every man and every woman. They share a world in which God lives in such close communion with them that God even walks in the garden during the cool of the day. But they also have a capacity for choice, and they exercise it in a fashion that alienates them from their creator.

The reality of choice is also the burden of story after story that describes God as deeply pained by the choices Israel makes, in spite of the relationship proffered Israel at Mount Sinai (see, for example, Exodus 34:6ff. and Numbers 14). Not only is the nation free to choose for good or for ill, but the sovereignty of God is not described in a predictable, linear fashion that ties reward to obedience and punishment to disobedience. Instead, although that language is used from time to time, God is also described as having a change of heart, and the nation's leaders are even described as averting judgment by reminding God of the covenant made with the nation.

None of this speaks directly, of course, to the issue of choice and the question of whether or not God has a list. As I have said, these stories do not explore those issues at length because they were not the issues of the people who told them; they are our issues. But another reason is that the people who told them presupposed a freedom to choose that makes these questions unnecessary.[11] As one Jewish exegete and philosopher observes:

Man is answerable for the universe! Man is answerable for others. His faithfulness or unfaithfulness to the Torah is not just a way of winning or losing his salvation: the being, elevation and light of the worlds are dependent upon it. Only indirectly, by virtue of the salvation or downfall of the worlds, does his own destiny depend upon it. As if through that responsibility, which constitutes man's very identity, each one of us were similar to *Elohim*.[12]

Those who are committed by their tradition to an obvious notion of divine sovereignty in which God determines all that we do will, of course, offer a very different reading of the biblical stories from the one I have described here. If you start with the assumption that the passages found in Scripture describing the power of God take precedence over everything else said about God, then this is a natural conclusion. But then an obvious notion of sovereignty also obligates those who see the stories that way to attribute the chaos and suffering of life to God—either by design or in response to the sinfulness of humankind. In that particular approach to filling in the gaps, the reassurance that God asserts that kind of control is at the heart of the picture that emerges.

But this approach is almost as problematic as it is reassuring. If God is love and in control, it is difficult to imagine why we are surrounded by the suffering and chaos that are so much a part of daily life. If, however, we assume that God's desire for a relationship with us also obligates God to grant the created order freedom, then it could be that God is forced to abandon that kind of control and assume considerable risk instead—in the name of creating men and women like you and me who are capable of loving and of being loved.

As with other relationships marked by such freedom, to-do lists cannot be made. The choices we make cannot be predicted, and beyond the broader ethical guidance that nurtures a creative space within which to work, the creation of lists works at cross-purposes with the freedom we have been given.

The Kind of Certainty We Can Have

Against this backdrop, Paul's appeal to the church in Rome that it *prove*—or as some translations have it, *discern*—the will of God may seem to contradict what I have just said.[13] Paul writes:

> I appeal to you therefore, brothers and sisters, by the mercies of God, to present your bodies as a living sacrifice, holy and acceptable to God, which is your spiritual worship. Do not be conformed to this world, but be transformed by the renewing of your minds, so that you may [prove or] discern what is the will of God—what is good and acceptable and perfect. (Romans 12:1–2)

Read in isolation, Paul's words in chapter 12 of the letter to the Roman church seem to be an invitation to find just this kind of to-do-list-type certainty. And the translated word *prove* seems to underline that invitation in explicit terms. Focusing on that choice of words, our science- and technology-oriented culture hears laboratory-like echoes of something that can be confirmed or falsified—something that can be found on a list or eliminated from consideration. We *prove* equations. We *prove* that this chemical will produce that reaction.

But that's our culture talking, not Paul. Throughout the first eleven chapters of his letter to the Romans, Paul is at great pains to bring together the Jewish and Gentile factions in the church at Rome. He accomplishes that task by insisting that both groups are debtors to the grace of God made available through the death and resurrection of Christ. The Law or Torah assumes a very different place in Paul's argument, however, than it did in his native Judaism.

It is difficult for most of us today to appreciate the issues that this difference raised for Paul. For Jews of the first century, as for Orthodox and Conservative Jews today, the Law not only informed the Jew-ish faith but was also the body of instruction that marked the social boundaries between the synagogue and the rest of the world. De-prived of the Temple more than once in their history, Jews had rede-fined what it meant to be the people of God, and the Law had served as the organizing center for that new self-understanding. If you wanted to know how to find and do the will of God, you looked to Torah.[14]

But Paul's argument had made it difficult to answer that question in quite the same way, and he struggled with it in the letters he wrote to the churches scattered around the Mediterranean.[15] Finally, in the last of his letters to survive, Paul gives this answer in the form of an exhortation: "I appeal to you, therefore, sisters and brothers, by the mercies of God, to present your bodies as a living sacrifice, holy and acceptable to God, which is your spiritual worship" (Romans 12:1).

Alert to his readers' needs and their background, Paul frames his answer in terms of worship. The sacrifices offered in the Temple that had set Judaism apart from other religions were prescribed in the Law. Now, Paul argues, the sacrifices they are called upon to offer are less tangible but nonetheless embrace the whole of life—body and mind. The Temple's Holy of Holies, where sacrifices were made, had been the sacred center of Jewish life. Now Paul calls for an approach to sac-rifice that embraces "human relationships in the everyday world."[16]

In some senses, however, the Law was written to guide the nation in living a life that reflected the will of God. For that reason, Paul could anticipate his readers' question: "What, then, distinguishes the Christian's life?"[17] In response, Paul follows the first exhortation with a second: "Do not be conformed to this world, but be transformed by the renewing of your minds, so that you may *prove* what is the will of God—what is good and acceptable and perfect" (Romans 12:2).

Paul, like Jesus before him, refuses to quantify what it means to do the will of God. A checklist morality is inadequate. Instead, Paul argues, the gospel begins with inward transformation. He is not urging his readers to practice a bit of baptized fatalism or focus on a Franklin Planner list. He is urging the open-ended exploration that follows on the experience of God's grace in Christ.[18]

The Greek word *dokimadzein*, which lies behind the English translations, does not mean "prove" in the scientific sense of "verify" or "confirm." It means to "probe," "explore," or "discover." The image is one of a mutual, open-ended process that is as yet incomplete. Understood in this way, Paul's exhortation is better understood if it is translated in this way:

> I exhort you, (my) brothers [and sisters], by the merciful acts of God, to present your bodies as a sacrifice living, holy and well-pleasing to God, (which is) your reasonable religion. And do not allow yourselves to be conformed to this age, but let yourselves be transformed by the renewal of (your) intellect, so that you (may be able to) *test* what the will of God is (*which means to discover*), the good and well-pleasing and perfect.[19]

Hand in hand with God, Paul invites his readers to "discover" the will of God. This does not mean that anything and everything can be the will of God. That which is to be discovered is still good, well-pleasing, and perfect. But the space for creativity matches the capacity of love and finds its source in God's love. The reassurance we are given is not the list but the love of God, and with it the reassurance of God's presence.

For those of you who are left-brained, perhaps the best image is a proving track. Designers develop and build a vehicle, but before they take it to the proving track, its capabilities are as yet unknown. By driving it at high speeds, bringing it to abrupt stops, and navigating hairpin turns, they prove, probe, or explore the unknown. For those of you who are right-brained, perhaps the best image is proving yeast. In preparing to use yeast, you put a bit of it in warm water to activate it. You are not sure of its properties, but you are about to find out.

When you think about it, this was true in ways that apply broadly to the experience of the church throughout its young life. In the space of just over a century, the church moved from being a sect within a sect to a sect in its own right. And finally it assumed the shape of an institution with its own religious consciousness. In making that transition, the church navigated new challenges—and did so with no religious texts of its own (other than the ones it inherited from Judaism), with no established leadership, and with no patterns of worship that were distinctively its own—and all in an environment in which its nearest religious relative understandably considered it heretical. To probe and explore was all that the members of the early church could do.[20] It is ironic in a way that the church in its most adventurous mode has become the model for Christians who want to reproduce the past.

Why This Kind of Certainty Is Enough

The problem for many of us, of course, lies in putting aside the Franklin Planner list and embracing that open-ended future. Suddenly there is not just one possible kind of world or one set of appropriate choices. We lose the one thing many of us long for most: the one and only right answer.

But if you struggle with that loss, then reflect on this: what you fear is not finally the loss of God, whose love Paul promises us is our gift in this exciting experiment we call life. What you fear is the loss of *the list*. In other words, what you fear losing is not at all where you should focus your faith—if you can call knowing the one and only answer "faith" at all. What you are losing is only a proximate authority—a substitute for trusting God.

Our faith should rest elsewhere, and the best image I can offer is this. Years ago my sister-in-law and her husband had five very young children. I was impressed. I am not a real parent. I have one child, and I have never had to say, "Stop touching your sister," or, "Leave your brother alone and stay on your own side of the car."

Their family room was the center of endless activity, with games, toys, and projects. Grape jam was occasionally smeared on the refrigerator door, and a sign over the kitchen cabinet read, "A CLEAN HOUSE IS A SIGN OF A MISSPENT LIFE." You never knew what was going to happen in that family room on any given day. There was endless proving, probing, and discovering. But this much was always clear. The things done, the mistakes made, and the lessons learned were embraced by the gracious and loving presence of the parents.

The same is true for those of us who are children of God. We make the wrong choices. Some of them are stupid or thoughtless. Others are willful and self-indulgent. We risk doing some things that fail, and we do other things that succeed so well that even we are surprised by the results. Sooner or later we fall and scrape our knees or smear grape jam on the refrigerator door. To expect more from life—to insist on perfection or certainty—is to live in a way that is deeply out of touch with our fallen and frail nature. Through it all, however, we are promised God's love, and that is enough. Freed to roam the family room that God has created for us, we are invited to laugh, love, seek, and discover that which is "good, well-pleasing, and perfect."

"Proving" the Will of God Without a To-Do List

This radically different way of living moves from a spirituality that is preoccupied with making the one right choice to a spirituality of creativity. And because that creativity is its hallmark, there is an open-ended character to it that resists narrow and formulaic definitions. Like an empty canvas, a blank page, or an untouched block of stone, there is no predicting or prescribing what may be painted, written, or chiseled on the surface of our lives.

Those possibilities are as endless as the number of souls who enter into life's dance. That is why an approach to discernment that reduces the adventure of life to a few steps or a method is fundamentally and dangerously misleading. Such an approach does not just promise more than it can deliver—it actually offers less than it should. By reducing both the responsibility and the freedom inherent in the invitation to discover the will of God, the person who might be described as a child of God is reduced to what Jesus might have called a hired hand (John 10:12). There are, however, some observations to be made that will help to sketch the creative landscape I have in mind.

> *Discernment is not a matter of getting the right answer. It is the invitation to create an answer.*

To be sure, there are choices that are morally unacceptable for a child of God. That is why Paul does not distinguish between ethical questions and doing the will of God. The two are of one piece in both Jewish and Christian understandings, and the literature of both traditions moves freely between the ethical and the spiritual for that reason. But within the life-giving boundaries provided by moral guidance, there is enormous freedom.

As such, moral and spiritual failure has less to do with making the wrong choice than with evading the responsibility to live creatively before God. A passivity that takes refuge in a baptized fatalism or a caution that feeds spiritual inertia can represent a far larger defection from what we are called to do than any choice we might make. In that regard, there is both an element of play and an element of responsibility in discerning the will of God, and the stories of the tradition highlight both elements.

Jewish tradition, for example, tells a story about stories—even in times of trial—that underlines the playful intention of God:

> When the founder of Hasidic Judaism, the great Rabbi Israel Shem Tov, saw misfortune threatening the Jews, it was his custom to go into a certain part of the forest to meditate. There he would light a fire, say a special prayer, and the miracle would be accomplished and the misfortune averted.
>
> Later, when his disciple, the celebrated Maggid of Mezritch, had occasion for the same reason to intercede with heaven, he would go to the same place in the forest and say, "Master of the Universe, listen! I do not know how to light the fire, but I am still able to say the prayer." Again the miracle would be accomplished.
>
> Still later, Rabbi Moshe-leib of Sasov, in order to save his people once more, would go into the forest and say, "I do not know how to light the fire. I do not know the prayer, but I know the place and this must be sufficient." It was sufficient, and the miracle was accomplished.
>
> Then it fell to Rabbi Israel of Rizhin to overcome misfortune. Sitting in his armchair, his head in his hands, he spoke to God, "I am unable to light the fire and I do not know the prayer and I cannot even find the place in the forest. All I can do is to tell the story, and this must be sufficient."[21]

"And it was sufficient," the story concludes, "for God made man because he loves stories." Each generation fails to perform some part of the ritual. But it doesn't matter. The intention endures, as does the relationship, and that is enough.

This does not mean that we are without responsibility, nor that in the moment the details do not matter. A story told by Jesus makes that clear:

For it is as if a man, going on a journey, summoned his slaves and entrusted his property to them; to one he gave five talents, to another two, to another one, to each according to his ability. Then he went away. The one who had received the five talents went off at once and traded with them, and made five more talents. In the same way, the one who had the two talents made two more talents. But the one who had received the one talent went off and dug a hole in the ground and hid his master's money. After a long time the master of those slaves came and settled accounts with them. Then the one who had received the five talents came forward, bringing five more talents, saying, "Master, you handed over to me five talents; see, I have made five more talents." His master said to him, "Well done, good and trustworthy slave; you have been trustworthy in a few things, I will put you in charge of many things; enter into the joy of your master." And the one with the two talents also came forward, saying, "Master, you handed over to me two talents; see, I have made two more talents." His master said to him, "Well done, good and trustworthy slave; you have been trustworthy in a few things, I will put you in charge of many things; enter into the joy of your master." Then the one who had received the one talent also came forward, saying, "Master, I knew that you were a harsh man, reaping where you did not sow, and gathering where you did not scatter seed; so I was afraid, and I went and hid your talent in the ground. Here you have what is yours." But his master replied, "You wicked and lazy slave! You knew, did you, that I reap where I did not sow, and gather where I did not scatter? Then you ought to have invested my money with the bankers, and on my return I would have received what was my own with interest. So take the talent from him, and give it to the one with the ten talents. For to all those who have, more will be given, and they will have an abundance; but from those who have nothing, even what they have will be taken away. As for this worthless slave, throw him into the outer darkness, where there will be weeping and gnashing of teeth. (Matthew 25:14–30; Luke 19:11–27)

But even here, the specifics of the performance are irrelevant. The servant is not chastised or punished for having failed to respond in a prescribed fashion. In that regard, the servants are utterly free to choose how they will invest their master's wealth. Instead, the servant is punished for having done nothing at all.[22]

A creative discovery of God's will is not a matter of self-actualization. Spiritual discovery is possible only if it is nurtured in a conversation with God marked by genuine humility.

As I said above, the problem, of course, is that humility has an all but completely negative connotation. To be humble—so we think—is to be servile and lacking in force of character. But nothing could be further from the truth. The word itself shares the Latin root *humus*, or "earth." To be humble, then, is to be in touch with our created nature and, as a consequence, to be fully aware of our dependence on God's grace.

The lives we live are possible thanks to the enlivening presence of God. The inspiration that lends genius to our work, skill to our hands, balance to our bodies, and grace to our bearing is God's gift.

But in acknowledging that gift—in receiving it with open hands—we also embrace incredible power. Indeed, one could argue that it is all but impossible to ask God-questions without the gift of humility. Joan Chittister observes:

> Humility and contemplation are the invisible twins of the spiritual life. One without the other is impossible. In the first place, there is no such thing as a contemplative life without the humility that takes us beyond the myth of our own grandeur to the cosmic grandeur of God. In the second, once we really know the grandeur of God we get the rest of life—ourselves included—in perspective.[23]

It is a shriveling of our souls, then, that experiences humility as oppression. Humility and only humility can guide us, protect us from excess, and alert us to the difference between the exercise of freedom that acknowledges our responsibility to God and one another and an exercise of freedom that brings attention to itself. The great failing of fundamentalism is its tendency to replace humility with laws that enforce divine direction. The great failing of fundamentalism's critics is often the spiritual pride that refuses to acknowledge that creativity arises out of humble discipline.

Humility is necessary because it safeguards and deepens a process of discovery that is never the same from moment to moment but requires the strength and wisdom to respond to ever changing circumstances.

When I taught New Testament studies on a regular basis, I had no small number of students who were anxious to understand the life of the early Christians as a key to understanding how they themselves should live. In one way, it was an admirable goal, and I was always reluctant to question them too quickly about their motives. In another way, of course, it was a fragile enterprise fraught with problems.

The distance between our cultural, social, and religious horizon and that of first-century Palestine is evident everywhere you turn in the biblical text, and there are often dramatic differences within the text itself as you turn from book to book. The differences range from basic assumptions about life—including the place of the individual and the role of community—to more mundane matters, such as diet. But as you begin to identify the differing threads that make up the fabric of their lives and ours, those things that appear to be profound and those that seem mundane slip and blur. Slowly and then abruptly, the features that lend the biblical stories an immediacy that speaks to us take their place alongside the considerable differences that lend those same stories a very foreign feeling.

As a result, it becomes clear that we may be able to talk about commonalities with the biblical stories from time to time and, more often, about the spirit of the text or trajectories of faith. But our own world keeps changing, and I came to see that my students were making sweeping and problematic assumptions about the guidance they could expect by simply holding up their Bibles against the lives that we live.

Whatever guidance we can find in the Bible and whatever measure of inspiration we ourselves can bring to the effort of finding and doing the will of God, spiritual humility is an indispensable key. A willingness to be led by God is part and parcel of what it means to be human, and the key to remaining fully human. This willingness need not be experienced as loss. Indeed, it is threaded through with wonder at being named God's daughter or son. But without it, there is no means of hearing God in the midst of life's noise and distractions.

The freedom to be creative is not an end itself. It is instead the vehicle through which the life of God deepens in us. Or to put it another way, the choices we make are not as important as the fact that we make them in response to God's love.

To be sure, in the moment that we make a particular decision it carries considerable significance. We need to be aware of the impact that our decision may have on others. We are obligated to consider the consequences of our actions. And we are obliged to make choices that are morally responsible.

There is another sense, however, in which the decisions we make have a transcendent significance that depends less on the choices we make than on the way in which we make them. We are not making decisions that are simply more or less charitable, more or less moral, or more or less responsible—we are also making decisions that either do or do not take our relationship with God seriously. Appropriately, then, Thomas Merton once prayed:

My Lord God, I have no idea where I am going. I do not see the road ahead of me. I cannot know for certain where it will end. Nor do I really know myself, and the fact that I think I am following your will does not mean that I am actually doing so. But I believe that the desire to please you does in fact please you. And I hope I have that desire in all that I am doing. I hope that I will never do anything apart from that desire. And I know that if I do this you will lead me by the right road, though I may know nothing about it. Therefore, I will trust you always though I may seem to be lost and in the shadow of death. I will not fear, for you are ever with me, and you will never leave me to face my perils alone.[24]

Acknowledging the inevitable ambiguity that is part and parcel of life, Merton underlines what is in fact most important: "But I believe that the desire to please you does in fact please you."

A children's story will help me make the point in a different way, although I cannot say for a certainty that its author had the point I am about to make in mind. Written in 1961, Norton Juster's book *The Phantom Tollbooth* is an intriguing children's story with a not-so-childlike message, based on the fanciful tale of a young boy, Milo, who unwraps a mysterious package marked "one genuine turnpike tollbooth." Passing through the tollbooth, Milo, accompanied by his dog Tock and a resident of the Kingdom of Wisdom called "the Humbug," begins a series of adventures that tell a story on two levels: one on the level of children's fantasy, and the other a sidelong commentary on life. The opening lines of chapter 9, entitled "It All Depends How You Look at Things," tell a story that is an important part of that commentary:

> Soon all traces of Dictionopolis had vanished in the distance and all those strange and unknown lands that lay between the kingdom of words and the kingdom of numbers stretched before them. It was late afternoon and the dark-orange sun floated heavily over the distant mountains. A friendly, cool breeze slapped playfully at the car, and the long shadows stretched out lazily from the trees and the bushes.
>
> "Ah, the open road!" exclaimed the Humbug, breathing deeply, for he now seemed happily resigned to the trip. "The spirit of adventure, the lure of the unknown, the thrill of a gallant quest. How very grand indeed." Then, pleased with himself, he folded his arms, sat back, and left it at that.
>
> In a few more minutes they had left the open countryside and driven into a dense forest. "THIS IS THE SCENIC ROUTE: STRAIGHT AHEAD TO POINT OF VIEW" announced a rather large road sign; but, contrary to its statement, all that could be seen were more trees. As the car rushed along, the trees

grew thicker and taller and leafier until just as they'd hidden the sky completely, the forest abruptly ended and the road bent itself around a broad promontory. Stretching below, to the left, the right, and straight ahead, as far as anyone could see, lay the rich green landscape through which they had been traveling.

"Remarkable view," announced the Humbug, bouncing from the car as if he were responsible for the whole thing.

"Isn't it beautiful?" gasped Milo.

"Oh, I don't know," answered a strange voice. "It all depends on how you look at things."

"I beg your pardon?" said Milo, for he didn't see who had spoken.

"I said it depends on how you look at things," repeated the voice.

Milo turned around and found himself staring at two very neatly polished brown shoes, for standing directly in front of him (if you can use the word "standing" for anyone suspended in mid-air) was another boy just about his age, whose feet were easily three feet off the ground. . . .

"How do you manage to stand up there?" asked Milo, for this was the subject which most interested him.

"I was about to ask you a similar question," answered the boy, "for you must be much older than you look to be standing on the ground."

"What do you mean?" Milo asked.

"Well," said the boy, "in my family everyone is born in the air, with his head at exactly the height it's going to be when he's an adult, and then we all grow towards the ground. When we're fully grown up or, as you can see, grown down, our feet finally touch. Of course there are a few of us whose feet never reach the ground no matter how old we get, but I suppose it's the same in every family."

He hopped a few steps in the air, skipped back to where he started, and then began again.

"You certainly must be very old to have reached the ground already."

"Oh no," said Milo seriously. "In my family we all start on the ground and grow up, and we never know how far until we actually get there."

"What a silly system." The boy laughed. "Then your head keeps changing its height and you always see things in a different way? Why, when you're fifteen things won't look at all the way they did when you were ten, and at twenty everything will change again."

"I suppose so," replied Milo, for he had never really thought about the matter.

"We always see things from the same angle," the boy continued. "It's much less trouble that way. Besides, it makes more sense to grow down and not up."[25]

The definition of "growing up" in our world shifts to some degree from culture to culture. But in general terms, the process is often marked by a similar set of values: achievement; the attainment of wealth, influence, and position; and the assumption of "adult" responsibilities. In some circles "growing up" takes on the added connotation of learning to cope with adult realities and losing a certain amount of innocence—taking on that slightly jaundiced, worldly-wise perspective that only someone who has "been there, done that, and got a T-shirt" can possess.

On this reading, wisdom comes with experience, initiation, and personal growth. A largely do-it-yourself affair, this notion of growing up is well in sync with the individualism of our culture. And there is no need to ground the process of growing up in anything larger than our own lives. It is a bit like becoming a member of a fraternity or sorority, only the club is much larger and everyone sagely agrees that the stakes are higher.

By contrast, proving the will of God is a matter of "growing down." The discerning woman or man is not one who knows more things but one who knows things, as it were, in the way that God knows things. In this sense, having been there and done that counts for very little if you haven't been there and done that with God. In fact, this version of maturity is something people can possess and, at the same time, appear to be a bit foolish, naive, or vulnerable in the face of "adult realities."

But don't be misled—this is not a milquetoast wisdom, a dull, vacuous, bumbling, "life's a box of chocolates" worldview. It can be tough, tenacious, and fully aware of the liabilities in living in this way. The person who grows down is alert to the losses that can be incurred, including the loss of all the other trappings that go along with choosing to grow down instead of up—influence, power, and the T-shirt. On a lifelong pilgrimage, the person who grows down is also one who waits patiently for wisdom, knowing that the one view from *above us* is God's.

The choices we make should be shaped by a love of God and others.

Given our finite nature, the choices we make are always flawed. The future is always in the making, and when it arrives, we may well discover that we have acted too hastily, misread the circumstances in which we find ourselves, or made a decision without enough information. There are far too many variables, far too many unknowns. A colleague of mine and I were talking one day about the task of advising students, and he mentioned that over thirty years ago he and his wife were involved in a program called Lifework Planning, designed to assist young married couples in planning their futures. These young people answered questions dealing with the number of children they might like to have, the kind of place they would like to live, and the kind of work they would like to do. The only thing that was predictable about the process was the fact that, in retrospect, there was nothing predictive about the "lifework planning" they did.

Such efforts are probably of some value—they do get us thinking. And answering the questions with another person can stimulate conversation. When it's all done, we probably know one another better. But to think that we can map out our lives or that we should be able to read a hidden agenda into the random character of the choices we make would be a mistake. It may well be that the most important lesson we can learn from life's dizzying freedom is utter dependence on God.

But that dependence is not a passive approach to life that waits for God's guidance to fall from heaven, as if it could be given independent of our thoughts and experiences. That dependence leads us to make choices that arise out of the love God has for us. As Augustine observes, "Love, and do what you will. If you keep silence, keep silence in love. Whether you exclaim, exclaim in love; whether you correct, correct in love; whether you forebear, forebear in love. Let love's root be within you, and from that root nothing but good can spring."[26] He is not talking about a vague, amorphous, or romantic notion of love. Rooted as it is in Augustine's own triage theology, the love he describes is one modeled by God and marked, for that reason, by an unconditional commitment that is much more demanding than the self-invested and fragile sense of attraction that dominates contemporary notions of love.

Love of this kind requires that we take responsibility for the ways in which our choices shape the world as the object of God's love. To do that, we need more than good intentions, a gentle spirit, or an ide-ology that describes the way we think things ought to be. Instead, we are called on to listen carefully for the movement of God's spirit in the world. Where that spirit is diminished or distorted, we are called on to make choices that resist the harm that is done as a result. Where there is an opportunity to make the spirit of God felt, we are called on to do what we can to be the bearers of God's presence in the world. It is almost like having been asked by God to gently cradle, preserve, and protect the world in the palms of our hands. On any given day, that delicate, daunting task takes shape in the people we meet and the situations in which we find ourselves.

Having grasped this, we can finally put aside yet another way in which we might have misunderstood what is meant by proving the will of God: we are not here to prove ourselves, to probe and discover our own needs. Instead, we are invited to ask: What do God and oth-ers need of us? To find the answers to that question is to find and do the will of God.

Spiritual Exercises for Proving the Will of God

- How important is certainty in your life? What experiences brought you to this place of needing certainty?

- What has been the impact of your desire for certainty on decisions you have made in the past? Give examples of how your decisions might have been framed differently had you concluded that God does not have a to-do list.

- If proving the will of God is an open-ended process, what are the emotional or intellectual obstacles in your life that keep you from living in this newfound freedom?

- Are those obstacles legitimate, or do they mask your need to surrender to proximate authorities rather than to God?

- Do you identify humility with weakness? If so, why? What would genuine humility look like in your life?

- Think of someone close to you right now. What are that person's needs, and how can you lovingly help meet those needs?

- In addressing those needs creatively, what do you feel called to "prove"?

Five

LISTENING FOR
THE VOICE OF GOD

Behold God beholding you . . . and smiling.
Anthony de Mello[1]

Listening for the voice of God has never been an easy task, and stories as well as theories abound about how, when, and where the voice
of God can be heard. Imbedded in the ancient Christian story that
follows are a number of the strategies that people have employed to
open themselves to God's leading:

One of the Egyptian fathers, seeking a sign of divine approval for his long years of monastic devotion, was told that
his sanctity was nothing compared to that of a common grocer in a nearby town. On going to study this man very carefully, the monk found him occupied with his vegetables
amid the noise and hurry of the city streets, attentive to the
needs of all those coming to him. Even as night came on,
with the people growing rowdy, singing loudly in the streets,
the man stayed at his task, helping latecomers with their
needs. In exasperation the monk finally blurted out, "How
can you ever pray with noise like this?" The grocer looked
around, feeling compassion for the people that made up his

ordinary life, and answered very simply. "I tell myself they're all going to the kingdom," he said. "They're concentrating with single-minded attention on what they do, singing songs with all the joy they can muster. See how they prepare for the kingdom of God without even knowing it! How can I do less myself than to praise in silence the God they inadvertently celebrate in song?" That night the old monk walked slowly back to his cell, knowing himself to have received— from a grocer, no less—an important lesson in the craft of desert attentiveness.[2]

The old monk expects to be recognized for his devotion, and he is surprised that he is not. In stressing his devotion, the story hints at the ever greater levels of self-denial that monastic orders have sometimes observed to ensure a closeness to God that their way of life by itself failed to achieve. More time in silence, more prayers said more often, lives lived with fewer and fewer of life's creature comforts— these and other approaches have shaped life in monasteries from time to time; and have often been at the heart of some efforts to found entirely new monastic communities. As the story implies, the practice of silence and a regular cycle of prayers have played an important role in the attempt to find and do the will of God. The old monk is appalled by the noise that surrounds the grocer, and he finds it impossible to believe that the man can hear or speak to God above the din of daily life. But he does.

In the Middle Ages there were also those who searched for an approach to listening for God that was structured around a rather more deliberate effort to examine the movement of one's inner emotions and to weigh the variables when making a decision in order to come as close as possible to a choice that might honor God. Probably the most significant example is the literature that has grown out of the approach used by the followers of Ignatius of Loyola in attempting to decide whether to found the new religious order that we know today as the Jesuits, or the Society of Jesus. Ignatius gave a great deal of attention to the task of naming the emotions that shape our inner lives. One could almost describe his spiritual exercises, as they are called, as ways to name and isloate the jealousy, anger, and a host of other deep-seated emotions that might mislead us in our perceptions of God's will.

But Ignatius paid less attention to the actual task of finding and doing the will of God. If there is an Ignatian method, as such, it arises instead out of the efforts of later scholars to distill an approach from the records we have of the conversations between Ignatius and his followers about founding the order. Based on that record, the Jesuit scholar Jules Toner, for example, has outlined "a method for communal discernment of God's will" that has nine steps—or more, depending on how you count them:

- The formulation of genuine alternatives

- An effort to become informed

- Prayerful reflection on the alternatives

- Private reflection by each participant in the decisionmaking process

- The presentation of reasons for each alternative

- Prayerful reflection on the reasons identified

- Evaluation of the reasons given

- Prayerful reflection on the evaluations and further evaluation

- Voting[3]

This Ignatian approach can be very helpful for groups, particularly when they are faced with making difficult or momentous decisions, because it provides a map for the process. Often in a group setting much of what causes anger, frustration, and suspicion has less to do with the decision made than with *how* the decision is made. If people feel that they have been treated unfairly, or if they have a different understanding of when and how a decision will be made, then the triumph of another point of view almost always generates ill will. Speaking as a veteran of both academic and ecclesiastical circles, I can say this with certainty. As I have often had occasion to say, and as I have often been told: "The politics in both institutions are so dirty (that is, the process of decisionmaking is violated so often) because the stakes are so small!"

The difficulty with the Ignatian process is that—with an occasional exception—most individuals cannot possibly carry on their daily lives relying on such a complex process. And of course, as Jesuit thinkers themselves observe, even the application of steps as thoughtful as these to complex group decisions can be useless unless the participants possess what we all intuitively seek—the freedom that emerges from a sense of connection with God and makes much if not all of what we do the product of a fluid and effortless inner conversation with God.[4]

It is that sense of *effortless inner conversation* that I am interested in helping you discover. So, in the pages that follow, I want to affirm a means of listening that nurtures that inner space in monk and grocer alike—in you and in me. The recommendations I make here cannot be described as steps. In fact, it is not as important to remember the suggestions outlined here as it is to remember the kind of listening they commend. They do not constitute a method, and they do not guarantee an answer.

As you already know from reading this far, I do not think that we are looking for items on a to-do list at all. Instead, it is my hope that these suggestions will nurture the kind of intimacy out of which you are able to exercise the freedom that belongs to the children of God—children who are invited to probe and explore, discovering the will of God in the process.

For that reason, the best way to think of this chapter is as a guide to creating space for the kind of intimacy that lets you listen in a way that gives you that freedom—not as a goal but as the energy that flows naturally from such intimacy. The suggestions, then, are these:

- Listen to God like someone in love.

- Listen to God for the sake of listening to God.

- Listen holistically.

- Listen with freedom.

- Listen with your life.

- Find a way to listen here and now.

Listen to God Like Someone in Love

In these days of strained relationships, to argue that we should listen to God like someone in love is to run any number of risks. We are so completely clueless about the nature of love that the mere suggestion that our relationship with God should be conditioned by it can strike us as outrageous, provocative, distracting, or innocuous.

Most of us would prefer to hold God at arm's length—close enough to help in a time of crisis, but far enough away to avoid the kind of attachment that might influence how we live our lives. And so for many of us the suggestion to listen to God as though we are in love with God will seem far too earnest.

Factor in the widespread idea that there is only one right way to show that love and many will instantly feel that it is beyond them. I see that happen a great deal in religious communities. A handful of people are outspoken about their faith or use positions of leadership to make a case for the way in which they love God as *the* way to love God. Instantly, people move away from the center, like the particles in a centrifuge.

Those pressing a singular way of showing love are convinced that the movement is part of an inevitable spiritual winnowing—the chaff being separated from the wheat, the wheat from the tares, the sheep from the goats. The self-congratulatory—if appropriately saddened—righteous few usually struggle very little with the process. Unfortunately, many of those driven away are alienated not by their own refusal to accept the truth—because the righteous remnant may not be right, or even reacting to the truth at all—but rather by the ugliness of what they see. Those who are driven away are also likely to be alienated by their impression that the model they have been given for loving God is the only model available. Sorrow and sometimes anger set in. Some move quietly away from their communities and traditions. Others, deeply hurt, strike out, attempting either to subvert their communities or to hurt them back by moving as far as possible in the other direction.

No race, no creed, no theological or social position is completely innocent of such brutal behavior. And of course, the great sadness is that, with the narrowing of the name of God, not only do we see less of God, but for many people it actually becomes very difficult to love God.

It is possible to love God in a variety of ways. Two, it is important to realize that our ability to find and do the will of God is deeply dependent on our capacity for loving God.

The first point ought to be evident, but often it isn't. Living in Jerusalem some years ago, I took a group of students to the Church of the Holy Sepulchre on at least two separate occasions—once to get a sense of the place in all its religious and archaeological complexity, and once as a part of the stations of the cross, a spiritual prayer exercise that moves from site to site along the probable route that Jesus walked on the way to the cross. Located today in the heart of the Old City, the Church of the Holy Sepulchre is the likely site of Jesus's death and burial.

Erected, destroyed, and rebuilt on that site over a period of centuries, the church is a jumble of chapels, altars, and candle stands; and in every part of it a different tradition is represented. On the roof are the Coptic and Ethiopian chapels; on what might be characterized as the main floor are chapels belonging to the Greek Orthodox and Latin or Roman Catholic traditions; and elsewhere is space devoted to the Syrian Orthodox and Armenian Orthodox Christians. Each displays its love of God in a unique way—differences in worship calendars, feast days, traditions, and rituals are intertwined with still other differences in language, skin color, and history.

Unfortunately, rather than this riot of diversity reflecting exploratory and free-wheeling expressions of love for God, the history of the place is enmeshed in long and storied cross-claims to preeminence. As a result, in 1852 leaders crafted a document called "The Status Quo of Holy Places"; still in effect to this day, it designates which chapels belong to whom and entrusts the key to the church to a Muslim family.[5]

Sad as it is to see all this jockeying for position, the fact remains that the ways in which we love God are not as singular as any one claimant to the church in the Old City might want to suggest. Marked by such dramatic diversity, the Holy Sepulchre is, in spite of itself, testimony to the fact that people can, do, and indeed *must* love God in ways that are radically different even within a single tradition. Such differences are deeply rooted and enmeshed in the shape of our lives, which differ radically from culture to culture and from life to life.

A love for God that reflects those differences is evidence of a relationship that is owned and experienced in much the same way that the relationship between two people is colored by specific memories and signs of affection. Truth be told, given the number of communal as well as individual differences that come into play, I am actually more surprised as time passes that we can gather at all around common understandings about how to love God than I am at the ways in which we differ over it.[6]

So here is the first point to be made: find a way to love God that harmonizes with the tradition in which you find yourself. In the final analysis, God is probably a bit like the best of valentines—not nearly so concerned about *how* she is remembered as about *being* remembered in the first place!

The second point to make is this: loving of God is not an optional extra or a passion for fanatics. It is a defining love out of which grows the peace, belonging, and sense of direction that we seek. As I put it earlier, our ability to find and do the will of God is deeply dependent on our capacity for loving God. A hunger for God's will cannot be grafted onto a life lived on other terms. It has to flow from a life lived in vital connection with God. Much of the frustration we experience in finding and doing God's will seems to originate here, and there are a number of reasons for it. But one in particular is worth noting: We blithely suppose that we can have the benefits of a relationship with God without the effort of nurturing the love in which it is grounded.

In a world marked by broken relationships of one kind or another, this expectation is not surprising. We want intimacy without sacrifice, relationships on our own terms, emotional highs without lows, getting without giving. These are not the patterns that foster love, however, and that is why many of our relationships flounder in the way they do.

It should not surprise us that the same is true of our relationship with God. When Jesus taught that in loving others we love God, I am convinced that he was not only urging his hearers to be loving but giving expression to a principle deeply at work in our lives. If we cannot comprehend that our lives are deeply dependent on not only receiving love but giving love, then we are not likely to recognize the same deep rhythm at work in our relationship with God.

So if we live our lives in a way that is uninformed by that kind of love and then we suddenly seek God in a crisis or at an important crossroad, it is small wonder that God seems remote and unmoved by our need. It is, if you will, a bit like accosting someone on a sidewalk and demanding, "Meet my need." If intimacy is missing, it may be because we have failed to nurture it.

Finding and doing the will of God is not a matter of locating that one thing on a divine to-do list with your name alongside it. Finding and doing the will of God is a creative, life-giving response to the world about you that flows from a love of God.

Deus Ex Machina or Divine Lover of Souls

In high school and then again in college, I was often assigned Greek dramas to read. Acted out in the ancient theaters of Athens and other major cities, these plays were originally produced on stages that were sparsely appointed, with very little scenery. Above the stage there often hung a crane, or *mechané*, that consisted of ropes and pulleys and allowed airborne characters to fly to and from the stage, often in a winged chariot. This was obviously a handy device for introducing gods into the play, and in due time the arrival of such divine figures became known as a *deus ex machina*, or "god from the machine." Because the sudden appearance of gods in a play often resolved a situation that was otherwise unresolvable, slowly the phrase came to refer to any artificial, improbable, or contrived resolution to a difficulty in a plot.

That device and its role in Greek tragedy describe, it seems to me, precisely the problem with how we relate to God. The plot in our lives goes on without reference to the divine. We make choices, climb the ladders that life provides, indulge our needs and fantasies. Then, in the midst of a crisis, we call out for the crane to lower God into the story—just long enough to resolve a kink in the plot that might otherwise go unresolved.

The skeptic is likely to argue that there is no God and that therefore the lesson to be drawn from the illustration is that hope in God is misplaced. In real life there is no crane and no God. But the absence of God is not the problem. God is there on the stage, from the beginning. The problem is that if we look for God at all we tend to look for a *deus ex machina* when we should be attentive to the movement of things on the stage of our lives all the time.

That is why organic metaphors for the spiritual life, including trees and other living organisms, are used in biblical literature, and that is why they are particularly apt. The person whose life is imbedded in and shaped by communion with God does the will of God by drawing on that experience and on that relationship with God, not on something from outside that occasionally intersects with his or her life. So, the Psalmist observes, "Happy are those . . . [whose] delight is in the law of the Lord . . . they are like trees planted by streams of water which yield their fruit in its season, and their leaves do not wither" (Psalm 1:1–3).[7]

And that is also why the Bible uses images of love and romance. It may well be that the Song of Songs was originally written as a love poem. But fully aware of its romantic content, both Jewish and Christian interpreters have long thought that it conveys appropriate images of the spiritual life as well.[8] Preaching from the Song and alluding to the same theme in Paul's letter to the Corinthians, Bernard of Clairvaux writes:

Who is it whom your soul loves, for whom you inquire? Has he no name? Who are you and who is he? I speak like this because of the strange manner of speech and extraordinary disregard for names, quite different from the rest of the Scriptures. But in this marriage-song it is not the words which are to be pondered, but the affections behind them. Why is this, except because the sacred love which is the subject of the whole canticle cannot be described in the words of any language, but are expressed in deed and truth? And love speaks everywhere; if anyone desires to grasp these writings, let him love. It is vain for anyone who does not love to listen to this song of love, or to read it, for a cold heart cannot catch fire from its eloquence. The man who does not know Greek cannot understand Greek, nor can anyone without Latin understand someone speaking Latin. . . . So, too, the language of love will be meaningless jangle to one who does not love, like sounding brass or tinkling cymbal.[9]

Listen to God for the Sake of Listening to God

In the search for the kind of intimacy that Bernard describes, there is no substitute for listening. But nothing could be more alien to us.

Serving as director of programs in religious education and spirituality at Washington National Cathedral, I had responsibility for a space on the crypt level of the cathedral devoted to silent prayer and meditation. Called the Center for Prayer and Pilgrimage, it is adjacent to Resurrection Chapel. Many of the self-selected volunteers who serve there understand the importance of listening to God. So they were frequently frustrated by how uninterested in the center the vast majority of visitors seemed to be.

We had a number of conversations that revolved around the question of how we might make the center's presence better known.

In truth, however, the difficulty never lay in "promoting" the center as much as it did in acknowledging the adverse angle at which an invitation to listen intersects with our culture. The distance from the streets of Washington to the center was not as great as the spiritual, social, and cultural distances between the world of contemplative prayer and the larger world of which we are a part.

Surrounded by a culture devoted to "getting the message across," North Americans and larger and larger parts of the rest of the Western world as well are bombarded with messages that everyone is sending and to which few are listening. Often referred to as the "information age," our era is unlikely ever to merit the label the "age of wisdom." Wisdom comes from listening, from observing. Wisdom presupposes a process of discernment, of weighing and sifting. By contrast, information is the mere collection of data, and our technological infrastructure is designed to record, transmit, and store more data than any human being can hope to use.

In self-defense, we have become adept at mining and selecting the information we need in order to accomplish our own specific goals. That is an understandable response to an avalanche of information. But if we move only between the two poles of the avalanche of information, on the one hand, and the immediate use we might make of that information, on the other, it is difficult, if not impossible, to break with that pattern when we want to listen for something deeper.[10] And an ever larger number of us are hardwired by our cultural surroundings to do anything but listen. At a retreat one man told the group, "The difference in my training and my wife's is obvious. As a school counselor, she sees a gap in a conversation as an opportunity to digest what has been said. Coming from the world of sales, I see it as a cue to say something."

His response was good-humored and self-deprecating. And if he had pointed to a difference that was confined to the professional behavior of sales agents and counselors, his comments might have had little significance. But in fact, the behavior he pointed to is far more widespread than that; the pace and volume of our lives are causing many people to forget how to listen. Those of us who are trained to listen, allowed to listen, or able to find time to listen are part of a smaller and smaller fraction of society. It has been argued in fact that the world in which we live is remapping our psyches, yielding "a Protean self"—a "many-sided self in constant motion" that mimics the behavior of the shape-shifting Greek god of the seas, Proteus.[11]

Some argue that this is a positive development and that our protean nature is evidence of our adaptability.[12] But it is interesting to note that even for the Proteus of Greek mythology, constant motion and shape-shifting was a means of escape, not a way of being. Hiding all that he knew, Proteus would begin to change form only when, during his midday slumber, someone seized him and tried to force him to answer a question.

Our fluid, shape-shifting character may be evidence of our ability to survive. But escape is not a substitute for living. If the only two poles that shape life are the random content of the avalanche coming our way and the pragmatic use that we make of that information, then the shape of our lives will be free-floating. We will react, but not reflect. We will "grow up," but not "down."[13] Although we may not be able to completely change the world around us, we can and must find a way to listen for God and listen for its own sake. To do otherwise would be to strip-mine our experience of God in the same way that we strip-mine the rest of life, looking for a fragment of something to use "here" and another to use "there."

Practically speaking, there are a number of ways in which we can try to listen to God, some of which fit more readily with our personalities, our schedules, our resources, or our prior experiences. I will make three suggestions on the subject here.

One way to begin is by finding a point in the day that permits time for listening. One of my students found that her day presented

her with just such an occasion during which silence was possible—
an odd wedge of time in the late afternoon before her children arrived home was an ideal time for prayer, given the shape of her
responsibilities.

Most of us, however, would be hard-pressed to find a moment of
silence in our day, if only because we have been conditioned to fill
our days with noise. Modern life has given us any number of means
for doing it. Radio, television, and cell phones have all pressed silence to the margins of our lives, and many of us are not aware of
how often we invite such noise to invade our lives. We spend a few
moments in reflective prayer, and we suddenly remember that there
is someone we should phone. We start our cars and turn on the radio
as if the car would not run without the radio on.

Another means of finding time to listen for the sake of listening is
to go on retreat. The word *retreat* has its origins in the fourteenth
century and originally meant to withdraw in the face of pressure
from an enemy on the field of battle. The earliest surviving references to *retreat* as an opportunity for spiritual practice date to the
eighteenth century. For that reason, it is not surprising that at least
some of those early references are laced with the rather more negative, or at least defensive, connotation of retreat from a spiritual
enemy.[14] But the kind of retreat I have in mind is much more expan-
sive and open-ended, in the same way that time spent with a good
friend is not necessarily dictated by crisis or an identifiable need.
One word of caution, however: not all retreats are equally good for
listening. Some retreats are really conferences in disguise and crowd
out the opportunity for prayer and reflection with workshops and lectures. Retreats shaped by the Benedictine and Ignatian traditions are
often good alternatives.

A third approach to listening is pilgrimage—travel to and from a
holy site with time at the site for prayer, reflection, and devotion. Pilgrimage can be taken to a shrine, a cathedral, or any place of special

spiritual and historical significance. The word *pilgrimage* has spiritual associations that are older and more basic than those of the word *retreat*, and the practice itself is older yet. Behind the walls of the Armenian Orthodox chapel in Jerusalem's Church of the Holy Sepulchre, for example, is evidence that Christians made pilgrimages to the site of Jesus's crucifixion very early in church history.[15] And the practice of pilgrimage is rooted even more deeply in the ancient Hebrew ritual of marking a place where God was encountered with a new name, a small shrine, or even a simple pile of stones.

Pilgrimage has a checkered history in the church, and some in the Protestant tradition in particular have felt that the practice is completely unnecessary considering that God is present everywhere.[16] But pilgrimage is not a matter of going to a special place in order to find God. Pilgrimage is a matter of going to a special place so that God can find us. Part of a "tactile spirituality," pilgrimage concentrates our senses so that God can get our attention in ways that might not otherwise be possible.[17] Over and over again during the time I spent in Jerusalem, I met people who heard God more clearly than they ever had before, thanks to the singular fashion in which the sights, sounds, and even smells of pilgrimage focused their attention. And though it is not necessary to bolster the value of pilgrimage, there are those who argue that the sheer struggle in prayer that marks pilgrimage places makes them powerful sites at which to do some listening.[18]

Alongside these three practices, allow me to offer three caveats, however, that might usefully shape our approach to listening. First, none of what I have suggested means that you need to travel far and wide in order to listen to God. I have a dear friend, now in his eighties, who owns an old and very simple prayer stall from a church that occupies a special place in his apartment. He is long retired from a psychiatric practice and a stint as a flight surgeon, and his health keeps him from traveling long distances now. But the simple way in which he has identified a space in his home provides the kind of physical reminder he needs for the delights of listening for listening's sake.

Second, look for the natural opportunities for listening provided by your life (and this observation, by the way, applies to place as well). Over the years I have had students whose passion for listening to God led them to extraordinary extremes in reorganizing their lives in order to find more time for prayer. I still remember one of my students presenting me with her academic planner, asking my advice about the new regimen she had established for ensuring that she would pray and do other things to deepen her spiritual life. The pace that she set for herself was anything but spacious and life-giving! Five A.M.: "get up, read my Bible." Five-thirty: "pray for a half-hour." Six A.M.: "get ready for class." Seven A.M.: "eat breakfast." The schedule was scripted in the same regimented fashion for every hour of the day, every day of the week. At the time, the schedule reminded me a bit of an interview that was conducted years ago with a U.S. senator:

> "What's it like to be a United States senator?"
>
> "My day is divided into ten- and fifteen-minute increments that are completely at the discretion of my administrative assistant, and if everything goes well, life is hell."[19]

A schedule of that kind is undoubtedly hard on a senator. The metaphor of a regimented schedule should never apply to our spiritual lives, and this student's schedule did look like hell.

A far healthier approach is to look for the seams in our lives. One of my colleagues tells a story about his father that is particularly apt. Bill Bryan is the director of our internship program. A longtime resident of Dallas, his father, Sonny, is well known as the founder of Sonny Bryan's Barbecue, a highly successful restaurant chain that even today, long after his death, continues to command the loyalty of barbecue aficionados. Bill and his brother often worked in their father's first restaurant near Parkland Hospital, and that gave them a chance to watch their father in action. One practice of his that puzzled them was taking personal responsibility for cleaning the restaurant's restrooms. They assumed that there might be a number of reasons he did this: perhaps he didn't feel that anyone else would do the job properly, or perhaps he wanted to demonstrate to those who worked for him that no job was beneath him. Years later, when they finally did ask their father about this practice, he responded: "Oh, I used that time to pray for you, your mother, and the people who worked in the restaurant. You know, no one ever interrupts you while you are cleaning restrooms!" Look for seams in your life.

Third, begin modestly. It is easy to look at the many stories of spiritual devotion and to conclude that you need to carve out extraordinary amounts of time for prayer. One of the mistakes that many people make early on is to set themselves to the task of listening to God for hours on end though they have little or no experience of listening at all. Or they talk to friends who have had the opportunity to go on extended retreats, and they simply despair of ever having the time to do that. Begin more modestly. As a friend of mine who is a spiritual director recommends to many of her directees, if you have never prayed, then begin with a timed electronic toothbrush that runs for a designated period of time. Holding it in your mouth will force you not to talk. You will get a better prayer life and better dental hygiene! It may be modest, but it is a beginning.

Listen Holistically and Not by Halves

"Hearing in halves" is a perennial spiritual challenge. Mark's gospel makes it clear that those around Jesus failed to understand his ministry and message because they listened to him selectively. They

watched him heal and concluded that his ministry was one of healing. They overlooked the fact that Jesus did not heal everyone. They
did not perceive that Jesus linked the healings he did do with the in-
breaking of the Kingdom. They did not grasp that he vigorously dis-
couraged their attempts to highlight those healings. They did not
register the fact that his message focused on the suffering that he
(and his disciples) were about to face.[20]

Our inability to listen holistically has not changed dramatically.
There are those who argue that some lives are not marked by enough
attention to the needs of others and others who argue that our lives
lack a depth of spirituality. There are those who argue that we can be
too cerebral and others who argue that we are not cerebral enough,
those who argue that our spirituality lacks a capacity for love and others who argue that our spirituality lacks a capacity for holiness. In debate after debate, we pit one choice against another.

In these and in other ways we choose to listen to only a part of the
insight our tradition has to offer us into the spiritual life and the will of
God. The spiritual journey inward leads to a journey outward and to
an engagement with the needs of the world. To choose between the
two is to miss something basic to what it might mean to live fully as a
child of God. Spirituality and a life attuned to the heart may keep theology from becoming dry and cerebral. But theology and a thoughtful
approach to one's interior life keep spirituality from becoming dangerous, errant nonsense. Holiness without love is devoid of saving
power—an arid and potentially abusive betrayal of the truth's own
best ends. And love without holiness is devoid of direction—a sentimentalism lacking the strength that renders love reliable.

Some years ago two colleagues of mine raised serious questions
about the way in which spiritual issues are discussed, even among
scholars. Arguing that far too many of us use either-or categories,
they pointed out that we often do our hearing "in halves." Left and
right, conservative and liberal, even those of us who are accustomed

to talking about spiritual and religious matters resort quickly to a simple picture of mutually exclusive choices. In the academic world, hearing in halves may make it easier to explain a given reality, but the price we pay is a loss of subtlety, accuracy, and, more critically, the truth.[21]

In the spiritual life, hearing in halves runs all of these risks and still others. When we fail to listen holistically, we inevitably distort and slow our own spiritual growth. So, for example, a deeply reflective spiritual life that is unaccompanied by an ability to see or respond to the needs of others can be impoverished and marked by a selfishness that erodes the value of our prayer life. Self-invested and self-absorbed, we become the only interesting subject in the center of a spiritual quest in which we figure as the only important participant in our quest, and those around us become little more than adjuncts to our spiritual needs.

By the same token, a life devoted to political work on behalf of others that lacks a contemplative dimension can lose its mooring in something deeper than our politics. And when confronted with setbacks and failures, mere activism can lead to compassion fatigue and a failure of nerve. Without a deeper dependence on God, we may find that caring for others even becomes a substitute for the inner needs that have gone unaddressed in our relationship with God.[22]

The greatest price we pay spiritually when we fail to listen holistically is that we receive so much less of what God has to give us. Like children with our hands full of toys on Christmas morning before the packages under the tree are even opened, our spiritual lives are dominated by half-hearing that makes full hearing more impossible. And when those half-heard truths harden and become our reality, they can, worse yet, become a substitute for God.

There are countless reasons for our failure to hear everything that God might want to tell us. For some, it may be a lack of spiritual and intellectual discipline. Many assume in fact that the spiritual life *ought* to be marked by ease and that any approach to it that bears the marks of something rather more daunting is the product of excessive zeal.

Additionally, we live in an increasingly "unconscious" society in which we live our lives at a pace that makes reflective, holistic hearing intrinsically more challenging. We haven't been taught to reflect. For those who do manage to make space for reflection, there are often very few conversation partners along the way and countless distractions.

On a more personal or autobiographical level, we can also harbor an unconscious desire to avoid the harder half of the listening we need to do. Thus, when we listen to this extent, it is tempting—in the strongest sense of that word—to identify half of the truth with all of it and avoid the hard truths we do not want to hear.

Years ago I spent a good deal of time in college competing in speech contests, and more often than not I was involved in debate or extemporaneous and impromptu speech events. At one university where we competed, they held a hearing contest. It consisted of three separate stages, each followed by a quiz on the material. In the first part of the competition, we listened to a tape of a short story read at a normal reading rate. That was not particularly difficult, and since we knew that we would be required to take a quiz, we were prepared to focus. In the second phase of the contest, we listened to another story read at twice the normal reading rate. That was a bit more challenging! Then, in the third part of the contest, the reading rate was dropped back to a normal speed, but this time we were introduced to two more stories read simultaneously. To make matters more difficult, we were instructed to focus on one of the stories, but we were quizzed on the content of both. In this way, they tested not only our ability to focus but our residual memory of the other story as well.

It is always great fun describing the details of this memorable contest, and in recent years it has occurred to me that the third stage of that contest is also an apt metaphor for the challenge we face in hearing God speak to us. In a sense, we live lives in which we have been told to focus on one story—the story that our culture tells, with its own plot, its own cast of characters, and a distinctive set of values. The story we really need to hear, however, is the other one, the one that is there all the time but to which we give only fragmentary attention—the story that God tells. Shaped by the fruits of the Spirit (love, peace, patience, and kindness), it is the story that never tires of the story in which we become more fully God's with each passing day (Galatians 5: 22–26.).

We can hear God's story. We need to hear God's story. But depending on the extent to which we allow other things to occupy our attention, we hear either more or less of what is said. There are times when we are drawn into the story. We are attracted by the way the plot unfolds. The central actors in the drama suggest a very different approach to life, and we are excited about the possibility of living life in a radically different way. But then the old story line—the one on which the authorities tell us we'll be quizzed—begins to assert itself, and God's story fades from consciousness. As a friend of mine points out, many of us don't need to know any more about the will of God than we already do because we already know more than we are prepared to do.

Finding and doing God's will entails profound change and a willingness to surrender other stories to which we have become deeply attached.[23] And surrender is one of the most difficult spiritual disciplines to practice—in part because surrender is, by definition, difficult, and in part because each time we live too deeply into the stories the world tells us, the need to surrender pulls at our lives in a different way. Pride, security, fear, the uncertainty of letting go—all carry a different kind of real and perceived loss.

The Ignatian tradition and others refer to that experience as desolation.[24] And while the tradition teaches that desolation can be a very good thing in the spiritual long run, it is almost always likely to spark resistance. The ability to name that resistance and its causes provides an opening for spiritual growth. That is why so much of the Ignatian tradition is devoted to the task of spiritual ground-clearing, focusing on movements within that might obstruct our ability to hear the voice of God.

Without the ability to name the causes of resistance, the specter of loss takes on a reality that can shape the flow of God's spirit just as surely as the larger rocks on the bed of a stream can shape and channel the water that flows around and over them. Submerged realities—the rocks of our resistance—exert an influence around which an entire life can take shape. Once our resistances are named and identified, it is possible to begin listening holistically.

But listening is not an end in itself. It is the gift that makes it possible to listen with freedom.

Listen with Freedom

At one time I taught Greek on a regular basis, so I have an eccentric interest in grammar. One of the classes I taught introduced students to the entire first year of Greek grammar in the space of six weeks. At the end of one class, two large ex-Marines presented me with a soccer ball signed by the class, and on one panel they had written, "You won't have us to kick around anymore." I counted it a charitable response coming from two Marines.

Of course, teachers often learn as much or more than their students do. One of the things I learned in the course of teaching Greek grammar is that prepositions can make a great deal of difference in the meaning of a phrase or word. That is no less true of English than it is of Greek, and prepositions make a striking difference in the way we use the words *freedom* and *God* (or *Christ*) in the same phrase.

Highlighting prepositions can help, for example, to make sense of the American spiritual landscape and other parts of the Western world. We vacillate between a desire to have "freedom *for* the worship of God" and "freedom *from* the worship of God." The history of spirituality in the United States and in other parts of the West could even be seen as a movement from the one preposition to the other.

The Bill of Rights and early convictions in colonial America about the separation of church and state reflect a desire to ensure freedom *for* worship, spiritual exploration, and devotion, just as struggles between the throne and the church in Rome reflected some of those same struggles in England. Today those struggles are memorialized and preserved in many of our laws. But culturally an increasing number of people talk far more often about freedom *from* those experiences. In fact, an increasing number of books and workshops are devoted to spiritualities that do not necessarily focus on a relationship with God at all.[25]

For and *from* language is also the language of objectification. The spiritual life or a relationship with God is something "out there." We can talk about it, if need be, as something separate from ourselves, and it is even necessary to do that if you are trying to distinguish between the roles of government and God.

Spiritually, however, the motives for using the language of objectification can be very different. There are times when you might want to talk in objective terms about your experience of God. Conversations between people of different faiths may call for that kind of language, and certainly some educational settings call for it. But in the spiritual life the same language can also be used to evade an encounter with God. We can be asked about our experience of God's forgiveness and choose instead to talk about the concept of God's forgiveness. We can be asked about our experience of God in prayer and choose to talk about a theology of prayer. We can even wax at length about the virtues of spiritual life without even talking about God, or having a spiritual life.

But the spiritual life as understood in the Christian tradition cannot thrive on objective language. It is shaped, instead, by a vision of freedom *in* God—or as Paul puts it, *in* Christ. It is subjective, not objective, in nature—an experience, not a topic. And instead of being something that we can simply observe, the spiritual life is a perspective that shapes, informs, and conditions everything else that we see, including our ability to find and do the will of God. The phrase also suggests that freedom is neither something that can be used to provide an opportunity *for* God nor something that can be achieved apart *from* God, but is instead an experience found *in* God.

In a world where our earliest understandings of God are often shaped by the mistaken notion that God is the angry, old (but cosmic!) authoritarian who imposes certain strictures on our lives from outside or above, finding and doing the will of God is shaped for many of us by one of two equally untenable choices.[26] One is an anxious conformity to the strictures that we believe God imposes on us. The other is frustrated or even angry rejection.

As different as those choices appear to be on the surface, they both objectify our relationship with God. God is still "out there," demanding something. As a result, the spiritual life is shaped either by an anxious effort to find the list and complete it (legalism) or by all-out resistance to anything that might present itself as the will of God (libertinism or lawlessness).

Neither approach, however, could be further from the truth. To allow our listening to be shaped by life "in Christ," as Paul suggests, is to listen in creative freedom. To be "in Christ" recognizes our release from guilt and from the painful imprisonment of our brokenness and sin. It is to find ourselves in that creative space. The practice of listening to God is not a matter of being chained to an onerous routine in which an infraction leads to punishment. It is instead the freedom to wade, paddle, splash, and luxuriate in a life-giving stream.

As I was teaching my class at the monastery, this realization recently struck me deeply in terms that I would not have used before. When I go there with the students, we arrive on Sunday evening and begin praying with the community. The first year I taught the course I was, like the students, distracted to some degree by the logistics of our visit.

It is easy for visitors to imagine that those prayers are part of a routine to which the community is chained. One can visualize the abbot taking attendance and throttling those who fail to appear at the appointed hours for prayer. In the first year, as we discussed monastic life, I pointed out that some monastic communities have effectively treated their prayer life in that fashion, but that doing so is not their intention.

The second year I taught the course I arrived ahead of the students and went to the evening prayers on my own. This time the surroundings were familiar, and I was undistracted by what lay ahead. Because the community is seated in the transepts, there was no one visible from the nave where I took my place. As the music and prayers began, it struck me: stepping back into that routine of prayer is like stepping into the stream of God's presence. It stretches endlessly into the past and far beyond into the future. Its message is not, "If you are here all the time, then you might be all right." Its message is one of loving embrace, of welcome, of release to listen without defensiveness, guilt, or fear. It says, effectively, as God has in the past, "Fear not, I am here."

The reason we find it so difficult to listen with freedom lies, I think, in our perception of authority. We instinctively resist the invitation to listen because many of us have been deeply shaped by the conviction that the exercise of authority—the authority of God, the implied authority of life in community, even the structure of spiritual practice—is, by definition, the exercise of control or power. And we have also learned that there are only two ways in which we can relate to that kind of authority. Either we wield power or we are subject to it. So the notion that freedom can be found *in* Christ is a contradiction in terms.

Properly understood, however, authority is not the exercise of power. It is the ability to nurture and preserve creative space. The promise, then, of life *in* Christ and in the space nurtured by prayerful listening is creative, not controlling. Like the scales practiced by a master cellist or the music theory studied by jazz musicians, the "authority" of those experiences is something that, far from crushing creativity, instead unleashes it.

If the boundaries loom large in our thinking from time to time, it is not because God is anxious to enforce those boundaries or narrow the creative space within them. They loom large because we choose to abandon the freedom we are offered in exchange for enslaving ourselves to other gods.

One of the blessings of my life over the last ten years has been the friendship of a number of men and women who are now in their sixties, seventies, and eighties. There is a great deal that you can learn from men and women of that age: they possess wisdom worth appropriating sooner rather than later in life. One example of that wisdom is the freedom they have found in the far larger creative space God has given them. Over and over again my friends have noted that they entered that space only by abandoning the counterfeit freedom they believed freedom *from* God would give them. Having escaped the unacknowledged tyranny of the workplace and its ambitions, as well as their own private obsessions, they have discovered new freedom.

I am sure that discoveries of this kind are partly rooted in the release that comes with retirement, although some of my friends were claiming this freedom long before they retired. Some spiritual experiences are the gift of the changes that come when one part of life ends and another begins. But there should be—and is—a means of claiming at least some of that freedom earlier in life.

In reflecting on the experience of my friends, I've seen that part of their ability to claim that freedom lay in setting aside the kind of time to listen that I have already described. The space we devote to reflection on God's will provides an important opportunity for values to take root in our lives that we would otherwise find it hard to maintain. My friends are people who have found that kind of time, and it has created space in their lives for listening to God.

Generally speaking, however, they are also people who have begun to reframe the way in which they think about life: they are reflecting not simply on the immediate future but on its final chapter. They are not morbid, and among the people I know, they are blessed with a love of life. But they are people who not only have grasped the transient character of much of what this life holds but have come to see it as a window into a deeper life that is already theirs *in* Christ. Their approach to finding and doing the will of God is much more of a piece with the thinking of Paul, who uses both the future and the present tenses to describe eternal life. As a result, in seeking to find and do the will of God, they reach out to people on the margins of their communities; they show interest in people who do not figure in the political calculus of the organizations in which they work; and they exhibit an independence of mind and strength of character that allow them to do what needs to be done. Theirs is the wisdom of an ancient Irish prayer:

> Three wishes I ask of the King
> when I shall part from my body:
> may I have nothing to confess,
> may I have no enemy,
> may I have nothing.[27]

Listen with Your Life

With the giving of the Law, the book of Deuteronomy compulsively adds phrases that underline the ancient Hebrew notion of knowledge. In chapter 5 alone, Moses tells the children of Israel, "You shall learn [the commandments] and *observe them diligently*" (verse 1). In turn, the children of Israel urge Moses, "Tell us everything that the Lord our God tells you, and we will listen *and do it*" (verse 27). And finally, God tells Moses to give the children of Israel the ordinances so that *they may do them in the land*" (verse 31). Listening is always completed in action. Knowledge requires transformation. The ancient Hebrews listened with their lives.

By contrast, for many of us knowledge and transformation are all but unrelated. We hear a great deal, but our lives do not reflect it. There are many reasons for the disconnect. Some of us intellectualize the spiritual life. We "live in our heads." We find it easier to talk about what we think of the spiritual life than to experience the spiritual life. As a result, the hearing we do remains largely abstract.

Others of us fail to embrace change because our capacity for spiritual transformation is diminished by other factors in our lives. Addictions, family history, and any number of other dynamics may make it difficult to respond to the direction that we find in prayer and reflection. This is not to suggest that addiction and other struggles are without a spiritual dimension. At root many of them are in fact spiritual dilemmas, and those who are able to create a space in which they can listen to God are able to do that only because they depend on their faith. But struggles of this kind are also deeply imbedded in problems that require psychological counseling as well as spiritual guidance.

Still others lack a supportive environment. None of us can be spiritual alone, and the effort to respond in a proactive fashion to the listening we do in prayer can be far more difficult if we are surrounded by people who are indifferent, unsympathetic, or hostile to those who value the spiritual life.

But there are other reasons rooted in the contemporary nature of knowing itself. We live in a world in which assimilating knowledge is more akin to sipping from a fire hose than to drinking deeply from a well. We are constantly exposed to information that yields no particular response and to information without a context in our own lives. As a result, much of what we "know" today is not the kind of information on which we can act, and some of it does not even deserve our attention. As sociologists observe, the contemporary challenge is not to acquire knowledge but to determine what is important.

The sheer volume of information to which we are exposed and the way in which it is manipulated has also fostered routine, defensive cynicism. That cynicism serves us well in fending off some of the distractions that contemporary culture throws our way, and it has other constructive functions as well. It can keep us from being misled and alert us to lies. We doubt the truth or sincerity of what we are told and so protect ourselves from being used.

But routine cynicism can also color our approach to listening more generally, ultimately poisoning our relationship with God and with others. A quintessential modern, the philosopher Jean-Paul Sartre, is an excellent, if tragic, example. Deeply scarred by the manipulative behavior of his extended family, Sartre describes the first ten years of his life as ones in which he and his widowed mother were "appendages" to life in the home of his strident and domineering grandfather. Sartre became convinced that expressions of love were designed to control him and that his success in life depended on his own efforts to do the same.[28]

So I'm a promising poodle; I prophesy. I make childish remarks, they are remembered, they are repeated to me. I learn to make others. I make grown-up remarks. I know how to say things "beyond my years" without meaning to. . . . The recipe is simple: you must trust to the Devil, to chance, to emptiness, you borrow whole sentences from grown-ups, you string them together and repeat them without understanding them. In short, I pronounce true oracles, and each adult interprets them as he wishes.[29]

One can easily hear the cynicism in Sartre's reminiscence. He doubts the sincerity of those with whom he lives, and he has been their victim. But he has also learned how to play the same game. As a result, his own words are now meaningless except as a means to an end, and he has become what he most despises.

Sartre's experience would be a matter of historical curiosity if the same corrosive forces that haunted his personal life had not gained wider influence. In many quarters cynicism has become the hallmark of contemporary life. Described by some as "the mud of everyday life," it dominates private and public discourse.[30]

In a social climate dominated by cynicism, our relationship with God cannot go unaffected. It begins to exercise what the monastic tradition calls "the despotism of hidden thoughts."[31] Lives that disintegrate in the wake of sexual misconduct, lies, and abuse are as much the evidence of deep-seated cynicism as they are the product of specific misdeeds. If knowledge is something to be manipulated in order to elicit a specific response from those around us, and if the truth is endlessly malleable, then we inevitably treat a knowledge of God's will in a similar fashion.

But *finding* and *doing* the will of God are two parts of a single phrase because both are inextricably related to one another. You cannot listen without listening with your life. And the two movements belong together in our world just as surely as they belonged together in ancient Israel.

Finding the will of God without doing it—or pretending to do the will of God without having sought it—nurtures lies, fosters pride, and deepens guilt. Like the manna given to the children of Israel in the book of Deuteronomy, if the truth is consumed and becomes a part of us on the day it is given to us, it nourishes us. But if we keep it without consuming it—without making it our own—it putrefies and poisons us.

It is perilously easy to traffic in unlived truths, and the sole antidote is an effort to listen faithfully by giving concrete expression in our lives to what we already know of God's will. This is not an exercise in self-justification or "works righteousness," as the old expression goes. But it is an acknowledgment that *finding* and *doing* the will of God are as inseparable in the spiritual life as breathing in and breathing out:

> You dare your Yes—and experience a meaning.
> You repeat your Yes—and all things acquire a meaning.
> When everything has a meaning, how can you live anything but a Yes.[32]

Listen Here and Now

The life of the artist is much like the life shaped by grace. The following story is told about a performance by the great violinist Itzhak Perlman.

On November 18, 1995, Perlman came onstage to give a concert at Avery Fisher Hall at the Lincoln Center in New York City. If you have ever been to a Perlman concert, you know that getting on stage is no small achievement for him. He was stricken with polio as a child, and so he has braces on both legs and walks with the aid of two crutches.

To see him walk across the stage one step at a time, painfully and slowly, is an unforgettable sight. He walks painfully, yet majestically, until he reaches his chair. Then he sits down slowly, puts his crutches on the floor, undoes the clasps on his legs, tucks one foot back, and extends the other foot forward. Then he bends down and picks up the violin, puts it under his chin, nods to the conductor, and proceeds to play.

Most audiences are accustomed to this ritual. They sit quietly while he makes his way across the stage to his chair. They remain reverently silent while he undoes the clasps on his legs, and they wait until he is ready to play.

But this time something went wrong. Just as he finished the first few bars, one of the strings on his violin broke. You could hear it snap—it went off like gunfire across the room. There was no mistaking what that sound meant.

There was no mistaking what he had to do. People who were there that night figured that he would have to get up, put on the clasps again, pick up the crutches, and limp his way offstage, to either find another violin or else find another string.

But he didn't. Instead, he waited a moment, closed his eyes, and then signaled the conductor to begin again. The orchestra began, and he played from where he had left off. And he played with such passion, power, and purity as had never been heard before.

Of course, anyone knows that it is impossible to play a symphonic work with just three strings, but that night Itzhak Perlman refused to acknowledge it. You could see him modulating, changing, recomposing the piece in his head. At one point it sounded like he was de-tuning the strings to get new sounds from them that they had never made before.

When he finished, there was an awesome silence in the room. And then people rose and cheered. There was an extraordinary outburst of applause from every corner of the auditorium. The audience were all on their feet, screaming and cheering, doing everything they could to show how much they appreciated what he had done.

He smiled, wiped the sweat from this brow, and raised his bow to quiet the audience. And then he said, not boastfully but in a quiet, pensive, reverent tone, "You know, sometimes it is the artist's task to find out how much music you can still make with what you have left."[33]

It is easy to imagine a different set of circumstances as the necessary preamble to listening for the voice of God: more time, a better place to listen, fewer responsibilities, distractions, and interruptions. But people of faith are artists of living, and Perlman is right—there are times when we are called on to find out how much music we can make with three strings instead of four.

There are few spiritual maxims that are found across the religious traditions, but the insistence that God is to be sought *now*, not later, is, as far as I am aware, an all but universal imperative. The Old Testament does not urge us, "Seek God next week." Jesus does not tell his followers, "Sufficient to tomorrow is the evil thereof." Tradition after tradition presses this point. As demanding and ever deepening as our ability to listen for God's voice might be, there is a very real sense in which it is enough to hear what we can hear in this moment.

In a book devoted to getting clear about what it means to find and do the will of God, this may be one of the more liberating observations that needs to be made. We live in a world bent on optimizing our lives. We thrive on techniques and regimens for achieving personal, social, and professional goals. Five steps to a better body, three steps to better relationships, seven steps to financial security. And along with those regimens go a host of other choices to be made: the ultimate gym, the latest in matchmaking, the best investment tools.

In a climate like ours, it is easy to imagine that the same self-help approach will maximize our spiritual lives. But while there is a great deal to be learned about finding and doing the will of God, in point of fact the only thing we can do in this moment is to give ourselves as fully to God as possible in the space available to us. For monk and grocer, for you and me, that much of God's will is easily known.

Spiritual Exercises for Listening for the Voice of God

- Evaluate your own prayer life, asking whether you:

  Listen to God like someone in love

  Listen to God for the sake of listening

  Listen holistically

  Listen with freedom

  Listen with your life

  Find a way to listen here and now

- Which one of these approaches is the most uncomfortable for you and why?

- Identify a specific way in which you could provide space for the Holy Spirit to nurture new growth in your life.

Six

WE-QUESTIONS

Two people, three people, ten people may be in living touch with one another through Him who underlies their separate lives. This is an astounding experience, which I can only describe but cannot explain in the language of science. But in vivid experience of divine Fellowship it is there. We know that these souls are with us, lifting their lives and ours continuously to God and opening themselves, with us, in steady and humble obedience to Him. It is as if the boundaries of our self were enlarged, as if we were within them and as if they were within us.

Thomas R. Kelly[1]

In 1985 the sociologist Robert Bellah and a handful of colleagues published *Habits of the Heart*, a book about the perils of individualism that proved to be something of a media event. The issues it raised continue to lie at the center of a debate about both modern and American life.[2] The book, in Bellah's own view, is both a political and implicitly theological work, and it earned him the National Humanities Medal in 2000.[3] Reflecting on Bellah's achievements, President Bill Clinton noted that the medal was given in recognition of Bellah's "efforts to illuminate the importance of community in American society. A distinguished sociologist and educator, he has raised our awareness of the values that are at the core of our democratic institutions and of the dangers of individualism unchecked by social responsibility."[4]

The literature spawned by *Habits of the Heart* refers repeatedly to "Sheilaism," a term coined by one of the people interviewed by the authors. A young nurse and a veteran of successive rounds of therapy, Sheila Larson used the word to describe her one-of-a-kind, personal faith, and the authors, in turn, broadened its use to describe any spirituality that focuses squarely on the individual and private needs of its adherent.[5]

As the subtitle of Bellah's book indicates, he and his colleagues were interested in individualism and commitment in modern American life. But in a lecture given a year after *Habit's* publication, Bellah noted that the roots of Sheilaism are older and more widespread than modern life. Lecturing to an audience in a Catholic parish, Bellah recounted the story of a play written in 1946 by Dorothy Sayers about a pilot in the Royal Air Force who is killed and then returns to his home in Litchfield, England. Welcomed by the past inhabitants of the city, he is told that he must claim his citizenship.[6] In describing the requirements for claiming that citizenship, the town recorder tells the young pilot, "What matters here is not so much what you did as why you did it. Can you recite your creed?" In response, the young man begins, "I believe in God. . . ." Instantly the town's population joins in, "The Father almighty, maker of heaven and earth and in Jesus Christ. . . ." Protesting, the airman shouts, "No! No! No! . . . I reacted automatically to the word creed. My *personal* creed is something totally different." "So," Bellah observes parenthetically, "here we have Sheila in England already in 1946." And then he goes on to quote the reaction of the town recorder:

> What is speaking in you is the voice of the city, the church
> and the household of Christ, your people and country from

whom you derive. Did you think you were unbegotten, un-franchised, with no community and no past? Out of the dark-ness of your unconscious memory, the stones of the city are crying out, "Go home."[7]

If God-questions and I-questions shape the more obvious tension in our quest to find and do the will of God, "we-questions"—the questions we ask with others about the nature of God's will—are all but invisible to us. Oh, we are aware of them in broadly therapeutic terms. We know it is important to have friends and a support group. And we are loosely aware of the shared responsibilities that we have for our faith communities and the society around us. Civics class back in high school alerted us to that obligation, and preachers are forever talking about the church.

But the notion that questions about the will of God can *only* be raised by raising them with others is an all but foreign concept. Even the books devoted to the subject are either about groups looking for group guidance or about groups giving individuals guidance. They are not about individual lives being shaped and informed by ques-tions that are only finally answered by the groups of which those in-dividuals are a part. And even the question of what others might contribute to our individual understanding of God's will for our life is a fairly obscure consideration for most of us.

So to that extent we-questions are largely invisible. And yet there is a case to be made that these are the questions that ought to be sec-ond only to God-questions. We cannot be spiritual alone, and we are among the first generations in human history to assume—mistak-enly—that we can be. The task of asking we-questions is in a sense, then, a task of reclamation—of retrieving something lost. That will be the focus in this chapter—the reclamation of we-questions with a view to also retrieving:

- The deeper nature of our relationship with God

- The significance of we-questions for how we define doing the will of God

- The responsibility we have for one another (rooted in our relationship with God)

- The gift of being part of something larger than ourselves

- The privilege and the opportunity of listening with others

The Deeper Nature of Our Relationship with God

In a utilitarian world in which even the search for God's will has its application or use, it might seem strange to begin this part of the conversation with the subject of relationships. After all, most of us look for the will of God because we are getting ready to *do* something and so we want to know what God wants us to *do*. To talk about retrieving the significance of relationships—even our relationship with God— may sound abstract and irrelevant.

But both here and later in the final chapter, I argue that it is not at all clear that *doing* the will of God—in the sense of doing this thing or that thing—is as important in the end as we think it is. In fact, one of the most important things about the doing might be that it brings us back into relationship with both God and one another.

As a Christian, I am convinced that this dynamic is rooted in the Trinitarian nature of God. At first blush, an assertion of this kind seems hopelessly abstract, if not a bit strange. The Trinity is a theological doctrine that lingers at the fringes of most people's faith and remains largely neglected and misunderstood. It's a lump in our religious porridge. It's there all the time, but it's alien and indigestible, and you wonder whether it should even be there at all.

Dorothy Sayers was not only a playwright but an able theologian, and in a now widely read catechism she parodied the misunderstandings that even Christians perpetuate about the Trinity:

Q.: What does the Church think of God the Father?

A.: He is omnipotent and holy. He created the world and imposed on man conditions impossible of fulfillment; He is very angry if these are not carried out. He sometimes interferes by means of arbitrary judgments and miracles, distributed with a good deal of favouritism. He likes to be truckled to and is always ready to pounce on anybody who trips up over a difficulty in the Law, or is having a bit of fun. He is rather like a dictator, only larger and more arbitrary.

Q.: What does the Church think of God the Son?

A.: He is in some way to be identified with Jesus of Nazareth. It was not His fault that the world was made like this, and, unlike God the Father, He is friendly to man and did His best to reconcile man to God (see *Atonement*). He has a good deal of influence with God, and if you want anything done, it is best to apply to Him.

Q.: What does the Church think of God the Holy Ghost?

A.: I don't know exactly. He was never seen or heard of till Whit-Sunday. There is a sin against Him which damns you for ever, but nobody knows what it is.

Q.: What is the doctrine of the Trinity?

A.: "The Father incomprehensible, the Son incomprehensible, and the whole thing incomprehensible." Something put in by theologians to make it more difficult—nothing to do with daily life or ethics.[8]

I've heard this kind of description of the Trinity far too often to believe that Sayers is simply overwrought. For many of us, the Trinity amounts to little more than a grab bag of esoteric assumptions about the inner nature of God in which one person of the Trinity plays the judgmental heavy, one patches up our relationship with God, and the other one serves as a cosmic gofer. For others, the Trinity has become a list of extras—"further beliefs"—that Christians hold to be true about God as opposed to the "further beliefs" about God held by, say, Jews and Muslims.[9] Against the backdrop of those assumptions, it is easy to see why the Trinity has little or no connection with our lives.

Properly understood, however, the doctrine of the Trinity is something very different. As one theologian puts it, "The doctrine of the Trinity simply *is* the Christian doctrine of God."[10] And far from assigning a series of roles in a strange redemptive transaction in which there is a job for everyone and everyone has a job, the Trinity emphasizes the profound passion that God possesses for each of us. It also teaches that the love God has for each of us grows out of the love the persons of the Trinity have for one another—a love both so pure and so strong that the three are one.[11]

We-questions, then, figure as prominently as they do because the mutual love that the three persons of the Trinity have for one another is the engine of God's passion for us. And driven as God is by that passion, we are drawn in love toward God and one another. In giving, God prompts us to give. In embracing us, God encourages us to embrace one another. In seeking God's will, we cannot fail but to seek God together.

Much of the contemporary search for the will of God does not recognize this dynamic as a part of what it means to find and do the will of God. For one thing, most people assume that a concept such as the Trinity is just that—a concept. It might be of significance to theologians and church bureaucrats. It might even have something to do with right belief. But in the minds of many, it could not possibly have any significance for the shape of our lives.[12]

Instead, for many people the spiritual life consists of two discrete experiences in which the nature of God counts only as a means of explaining why God would seek to redeem us at all. One experience is that of salvation, the other a search for direction.[13] Moving as we do from one experience to the other, many of our lives are marked by a fairly private interaction with God in which our spiritual status is changed (salvation) and our lives are then given purpose (direction).

A relationship with God is considered necessary to this process. Many in fact urge that a *personal* relationship is necessary. Just how personal a relationship that is, is a matter of question. For many of us, even a personal relationship with Christ amounts to little more than accepting him as our savior. And relationship, in that context, can and often does amount to little more than acknowledging the saving intention of God. It is at heart an "I-question." How do *I* respond to God's saving grace for *me*? The nature of God in and of itself remains largely empty of significance.

But what if the spiritual life is about entering deeply into the life of God, and the life of God is marked in turn by mutual love? Then, as important as our redemption might be, it would never be enough to simply register that we accept the saving intention of God. The ultimate goal of our redemption would take us far deeper into the life of God, and doing the will of God would involve a far more subtle transformation of our lives.

The church has struggled historically to find a vocabulary that helps to bring that expectation alive. The struggle to do that in a widely intelligible way probably helps to explain why conversation about the nature of God has, from time to time, dropped almost completely from sight. Laypeople have not always been patient with theological language. "I just believe in love," people frequently tell me. And theologians have, from time to time, used the technical language of their discipline in such divisive and abusive ways that those who "just believe in love" are justified in their suspicions about anything more one might want to say about God. Along the way, however, powerful images of God have surfaced through the Christian tradition that might help us to picture what I have in mind.

One of the earliest images appears in chapter 17 of John's gospel in what is called "the high priestly prayer of Jesus," or "the Farewell Discourse." Described as a prayer that Jesus said aloud in front of the disciples, it is as much revelation as it is petition. And it is described as a conversation between the members of the "heavenly family." The language used there, particularly in the last part of the chapter, focuses on a prayer for unity.[14]

Historically John's prayer has been used to stress ecumenical and ecclesiastical unity, but it is unlikely that the evangelist had that in mind.[15] Instead, the passage stresses an intimacy and "community of life" shared by the members of the Trinity and entered into by those who follow Christ. The experience of unity is not an impersonal absorption into the life of God, nor does it require an ecstatic experience of some kind.[16] As John describes it, unity is instead a matter of entering into a communion with God that allows the one who shares God's life to both speak and do the work of God. It is both spiritual and moral in its expression, but it is not something we achieve.[17]

Over two centuries later Augustine developed a similar argument. In Augustine, the place of the Trinity is far more developed, of course, and unlike John, Augustine relies on prose and argument, not on story. But nonetheless, for Augustine, "salvation is dwelling in the fullness of God," and that fullness is given expression in the Trinity.[18] As one theologian notes, Augustine's purpose in describing God is "artegenic": it is meant to develop virtues in the seeker who, knowing God's nature, participates in God's virtues.[19]

In describing the Trinity, other theologians—including Gregory of Nazianzus, Irenaeus of Lyons, Basil of Caesarea, Dionysius the Areopogite, and Clement of Alexandria—have attempted to express the same conviction. To capture the nature of God and the nature of God's relationship with us, they have used a variety of images, liken-

ing the Trinity to life, living water, breath, Father and Son, and Father and Mother.[20] Julian of Norwich wrote:

> God is God, and our essential being is a creation within
> God; for the almighty truth of the Trinity is our father, he
> who made us and keeps us within him; and the deep wisdom
> of the Trinity is our mother, in whom we are all enclosed;
> and the great goodness of the Trinity is our lord and in him
> we are enclosed and he in us.[21]

Roughly a millennium after Augustine, the Russian iconogra-
pher Andrei Rublev made a similar effort in a completely different
medium, painting one of history's greatest icons. Drawing on a passage from Genesis, but eliciting obvious parallels with John's gospel,
Rublev depicted the Trinity as a circle of three figures in which we
are invited to participate as the fourth member of the circle. Describing the icon as a glimpse into "the house of perfect love," Henri
Nouwen observes:

> Within the circle of the Holy Trinity, all true knowledge de-
> scends into the heart. The Russian mystics describe prayer as
> descending with the mind into the heart and standing there
> in the presence of God. Prayer takes place where heart
> speaks to heart, that is, where the heart of God is united with
> the heart that prays. Thus knowing God becomes loving
> God, just as being known by God is being loved by God.[22]

In a very important sense, then, finding and doing the will of
God is a matter of spending time in God's presence, rejoicing in the
love and acceptance we find there, and listening to what we may
learn by spending time with God. Like the practice of reflecting on

an icon itself, the spiritual realities we see in the presence of God are experiences we take back into our world. And when we do, how we relate to the world is changed, often in ways we cannot articulate. The change, however, lies not just in seeing per se but in having seen God.

Returning from a retreat at a monastery in New Mexico, a friend observed, "I witnessed an easy grace and ready love in some of the people I met there. They did not have anything special to say. But you just got the feeling that they knew something you did not know, or maybe I should say, they knew some*one*."

The Responsibility We Have for One Another

At first blush, a preoccupation with God and communion with God may seem to take us right out of the world and off to a spiritual plane where we are too otherworldly to be of any earthly good. And there can be no doubt that some have read and reacted to the literature I have mentioned in this fashion. Contemporary spirituality is often marked by a quietism and retreat from life's realities. It is so common in fact that in some circles an introverted and quietist lifestyle has become all but synonymous with legitimate spirituality.[23]

But far from taking us out of the world, an awareness of the relationship we share with God takes us back into the deeper connections we share with the world and forces us to look anew for the will of God in our relationships with others.[24] Indeed, it could be argued that a sense of unity with God of the kind described in John's gospel is the only unassailable argument for struggling with those relationships. The activists among us are often unconsciously sustained by the myth of social improvement. But in point of fact, engagement with the world and its needs is marked by anything but linear progress.[25]

Many of the challenges we seem to have conquered reinvent themselves. Old enemies are replaced by new enemies, old perils are replaced by new perils, and solutions to one problem often create new problems. And there are countless perennial challenges that never yield to a final solution, including disease, poverty, and ignorance. Somewhat forlorn, a grandfather and business executive confessed to me recently, "You know, there was a time when I was deeply consoled by the conviction that in the wake of the Second World War and the cold war I was—at last—leaving my grandchildren a safer world. Sadly, I now feel that the world I am leaving to them is actually more dangerous than the one in which I have lived."

The frank admission that we live in a world marked by such ambiguity and genuine grief can drive us to withdraw from others as much as possible, and it can leave us without a clear reason to continue striving with the world. But the realization that our relationship with God takes us right back into the world is reason enough. If, as Rublev's icon suggests, we are meant to sit in the circle with the God who is one in three, we draw our motivation from a place where the specter of setback and loss holds no sway.[26]

This is not to say that relating to the world or seeking the will of God in the midst of our relationships with the world is always easy! In fact, John's gospel casts the relationship with the world in dualistic terms, shaped in part no doubt by the contentious religious atmosphere of his own day. Using the word *world* to mean the domain that refuses to acknowledge God's will, John frames at least part of the high priestly prayer I have already mentioned in terms that many commentators have tried to soften. Describing the nature of his petition, Jesus is said to have prayed: "I am asking on their behalf; *I am not asking on behalf of the world*" (John 17:9a, emphasis mine). The commentator C. K. Barrett is right. From John's point of view "the only hope for the *kosmos* [world] is precisely that it should cease to be the *kosmos*."[27]

There can be little doubt that at times finding and doing the will of God in the world is marked by just such tension. Viktor Frankl, the author and psychiatrist who survived the Nazi death camps, notes that the process of selecting capos—the prisoners who acted as trustees and, as a result, enjoyed special privileges—created a world within a world where the choices produced just this kind of dualism. Apart from the prisoners chosen by the SS itself, Frankl notes that a process of self-selection was also at work: many prisoners used "force, theft, and betrayal" to survive. "We who have come back," he writes, "by the aid of many lucky chances or miracles—whatever one may choose to call them—we know: the best of us did not return."[28]

There are other times and places in life where the tensions are neither as great nor as blatant. Perhaps we are seeking to discern the will of God in a climate that is supportive or sympathetic. We may find ourselves surrounded by like-minded friends, or we may be engaged in an effort to do the will of God that galvanizes our community. If we are fortunate, all of us have known times when one or all of these conditions have prevailed.

On other occasions what may appear to be a relatively benign environment turns out to be dangerously seductive. Or we may be betrayed by a struggle deep within ourselves. Reflecting on what he describes as "the preservation of the soul in corporate America," the poet and consultant David Whyte tells a story of hiking alone in the Himalayas. After traveling several days with fellow climbers, he decided to go it alone, and after a day or two he came to a deteriorated bridge that spanned a chasm almost four hundred feet deep. He found himself paralyzed by the prospect of trying to cross it and sat for hours on end simply staring, first at the bridge and then at the chasm below. Finally, an elderly woman from the region emerged from the mist and fog on the mountain, greeted him briefly, and crossed the bridge. In several frightened steps, Whyte crossed behind her as she disappeared from sight.[29]

Reflecting on modern corporate life, Whyte observes: "It seems to me every man or woman comes to such a bridge at one time or another in their life." Just as we begin to take a new step, "we . . . suddenly feel that the chasm is insurmountable and the bridge we had hoped to cross is down. . . . Our demons rise to meet us at the prospect of a fall: visions of ourselves thrown onto the street; . . . a sudden emptiness, a lack of confidence in our ability to do without all those many luxuries on which we have come to depend."[30]

Nevertheless, whether we find ourselves in an entirely hostile situation or one that is supportive, we are, by virtue of our relationship with God, in relationship with the world around us. Our task is to "forget ourselves on purpose" and to embrace the larger vision that only God can grant. Rublev's icon is an important reminder that, when we do, we cannot navigate the question of God's will as a simple transaction in which only God and our lives figure as significant considerations.

In fact, approaches to mapping out our lives by asking only simple questions of personal ambition or desire are deeply defective. Raised to the first order of importance, such questions are largely a private transaction, even if it is God we are looking to for answers to those questions. Listen to a life shaped by those transactions and it becomes clear that a person whose spiritual life is dominated by I-questions may *visit* Rublev's circle, asking for a favor now and then, but never really *sits* in the circle. This person tells stories about the ways in which God has blessed his or her life, but the stories are largely self-referential, lacking in any real attention to God or to the way in which God is at work in the world.

To be sure, I-questions have a place, and we will address those in due course. But they find a healthy balance only if they are raised in the context of a worldview shaped first by God-questions and then by we-questions. By failing to take our place in the circle of perfect love imagined in Rublev's icon, we do not gain greater control over our own lives or an added measure of autonomy. Instead, when we hide from God we diminish our lives and arrest our spiritual development.

In this regard, I am convinced that healthy spiritual and psychological development mirror and influence one another. For that reason, taking our place in Rublev's circle is not only akin to development of the self but actually deeply related to it.[31]

As infants, we are unaware of any distinction between ourselves and the world around us. We have no sense of where our hand ends and the world begins. Babies are bundles of undifferentiated perceptions, most of which revolve around basic bodily needs. As time goes on we become aware of the difference between our selves and the world around us. But we continue to think of the world as that which serves our needs. We are thoroughly self-involved and self-centered.

It is only with time that we discover that those around us have their own needs. Even then, however, the needs of others may constitute little more than obstacles to the achievement of our own goals. It may only be under duress that we grudgingly concede that the needs of others must be accommodated, but even then such concessions may be no more than part of a negotiating position as we continue to attempt to achieve our own goals.

Those who develop emotionally, however, learn that it is important to do more than negotiate. We learn that we share the world with others and that ours are not the only legitimate needs. When we learn this, some us may begin to think in terms of win-win relationships in which the needs of all concerned are met.

But as developmental psychologists note, there is a level beyond even this, and very few people reach it. Described as "interindividual," this higher stage of development is marked by a capacity for self-surrender and intimacy. Those who reach this stage discover that together—even in moments of sharp disagreement—we shape a reality with which we all live.[32]

We do not define our lives in isolation. We define them in dependence on one another—even when we find ourselves locked in dispute or, worse yet, at war. We learn that our deep yearning for self-expression is not possible apart from the relationships we forge with others, and we cannot hope to end our sense of isolation without surrendering something of ourselves to others, be it time, energy, or advantage. In an absolute sense, then, there is no such thing as a win-lose relationship, or even a win-win relationship. Our lives are inevitably touched by those with whom we live.

I once knew a man, for example, who lived and worked in a highly toxic setting in which, as far as I could tell, he responded to his colleagues with grace and character. Puzzled, however, by his willingness to endure the circumstances with which he lived day in and day out, I asked him, "How can you survive?" His answer was marked by the same candor that marked the rest of his relationships. "The man I work with is ill, and because I work with him day in and day out, I am sick." He was not seeking sympathy. There was no sense of veiled criticism in his comment. There was the simple and yet profound acknowledgment that together—as difficult as their relationship appeared to be—they lived in a world that shaped them both.

Not surprisingly, the desire for self-expression and the desire for a sense of belonging are both found in religious language and history. The German theologian Friedrich Schleiermacher talks about "ultimate dependence," while the reformer Martin Luther declares: "Here I stand!" The Hasidim of the Jewish tradition advocate a radical emphasis on communalism, while Job finds himself alone, talking to God.[33]

The need for self-expression and belonging cannot be fulfilled by pursuing only one or the other but in recognizing the deep inner connection between them. Like the lover or the friend who completes your thoughts before you speak them, the question of what is my thought and what is a thought from someone else is all but impossible to answer. Some have even argued that this is the deeper logic of the Trinity. It resists the logic by which we are so often captured: that there is only you and me, the known and the other.

Anyone who has ever known true friendship knows that this is the case. Augustine writes:

> Each of us has something to learn from the others and something to teach in return. If any are away, we miss them with regret and gladly welcome them when they come home. Such things as these are heartfelt tokens of affection between friends. They are signs to be read on the face and in the eyes, spoken by the tongue and displayed in countless acts of kindness. They can kindle a blaze to melt our hearts and weld them into one. This is what we cherish in friendship, and we cherish so dearly that in conscience we feel guilty if we do not return love for love, asking no more of our friends than these expressions of goodwill. This is why we mourn their death, which shrouds us in sorrow and turns joy into bitterness, so that the heart is drenched in tears and life becomes a living death because a friend is lost. Blessed are those who love you, O God, and love their friends in you and their enemies for your sake. They alone will never lose those who are dear to them, for they love them in the One who is never lost, in God, our God who made heaven and earth and fills them with his presence, because by filling them, he made them. No one can lose you, my God.[34]

We-Questions and Defining the Will of God

It would be a mistake, however, to think of the experience of intimacy with God and one another exclusively in terms of responsibility. In all giving there is a great deal to be received.

God has urged us to care for one another not just as a means of getting clear about the nature of love, God's love for us, or even our love for God. We have been invited into the relationships we share with other people because loving others is a part of what God intends. Passionate for relationship, God does not simply seek out each of us but gives us relationships shaped by love as a piece of what it means to be human.

I have conversations with my friends from time to time about devotion to God, and some of them are convinced that devotion to spouses, families, and all of the domestic demands that life makes on us renders it impossible to love God as fully as one who lives in a hermitage or a monastery. And certainly there are those who believe that is the case.[35] I do not. I won't argue that monastic life lacks any kind of virtue. There is a great deal to learn from monastic spirituality, even if you are not a monk. But I am *not* convinced that it rests at the top of some sort of imaginary pyramid and represents the pinnacle of devotion.

To get sidetracked—as some would put it—with changing diapers, running errands, or buying flowers is to learn how to love. And while loving the one for whom we bought the flowers will open spiritual windows into a love for God, it is not *just* a matter of loving God. It is, in the first place, about doing a bit of the loving for which God created us, and for that reason it is a matter of doing the will of God.

What is profoundly important to grasp, then, is that doing the will of God is not a matter of grand designs but of daily, commonplace investment in the lives of others. It is what another generation would have called "homely" activity—simple, domestic kindnesses by which we reach beyond the world of our own needs to touch the needs of others. Moreover, doing the will of God does not require the elaborate ceremonies of prayer and reflection that so many of us have come to see as integral to the practice of discernment. Much of what needs to be done follows easily and obviously from the needs of others as they surface—minute to minute, day to day.

Don't misunderstand: I am not suggesting that we should live unreflectively or without the discipline of regular prayer. Some decisions present themselves in a rather more obvious fashion only because we have already consciously given ourselves to the work of God's spirit. It can be a little bit like tuning your ear to music. If you have studied it or have an appreciation for it, you can hear the notes fit together. If you have no such appreciation or you are tone-deaf, you won't hear them fitting together. Similarly, if our lives are attuned to the work of God's spirit, we recognize God's will quite often as a matter of course. But without that basic change, we don't recognize God's will so readily.

Nor am I suggesting that life is without significant choices that need to be made deliberately, prayerfully, and without haste. But it is a mistake to believe that those decisions are the only important ones we make. Aside from our choice of a career or a spouse, which may frame our lives, such choices do not have the same cumulative significance as the choices we make on a daily basis. Life lived freely, moment to moment and in response to others, has as much significance as any of the other decisions we make—even the "big" decisions.

There is perhaps no more certain evidence of this than the way in which people respond to the death of someone they love. Oh, to be sure, there are eulogies and obituaries that outline a person's life and mention what they did. But what is interesting is how little information of that kind figures in the comments made by those who loved the person who has died. As I've sat with families who have lost someone they loved, what surfaces over and over again are the hundred and one ways in which they remember the love that was exchanged in simple, commonplace ways. It's the homely stuff that matters. Tears and laughter, not degrees and accomplishments, dominate such conversations, and they are the memories that families cherish at such moments.

Given the "radical simplification" that takes place at such a time, what survives feels a bit like the results of a refiner's fire (although I don't believe that death as such is God's will for us).[36] The gold surfaces. The foreign, less enduring elements burn away. And as a result, I am convinced that experiences such as the death of someone we have loved reveal a part of what is finally important in our efforts to do the will of God—the nurture and growth of love.

Born in Nantes, France, in 1874, Gabrielle Bossis was, according to her contemporaries, a bright, active woman who lived very much in the world and for some years wrote and acted in a number of plays. Her contemporaries also describe her as a contemplative whose life was marked by a deep passion to know God. A Franciscan monk even attempted to convince her to enter the convent, but Bossis resisted the suggestion.

Her life was just as busy as mine or yours, but interwoven with the busyness of her daily life was prayerful reflection. The journal she kept was written in a simple and direct fashion that alternates between a question and a note about the activity in which she was engaged at the time, and then the voice of Christ as she heard it in the moment. So her journal reads very much like the work of the medieval mystics who preceded her. At one point her journal simply notes: "While I was digging about the hydrangeas." This comment is followed by: "Be one with Me in My toil as a carpenter. It is not what you do that matters, but the way you love Me while you work. And love is oneness. Give Me the spectacle of a soul engulfed in its Savior, and this will be joy, My joy."[37]

The Gift of Being Part of Something Larger Than Ourselves

When we ask we-questions, we are given the gift of being part of something larger than ourselves. We begin to ask other-directed questions that take us beyond our narrow self-interest, and we begin to think instead of what we might do or say that will nurture the well-being of those around us and even those who will follow us in this life.

This is why Paul, in his letters to the first Christians, used the imagery of the body as a means of describing the human relationships that ought to exist by virtue of our relationship with God. Writing to the church in Corinth, he observes:

For just as the body is one and has many members, and all the members of the body, though many, are one body, so it is with Christ. For in the one Spirit we were all baptized into one body—Jews or Greeks, slaves or free—and we were all made to drink of one Spirit. Indeed, the body does not consist of one member but of many. If the foot would say, "Because I am not a hand, I do not belong to the body," that would not make it any less a part of the body. And if the ear would say, "Because I am not an eye, I do not belong to the body," that would not make it any less a part of the body. If the whole body were an eye, where would the hearing be? If the whole body were hearing, where would the sense of smell be? But as it is, God arranged the members in the body, each one of them, as he chose. If all were a single member, where would the body be? As it is, there are many members, yet one body. The eye cannot say to the hand, "I have no need of you," nor again the head to the feet, "I have no need of you." On the contrary, the members of the body that seem to be weaker are indispensable, and those members of the body that we think less honorable we clothe with greater honor, and our less respectable members are treated with greater respect; whereas our more respectable members do not need this. But God has so arranged the body, giving the greater honor to the inferior member, that there may be no dissension within the body, but the members may have the same care for one another. If one member suffers, all suffer together with it; if one member is honored, all rejoice together with it. (1 Corinthians 12:12–26)

I am convinced that most of us think of Paul's use of body language as a means of affirming the star-quality of the individual. We hear, "You have a gift *and so do I.*" Like so much of the motivational language we use today, to our ears Paul seems be lending religious justification to the pursuit of our individual ambitions. Or at a minimum, we assume that he is affirming our value as individuals in the eyes of God.

But Paul lived in a world in which the collective identity of people was far more important than the individual. In using the body metaphor, he sets aside the emphasis placed on the subordination of some parts to others that appears so often in Greco-Roman speeches and literature.[38] It is clear that Paul has a very different message in mind: "You have a gift and *we* are incomplete without it." Paul is not interested in affirming our star-quality. Instead, he emphasizes our dependence on one another, asserting that the body cannot be without any of its parts and noting that no one part of the body can claim pride of place.[39]

Paul's readers had elected to be part of the community to which he refers, and baptism was the sacrament that marked their entrance into that community. In a very real sense, baptism is for Christians the one true vocational choice we make; everything else amounts to little more than details. Doing the will of God, however, is for that reason a matter of being a part of the body. As the theologian Robert Barron notes, the Christian life is all about discovering it's not all about you.[40]

On the other hand, Paul's observation is also rooted in the conviction that God has placed us in a world where our interdependence is a given. Hillel, the great representative of first-century

Judaism, is said to have declared: "If I am not for myself, who will be for me? And if I am only for myself, what am I? And if not now, when?" (Avot 1:14).[41]

Absolute freedom is illusory. We are defined in community with one another. It is there that we are nurtured. It is there that we find meaning in life. Even when we are in sharp conflict with one another, our self-understanding and place in the world are shaped by that conflict and by the people with whom we differ. In one sense, then, the "gift" of seeking God together lies not so much in being part of something larger than ourselves as in recognizing that we are *already* part of something larger than ourselves.

With good reason, then, do some argue that when Paul talks about "the gifts of the Spirit," he is talking less about "individual endowments" than about ways in which our mutual dependence on one another is demonstrated and the larger significance of our life together receives expression.[42]

Hillel puts it this way: neglect the community and you cease to exist. So to ask we-questions is to invest ourselves in an effort that, quite apart from the results, is in and of itself of enormous value. In asking those questions and in striving together, we *are* doing the will of God, regardless of the results or the specifics of our pilgrimage.

The Privilege and Opportunity to Listen with Others

When we reach the stage where I-questions are finally appropriate, listening with others also proves to be important because no one of us can hear the whole of God's voice. Our perspectives are shaped by the circumstances of our lives: our social position, educational opportunities, economic advantages, and other cultural and social experiences. To listen well is to listen with the ears of others as well as our own. Listening with others surfaces deficiencies in our own perspective that would be impossible to detect in any other way. The voices of others alert us to the things we don't know we don't know.

Some of what we learn about the will of God is corrective in nature. We find that blind spots and defensiveness have limited what we can see of God's will. But some of what we learn from listening with others is positive, even defining, for us. Years ago, when I was serving a church in northeastern Ohio, an elderly lady with a knowing look on her face sidled up to me and declared, "You're kind of a teacher-preacher, aren't you?" The comment has stuck with me for years because she named two influences on my life that probably shape much of what I do in both the classroom and the pulpit. I recognized the characterization right away, but the label has helped me to define much of my life's work. Her observation was an unexpected gift.

Casual observers, our family members, our spiritual directors, members of the communities with which we worship, the people who love us but aren't impressed with us—chance conversations with any of these people can open windows and show us the shape of God's will for our lives. And if we cultivate careful listening, we can return the favor.

But a careful listener is not simply adept at saying the right thing. The careful listener asks gentle but probing questions while listening to the shape of the speaker's life story and reflecting with that person on the deeper nature of their life narrative—the cares, the concerns, the struggles, the longings.

That is an effort that takes time and patience. An African friend of mine once asked, "When people in your country ask, 'How are you?' do they really want to know? Because they never stop long enough to get an answer to the question." I was pained to admit that, on the whole, we do not. The best reading of our behavior is that the phrase no longer performs the function that the words suggest and has become shorthand for "Hello." On another level, I am also sure that how we ask and respond to this question reveals the perfunctory character of the care we extend to one another and the breathless pace at which we live. Chained to a cosmic gerbil wheel, we are robbed of community, and impoverished by its absence, we are, in turn, ever more poorly equipped to live in community.

The requisites of careful listening to and with others are not difficult to grasp or practice, but they are hard for us to value. Listening requires time and attention. It requires us to be present, here and now. To listen carefully is to listen reflectively and with patience, trying to tune in to the passion behind the position that the speaker takes, the true cause of the pain in his or her life's story, and the deeper longing in its telling. This kind of listening cannot bear fruit unless we are willing to abandon our own pride and the need to demonstrate or defend our competence. It thrives on the freedom to sacrifice our need for love in the name of giving it and on our ability to ask ourselves why we find it difficult to say or hear something rather than blame another.

Through it all, listening with one another demands the courage to speak the truth in love, knowing that the two complement one another. What I said earlier about holiness and love could also be said about truth and love: Truth without love is devoid of saving power—an arid and potentially abusive betrayal of the truth's own best ends. And love without truth is devoid of direction—a sentimentalism lacking the strength that renders love reliable.

A Dramatic Postscript

Robert Bellah says nothing further about the play by Dorothy Sayers and the fate of the young RAF pilot described at the beginning of this chapter. A look at the play itself, however, reveals that each time the

pilot tries to say something more about what he believes, he triggers
the response of the city, which in unison recites yet another part of
the Apostle's Creed. Finally, in frustration the airman protests,

> The past is dead. We must turn our backs on it,
> Forget it, bury it. I denounce the past,
> The past has turned the world to a living hell,
> We must build for the future.

To which the town's recorder responds, "*You* are the dead and
the past. Must *you* be forgotten?"[43]

So, as it turns out, the "perfect circle of love" in Rublev's icon
and Paul's image of the body of Christ is a far more complex gathering than we might have imagined. Included in both are not just the
people around us and visible to us but also those who have gone before us and those who will follow. For that reason, asking we-
questions is about listening not just to those who share our present
but also to those of the past and the future—to what that same creed
calls "the communion of saints."

Without that capacity, we isolate ourselves, and the meaning and
direction we hoped to find in doing the will of God is lost. Sayers understood this well. The town, rebuffed by the young airman, declares: "You have no part in us—No part in the dead, no part in the
living city."[44]

Spiritual Exercises for Asking We-Questions

- Identify some specific periods in your life when you felt both the positive and negative impact of the community on your spirituality. What made them positive and/or negative experiences?

- From whom do you seek spiritual counsel today and why? Do these persons *really challenge* you in love, or do they serve another purpose for you?

- Granted the doctrine of the Trinity can be theologically complex, what can this relationship tell us about God and about ourselves?

- Do you want to live in God's presence? When your answer is yes, why do you envision God's presence as life-giving? And when your answer is no, what images or names of God keep you from saying yes?

- How do you tend to view the world, its desires, and its values? Are you at odds with the world or in partnership with it? What are the strengths and pitfalls of each approach?

- Are you a Lone Ranger in your approach to spirituality, convinced you can go it alone? Or do you depend on a church or community to give you permission and validation for your spiritual life? How might either of these spiritual paths obscure the radical Christian claim that the Holy Spirit has taken up residence in you?[45]

◆—◆

Seven

GIFTS AND GRACES

> Only a kind of perversity can oblige God's friends to deprive
> themselves of having genius, since to receive it in superabun-
> dance they only need to ask.
>
> Simone Weil[1]

Once we turn our attention to asking I-questions, the issue of gifts
and graces surfaces quickly. By gifts I mean the specific talents or
strengths that each of us possess. It could be an ability to play a musi-
cal instrument or to sing. It could be a capacity for problem-solving
or for teaching and mentoring. It could be a facility for using numbers or for crafting something by hand. The list of possible gifts—the
kind of ability that usually surfaces in a job description or as part of a
skill set—is almost endless.

By graces I refer to those harder-to-define qualities that are more
immediately a function of our personality or that arise out of formative experiences. These capacities are more a matter of temperament
than of skill. Having the patience it takes to listen attentively is a
grace, as is the aesthetic sense required to detect when balance and
color are right. Graces would include qualities such as the emotional
sensitivity and maturity needed to gently nurture someone who is
struggling physically or emotionally, the tenacity needed to persist in
a difficult task, or a demeanor that instantly invites the complete trust
of others.[2]

Most of us are accustomed to thinking about spiritual gifts according to the list that Paul provides in 1 Corinthians 12, including healing, the working of miracles, prophecy, knowledge and discernment of spirits, interpretation of words, and the gift of tongues. Others have expanded this notion of gifts and graces to include what many would refer to as virtues, including justice, humility, faith, prudence, temperance, patience, and courage. Debates about whether these characteristics are direct, supernatural gifts from God or the natural products of the familial and social environments in which we are raised are beside the point. Once we have identified our personal gifts, the burning questions remain the same: To whom do my gifts ultimately belong? And what do my gifts and graces tell me about the will of God?

There is the potentially deceptive notion that we own what are in fact gifts. If you possess something, you may hold on to it very tightly, and you may rightly feel entitled to dispose of it as you see fit. But if you have been given something and entrusted with it, your sense of responsibility may loom larger than your sense of ownership, and your hold on it may be far lighter. Having been given a gift, we can only look to the one who has blessed us, anxious to understand how the blessing might be used and willing to ask both the God-questions and we-questions I have already described.

But even if we recognize the gifted and graced character of our lives, what does that tell us about the way we should live in response? That question is the burden of this chapter, and it revolves around three issues:

1. Where do I start?

2. What kind of I-questions will help me make concrete decisions in my daily life?

3. What do the answers to my deepest questions look like when my I-questions are informed by a newfound commitment to discerning God's will in the context of community?

Answers at the Extremes

At the extremes, the answers the church has often given to questions about finding God's will have been shaped by one of two foundational convictions, and they possess both the strengths and weaknesses of our bipolar approach to seeking answers to life's bigger conundrums.

One answer has been to suggest that our gifts and graces *are* the clue to what we ought to be doing. We should draw on them, celebrate them, live into them. The will of God is to be found in our comfort zone.

The language I am using is fairly contemporary, but this notion about the use of our talents and skills is fairly old, and it is common enough that a few illustrations will suffice. Much of its most ancient expression is imbedded in notions of fate or destiny, and Plato's *Republic* provides an excellent example. The Greek mythology of Plato's day held that human fate and, in particular, the duration of a person's life and the suffering he or she would experience were determined by gods. Referred to collectively as the Fates, or *Moirai*, they were thought of as three extraordinarily old women who spun the fabric of a person's destiny: Lachesis (the Alotter), Clotho (the Spinner), and Atropos (the Inflexible One). As Plato describes it, life flowed inexorably from a single choice:

When all the souls had chosen their lives, they approached Lachesis in the same order they had made their choices. She gave each the guardian spirit it had chosen, to go with it, watch over its life and fulfil its choices. This spirit first brought the soul before Clotho, passing beneath her hand and the whirl of the revolving spindle, to confirm the fate which the lot had allowed it to choose. When the soul had touched her, the spirit took it to where Atropos was spinning, so making the spun thread impossible to unwind. And from there, without turning back, it went beneath the throne of Necessity.[3]

This widely held notion in the ancient world—the tendency to identify the gifts and graces of one's life with the will of God and, by extension, to think of life as fated in one way or another—held equal sway elsewhere. The philosopher Plotinus, clearly depending on Plato, resurrected the same themes in the third century C.E.[4] Shakespeare alluded to the idea in his plays.[5] And a wide array of spiritual, philosophical, scientific, and psychological literature continues to revisit the notion in one form or another.

The psychologist James Hillman, for example, cites these and other epigraphs in the preface to his book *The Soul's Code* and uses the metaphor of the acorn to capture the notion that each of us possesses a destiny. He explicitly rejects the notion of "fatal-*ism*," which he defines as life lived "straight from the lap of Necessity."[6] But elsewhere he insists so strongly on the notion that each person has a "lot your soul chose before you ever took a breath" that it is difficult to imagine that his notion of destiny is any less determinative than the one shaped by Platonic categories.[7]

Relying on language that is somewhat more theological in character, the writer Parker Palmer quotes the poetry of William Stafford and begins, "'Ask me whether what I have done is my life.'" Noting that the line reminds him of moments when it is clear that he is not living the life that wants to live in him, Palmer urges his readers, "Before you tell your life what you intend to do with it, listen for what it intends to do with you."[8]

Although these writers hold widely disparate points of view and some are not at all concerned with a definable spirituality—never mind theology—each of them makes much the same point. Your gifts and graces are the critical clue to what it means for you to do the will of God.

The other answer offered by our bipolar struggle with this question about doing the will of God has less going for it in the way of published points of view. Fewer writers come right out and say, "Forget what your untrustworthy heart tells you! God wants you to strain, to struggle, and to embrace a life shaped by choices that may mitigate *against* your gifts and graces." But in many ways this has been no less popular or enduring an approach, even if it has received endorsement of a less direct nature—particularly of late.

One seedbed for this tradition lies in the monastic and spiritual practice of early and medieval Christianity, although it ranges across religious traditions and much further back in history. Sometimes referred to as "asceticism," it is predicated on the conviction that God is to be found and followed through rigorous spiritual practice and, according to some, "extreme austerities" or "self-denial."[9] As for many early monastics, asceticism is the key to the freedom needed to follow God.

But in many cases the price of that freedom is the withdrawal from society that often epitomizes the life of an ascetic. So, for example, Palladius, a monk and historian, recalls that early in his experience he asked Abba Macarius of Alexandria, "Abba, what shall I do? For my thoughts afflict me, saying: 'You are making no progress; go away from here.'" Macarius is said to have responded, "Tell them: 'For Christ's sake I am guarding the walls.'"[10] Withdrawal behind the walls has become something of a visual image for monastic life.[11]

Within those walls, the degree of asceticism required varied. For some, the demands of ascetic life were without boundary. Macarius urged his followers to "flee from humans . . . sit in your cell and weep for your sins."[12] But for others, the journey inward entailed a journey outward as well. Saint Anthony of Egypt is said to have spent two decades in complete isolation but then emerged at age fifty-five to spend the remainder of his long life counseling those who sought him out and training disciples.[13]

The ascetical tradition has also differed in the degree of self-denial thought to be necessary. In the convent where the writer Karen Armstrong lived for seven years, a text on the wall declared, "I would grind myself to powder if by doing so I could accomplish God's will."[14] The history of life in both convents and monasteries is replete with stories of communities founded or reformed to ensure that more time in prayer and spiritual practice is created. By contrast, other communities have observed a measure of ascetic practice, but have tempered their approach, insisting that the practice is a means of achieving communion with God and is not an end in itself.

The rigor of this approach to our question might have confined its advocates to a courageous few. But monasticism and asceticism have had a profound impact on spiritual disciplines, which came to be seen as important keys to spiritual growth. So the logic of monastic life has found its way into the larger conversation about spirituality, spawning books devoted to finding a "rule" for your life[15] and exploring the notion of "ordinary people as monks and mystics."[16] The writings of the monastic giants have also slowly earned a wider readership, and that has played a part in keeping the denial of self alive as a means of exploring what it means to find and do the will of God.[17] But probably the most important factors in keeping the ideal of self-denial alive have been the example of Jesus, the teaching of Paul, and the lives of the martyrs. Etched into the DNA of the Christian tradition, sacrifice is difficult to ignore if it is at the heart of your faith.

The Logic of Life at the Extremes

Broadly speaking, the logic of life at the two extremes can be traced to fundamentally different views of humankind, and therefore to very different starting points. The view that doing the will of God has almost completely to do with the shape of one's own life is rooted in a higher view of people in their "natural state" than is taken by the other pole. The second view is arguably more sensitive to human sin and frailty. For that reason, its advocates are convinced that spiritual discipline is central to discerning the will of God. Convinced that our lives and perceptions have been misshapen, those who take this view believe that self-denial creates a space within which God can work in our lives and give them direction.

Each view has its strengths and weaknesses. The view that our gifts and graces are the significant clue to God's will for our lives starts by acknowledging that those lives are gifts. That is certainly a positive and life-affirming place to begin, and it avoids a fretful, self-deprecating spirituality that is never at rest. It is also the kind of starting point that provides the person who is anxious to do God's will with a concrete and particular place to begin reflecting. It is far easier to imagine what to do with the life you have than it is to imagine what to do with a life you do not have!

This view has its disadvantages, however. Those who take their "comfort zone" to be a clue to God's will for their lives can also "hide out," evading challenge or risk. Although it is spiritually and psychologically healthy to practice self-acceptance, a spirituality shaped exclusively by that point of view is likely to overlook some very real shortcomings.

By contrast, the view that ascetical practice is the key to finding God's will displays its strength at precisely this point. Keenly aware of our capacity for self-deception, the ascetical approach eschews an easy reliance on life-as-it-is. It is aware of God's grace, but it is also aware of the potentially yawning chasm between the way things are and what God intends.

But taken alone, it is a view that can feed brokenness of another kind. For example, some who hold this view are so suspicious about the goodness of life that it is quite clear they do not really believe in God's grace. For such people, spiritual practice often becomes self-flagellation, and the space provided by spiritual practice to listen for God's voice becomes instead the arena in which they attempt to demonstrate their own worthiness.

If the self-indulgent hide out at one extreme, those who consider themselves unlovable reside at the other. If we want to do the will of God, then, plainly it is impossible to rely on the logic of life at either extreme. There is no way to avoid the struggle of proving, probing, and exploring the will of God—and then living with the consequences. Any simple formula fosters and shelters a spiritual brokenness that, while different in nature, is no less destructive.

Our "Natural Business"

How, then, do we navigate the choices that we make? There is no single answer, but there is a guiding principle. Some years ago, Robert Bolt wrote a play called A Man for All Seasons. The play tells the story of Thomas More, who from 1529 to 1532 served as lord chancellor of England under King Henry VIII. More was a devout Roman Catholic and a lawyer, and he commanded the respect of both the king and a good many of his countrymen.

Henry was anxious to have a male heir, and without the benefit of modern genetic counseling, he labored under the mistaken assumption that his lack of a son had something to do with his wife, Catherine of Aragon. And so he sought an annulment from the pope. When the Holy See denied Henry's request, he looked to More for help. But the lord chancellor was reluctant to help the king, "for conscience' sake," and declined.

The king persisted—in part because he wanted an annulment and in part because he deeply desired More's approval and was conscience-smitten by More's refusal to assist him. When it became clear that the king would not allow More to remain uninvolved in this venture, More resigned his post and retired to his country estate. But the king could not stand to be without More's endorsement. So Henry issued a decree approving of his separation from Catherine, and he required that everyone sign it. The one signature he really wanted, of course, was that of his onetime lord chancellor.

For his part, More declined to sign and also declined to give an explanation for his refusal. Knowing English law as he did, his response was part of a delicate strategy. By refusing to sign the decree, More obeyed his conscience and made his position on the king's divorce from his wife perfectly clear to anyone who knew More. But by refusing to say why he would not sign the decree, he also evaded charges of treason and execution, because English law held that a person's silence had to be construed as approval of whatever it was he or she was being silent about.

Eventually, in both the play and real life, More was betrayed by a young courtier who committed perjury in exchange for a court appointment and reported that More had voiced his disapproval of the king's divorce. But long before that happens in the play, there is an extended struggle to extract a statement from More of his own volition. In a poignant exchange with his daughter Meg and her husband Will, Meg asks her father whether they are going to sign the document or refuse and make their reasons for refusing publicly known. In response, More urges:

Now listen, Will. And, Meg, you listen, too, you know I know
you well. God made the *angels* to show him splendor—as he

made animals for innocence and plants for their simplicity. But Man he made to serve him wittily, in the tangle of his mind! If he suffers us to fall to such a case that there is no escaping, then we may stand to our tackle as best we can, and yes, Will, then we may clamor like champions . . . if we have the spittle for it. And no doubt it delights God to see splendor where He only looked for complexity. *But it's God's part, not our own, to bring ourselves to that extremity! Our natural business lies in escaping.*[18]

Few of us will face martyrdom of the kind that More faced, but the logic of his statement is nevertheless of interest to us. Our "natural business" is to be the people we were born to be. Our abilities, skills, strengths, and temperament, the experiences that have shaped our lives, the circle of family and friends around us—these are God's gifts to us. We, in turn, are God's gift to the world, and "our natural business" is to be that gift. *It is spiritually perverse to assume that the one thing God most wants from you is what you do not have.* There may be many things that drive us to believe this, including a sense of inferiority or insecurity, greed or pride, *but it is not God.*

So, in our seeking to do the will of God, our gifts and graces are indeed the natural place to begin thinking about the answers we might give to the I-questions in our lives. Taking inventory of our own temperament and skill set is a necessary starting point. For example, if you are uncomfortable with open wounds, you probably do not have a future as a surgeon. If you know how to bridge the gaps in people's grasp of the information they are given, you may have a future as a teacher. Whatever the specifics of your gifts, it is an important part of spiritual discipline to become aware of those gifts and graces and then to ask yourself whether your choices are conserving and nurturing their growth in service to God and others.

This is not to say that we may not find ourselves called to stretch our capabilities beyond those gifts. That is we must not only conserve our gifts but nurture them, and why we must not only nurture them to our own satisfaction but in service to God and others. Our gifts are meant to be spent and risked.

It is perilously easy, however, to risk them in the name of self-aggrandizement. We need to be mindful of More's caution: "It's God's part, not our own, to bring ourselves to that extremity!" It is only when circumstances make it necessary or we are theologically and morally obliged to face martyrdom—major or minor—that we should abandon our "natural business" to face the demands of the moment.

Nurturing Gifts and Graces

Because our natural business is nurturing the gifts we have been given, the siren song of success is just as much a source of temptation as is the tendency to look for martyrdom. In fact, for most of us that may be the far more common problem. Living our lives incrementally, accepting the challenges as they come, it is easy to let ourselves be shaped by the values and assumptions of the world around us rather than to attend to the shape of our lives in a reflective fashion.

Contemporary life is filled with stories of teachers who connected with children successfully and were then asked to work as administrators, physicians who abandoned the practice of medicine to provide leadership for a hospital, gifted students who were lured away from their life's passion to work for a company offering a lucrative salary—just to give a few examples. None of those choices are wrong in and of themselves. Capable teachers and physicians understand their respective cultures well, and often the people who can provide the creative leadership needed in such settings are those who have worked in them. Nor is there anything wrong with finding a job that pays well after finishing an undergraduate education. But such decisions can be wrong when they are made unreflectively, without attention to nurturing the gifts and graces we have been given.[19]

What is needed, then, is a spiritual life marked by the kind of reflective and prayerful space that makes that maturation possible. This includes taking the time to surface and name our gifts and graces, weigh their significance for our lives, and judge whether they are adequately expressed in the way we live our lives. Only with that depth of self-understanding can we evaluate our choices, and such self-understanding comes only through attentive and deliberate listening and self-examination.

The Doing Is in the Being

Beneath the question of what I should do and how I should nurture my gifts and graces lies a deeper question: Who am I before God and what am I becoming? To recognize the significance of that question changes everything. Asking that question not only brings up an issue that demands our attention but also places every other I-question in perspective.

It becomes clear, for example, that some decisions matter very little or not at all. Many of the choices we describe as preferences *may* fall into this category (I'll say more on this point later), but the maxim "You are what you eat" notwithstanding, our tastes in food, art, and music may not deeply shape what we become.

Sometimes what we choose does not matter nearly as much as the fact that we choose to do something. That we choose to demonstrate our love and concern for one another, for example, is often more important than how we choose to express it. The memory that we cared may in fact be all that endures.

In other cases, it is not so much a single choice as a pattern of choices that is determinative for our lives. "A virtue is a capacity to do what is right," and a capacity to do what is right can only be cultivated over years of experience.[20] A person who epitomizes a specific virtue cannot do that by making a single decision but by making the same kind of decision over and over again.

If we want to know and do the will of God, we will be able to talk reflectively not only about the choices we have made but about the relationship between those choices and the lives we are living. Our inner conversation with God about the shape of our lives brings up the questions that ultimately are the only ones to which we can give our full attention. We can reflect prayerfully on the choices we make. Out of a life of prayer, we can speak to how those choices have or have not nurtured our relationship with God and others. And against the backdrop of that conversation, we can probe and explore further what is "good and acceptable and perfect." We cannot vouch for the results, nor do we need to.

Anne Lamott tells the story of building a sand castle with her son just before a birthday party and being forced to tell him that it was time to go:

> "We have to go," I told him. The party at our friends' house was going to start in an hour or so.
>
> "No!" he wailed. "We can't. What about . . . our creation? We can't just leave it here. We have to stay and protect it. We've worked so hard on it! The waves will come and wash it away."
>
> "Honey," I said, "it was never meant to be permanent. You must have known the tide would come back in."
>
> He thought about this for a minute. "I'm going to kick it all over then," he said. "And I *hate* you," he added. "And I

hate *everything*." I didn't say anything. He walked away from me and the altar, world weary, shuffling with dejection, head down. Sam, I wanted to explain, making the altar was a way to celebrate, to honor you today. The fact that it's going to wash away heightens how wonderful our *making* it was. The altar didn't hold as much animating spirit as our *making* it did, the gathering, the choices. It's like: We made it, we love it—oops, it's gone. But the best part is still here.[21]

What Anne Lamott would have liked to tell her son is what God wants to tell us about our lives and the choices we make: our struggle to "get it right" and our anguish about preserving the results are a distraction. Whatever happens "the best part is still here."

Spiritual Exercises for Discerning Our Gifts and Graces

- Have the spiritual influences on your life ever led you to believe that life should be lived at one of the two extremes of self-indulgence or self-flagellation?

- How would you evaluate the impact of those influences?

- Do they linger as an influence on the shape of your life?

- List your defining gifts and graces in a single column.

- In a second column, identify one way in which you give expression to each of those gifts and graces.

- Are there defining gifts and graces that are unexpressed in the shape of your life?

- Identify a single step you can and will take to give those gifts and graces expression.

Eight

PUTTING IT ALL TOGETHER: ENVISIONING A NEW LIFE IN GOD

Only a few achieve the colossal task of holding together, without being split asunder, the clarity of their vision alongside an ability to take their place in a materialistic world. They are the modern heroes. . . . Artists at least have a form within which they can hold their own conflicting opposites together. But there are some who have no recognized artistic form to serve this purpose, they are artists of the living. To my mind these last are the supreme heroes in our soulless society.

Irene Claremont de Castillejo[1]

What does God want for our lives? There is, in one sense, no substitute for simply answering, "Getting on with it," as my British friends are accustomed to saying. There is also no substitute for asking the God-questions, the we-questions, and the I-questions that are basic to the task of discernment. And there is no probationary period that needs to be observed before we embrace the work of a triage theologian that is ours, by definition. Even what we take to be blind alleys and cul-de-sacs, which we are sure to encounter, are in fact part of that exciting adventure we call finding and doing the will of God. My description of that adventure will intersect with your own life in ways that neither you nor I can anticipate. Such is the advice of one pilgrim, given to another.

But I would be remiss in my responsibility to you if at this juncture I did not try to put it all together in a way that helps you to envision the new life in God that I have in mind. In this last chapter, I hope to do that in two ways. First, by offering you a few snapshots of how the approach I have described might work out in "real life," and then by giving you something of a bird's-eye view or "executive summary" of the ground we have covered. As with a family photo album, I'll describe the snapshots of life and then offer some suggestions about how the stories they embody help to illustrate the issues we've been considering.

A Snapshot of Vocational Choices

Stephen and his father, Don, are a lot alike. Both are quiet, introverted men, but both make friends easily. They sail and run for recreation; they are both trained as engineers; and they both possess the analytical and mathematical gifts their work requires. Their ties are deep to the family of seven of which they are both a part, and they are both devout Roman Catholics, so there are more than a few similarities in their triage theologies. They even look a bit alike. So, on the face of it, you might assume that they would see God's will for their lives in very similar ways. But they are, and are becoming, very different people.

While still in his early twenties, Don inherited a small engineering firm from his father that designs and produces metal parts, primarily for automobiles. Any other young man might have embraced the opportunity as a ready-made career and a chance to "be his own boss." Or he might have seen it as an obligation to preserve the family legacy. Those were certainly some of the I-questions that Don eventually asked.

But he had very different reasons for running his father's company, reasons shaped by larger God-questions. Can a business be a divine gift or trust? What does a company look like when its owner gives it back to God? Those questions took on greater focus as Don sought advice from his parish priest, Father Breznihan.

In his conversations with "Father B," Don found it relatively easy to see the way in which God might work through his efforts to take his father's company into the future. Don had a matter-of-fact approach to life that was largely uncomplicated by the desires and ambitions that others need to name before they can clearly discern the will of God. What surfaced rather quickly instead was a conversation about the chance to nurture a community of people who worked and played together and the opportunity to provide for the welfare not only of his own family but of those who worked in the shop. It was this vision that Don began to see as part of a God-given call that was larger than the considerations that shaped the day-to-day dynamics of a family-run business, and it was this vision that led him to take substantial cuts in his salary when times were tough.

Deeply influenced by his father's faith, Stephen was also predisposed to ask God-questions. But owing to the work he did with the nonprofit group Habitat for Humanity and the influence of his mother, Stephen was restive about joining the family business and found that the day-to-day demands of the firm left him longing for the hands-on sense of fulfillment he needed. For Stephen, the questions about where God was at work in the world were focused a world away and blessed with the leisure of years spent in study.

As a result, when Stephen finished his engineering degree at Purdue University, he found the choices that lay ahead less obvious. He considered returning home to work in the family firm, but he also applied to other companies nearby, thinking that the opportunity to work somewhere else would give him the space needed to "find his own way." Meanwhile, his work with Habitat had surfaced new passions, and as Stephen began talking with his friends and one of his uncles, who was also a priest, it became clear to him that there were deeper parts of his life that responded to the creative call of God. A desire to work more immediately with people, one-on-one, a heart for those living on the fringes of society, and the satisfaction of interacting with people individually came to characterize what seemed to be the natural business of his life. And yet he remained interested in engineering, and he realized that his analytical and mathematical skills were a large part of what he had to offer. A semester overseas provided the missing piece in his search for a means of translating his growing sense of who he was into something he might do. Instead of returning to his home in Detroit after graduation, Stephen joined the Peace Corps, and today he teaches math and engineering courses in Tanzania.

Don's and Stephen's experiences are instructive. Father and son share similar gifts and graces, both are triage theologians with a similar spiritual heritage, and both have asked God-questions. They have answered those questions in ways that are shaped by not only a deep desire to know what God wants for their lives but a willingness to do something about it. They have asked we-questions, even though the communities they have involved in those conversations differ in character.

Yet the answers they have found are significantly different. As different as their questions and answers have been, however, one is not right and the other wrong. Their spiritual pilgrimages diverge just enough that their answers to life's God-questions are necessarily different. In a way, Don did not have the opportunity to ask the questions his son has had to ask. Don's father died suddenly—his opportunities to weigh his choices were attenuated by his loss. Stephen was blessed with space to ask a wide range of questions, unhurried by the circumstances of life.

But father and son are different people as well. Don's "natural business" is not Stephen's, and the work that gives Stephen the sense of being in the center of God's will is not the kind of work that gives Don that same sense. The answers do not matter nearly as much as the inner conversation each one has had with God about his choices, and what they have chosen to do does not matter nearly as much as the kind of people they are becoming.

A Snapshot of Marital Choices

As someone who has celebrated a significant anniversary or two, I have always recommended premarital counseling to couples who approach me about officiating at their wedding. I am convinced that the more couples understand about one another and about the challenges of nurturing their love, the more likely they are to find the kind of joy and fulfillment that ought to be part of one of life's more extraordinary relationships. So when I first heard about Sara and Derrick, I was struck by how appropriate their decision was, but I also realized that their choice illustrated a serious and reflective approach to matrimony that is not easy to find.

Sara and Derrick have been friends for a long time. They had never been what one would call "high school sweethearts," but through the ups and downs of adolescence their friendship was one of the constants in both of their lives. Raised in the Episcopal church, they attended the same schools, were part of the same confirmation class, and attended universities that were not particularly far apart. As a result, the conversations they had with one another as teenagers continued into adulthood. Both of them entered professions that made huge demands on their time, and as with a growing number of young adults, their work dominated their lives well into their late twenties. Nonetheless, they stayed in touch.

In one lengthy e-mail exchange, the question of God's will for their lives spilled over into questions about marriage. They had talked at length about the vocational choices they faced, but this was a first. The whole conversation took yet another unexpected turn when Derrick observed that he had never felt as close to anyone as he did to Sara. The observation brought him up short, and it surprised Sara. She had "better luck" with friendships than Derrick, but it was difficult to remember a time when they had not "been there" for one another.

As the conversation continued, they inevitably began discussing the shape of their own families and the experiences of their friends. Both sets of parents were divorced and remarried, and it occurred to them that they knew very few people who had been married for over twenty years. While they could both think of rare cases in which divorce had been tragically unavoidable—marriages in which abuse or remorseless infidelity had figured prominently—the divorces their friends had experienced seemed to have been rooted far more often in an unreflective approach to marriage and in the assumption that even the marital relationship is largely disposable.

Agreeing that neither of them was interested in "going down that road," as Derrick put it, they began asking themselves how they could approach marital choices in a different way. Premarital counseling was certainly an option. Both Sara and Derrick felt that knowing a bit more about themselves and about anyone they might consider marrying was a matter of common sense. That step seemed premature, however, and they also instinctively felt that there ought to be more—something more deeply resonant with their spiritual lives.

Over the course of the summer they told their rector, Susan, about their conversation. Susan had considerable experience in spiritual direction and was familiar in particular with Ignatian spirituality. She talked at length about how the spiritual exercises designed by Ignatius were developed to help seekers examine their inner lives and, in particular, the attachments that might make it difficult to give themselves completely to God. Derrick and Sara realized that the attachments that were potential obstacles in the spiritual life—the need for acceptance, the search for self-worth, the desire to be loved—were potential obstacles to a healthy marriage as well. "Mixed motives" and "unrealistic expectations" had led some people, it seemed to them, to get married for "all the wrong reasons," and as a result divorce was all but inevitable.

In exploring the subject further with Susan, Sara and Derrick decided to do something that surprised her as much as it did me. They agreed that if self-examination was that useful in weighing other spiritual choices, it might be equally valuable in weighing the prospect of marriage—not because either one of them was particularly serious about someone, but because so many other motives could shape such choices. So they agreed that they would go on retreat, during different weeks, at a nearby monastery that offered its visitors spiritual direction.

When they returned, the conversation that ensued deepened the benefits of the retreats they had taken. Derrick, whose father had been less successful in staying in touch with him, surfaced a good deal of anger with his father that had made it difficult to understand the complex set of factors that led to his parents' divorce. The retreat helped him not only to forgive his father and let go of his anger but to see more clearly what had undermined his parents' relationship and the factors that might have otherwise governed his own marital choices.

Sara had fewer struggles of that kind, but she learned a great deal more about her own motives for wanting to get married. In some ways, though, the benefit to Sara was increasing her awareness of the ways in which those same spiritual forces were at work in the lives of people she knew. Sara had become good friends with Jason, a colleague at work, and she wondered from time to time whether her friendship might develop in another way. But the retreat had raised serious questions for her about that possibility. She realized on reflection that Jason had his own attachments and needs and that those attachments made it difficult for him to love either her or God with any kind of genuine freedom.

Both Derrick and Sara were sure, however, that much of the language they had heard about marriage was deeply misleading. There is no Mr. or Miss Right; marriage is a real choice; and love is something that deepens by choosing—again and again—the person you chose to love, honor, and cherish in the first place. They also learned that marriage, like many other dimensions of life, is as much a spiritual choice as it is an emotional or personal decision. This realization and the conscious attention they gave to the process of discernment were far more important than the decision they finally made about whether or not—or when—to marry.

A Snapshot of Choice in the Face of Adversity

Charlotte is a bright, thin woman with gentle eyes and a tender manner. Her appearance and demeanor are in sharp contrast to the work she did as a corporate lawyer when she was younger. In those days she combed through federal and state regulations, trouble-shooting for her clients. She responded to threats of product liability, taking full advantage of the law to protect her clients' interests, and she established her prowess in a profession that "takes no prisoners."

The long hours she invested at work earned her the recognition of her firm, and in time she achieved the partnership she had long coveted. A rite of passage that acknowledged her contribution, her rise to partner also signaled the opportunity to find new directions for her time and energy. She had found it easier to accept the demands placed on her early in her career, in part because the partners in the firm looked to the younger associates for the same dedication and long hours they themselves had once devoted to their work. It was a moment she savored, since she and her husband, Jeff, had both devoted long hours to their respective professions, and now, at midlife, they looked forward to having more time for one another.

But then, like a thin mist encroaching on an otherwise clear day, a very different future began to take shape. At first, Charlotte barely noticed it. She would fumble the occasional button on her blouse, or one foot would not completely clear the step ahead on her way to the courthouse door. "I'm becoming something of a middle-aged klutz," she joked with her colleagues. But over time the missed steps and the difficulty with her hands became more pronounced, and a more generalized sense of weakness began to creep in at the end of particularly long days.

Still, relatively unconcerned, Charlotte was inclined to chalk up her symptoms to the long hours at work and the stress that the pleasant but significant changes in her work had created. So she decided to schedule the physical she had been postponing. No harm, she thought, in letting the doctor know. It's probably a vitamin deficiency or passing fatigue. In the run-up to her appointment, she actually worried more about the inevitable lectures her physician would give her about her frenetic lifestyle.

The first appointment with her doctor ran true to her expectations. Charlotte seemed otherwise healthy, and her doctor made some fairly predictable recommendations, some of which she knew would be difficult to accommodate. But in the weeks that followed the symptoms she had been experiencing became constant companions, and she quietly made some adjustments in her schedule that honored her physician's recommendations without sacrificing her clients' interests. The adjustments she made, however, seemed to have little or no impact. So she made a second appointment.

This time her physician was rather more concerned. Charlotte had clearly taken his suggestions to heart, but the transient symptoms she had been experiencing had settled in as a permanent part of her physiology. So he arranged for a battery of tests and referred Charlotte to a trusted neurologist. That part of the process took far longer than the earlier conversations with her general practitioner. CTs, an MRI, an EMG, and a muscle biopsy were all eventually scheduled. The neurologist talked about nerve conduction, upper and lower motor neurons, and muscle atrophy. But after weeks of probing and prodding, the one abbreviation that was vaguely familiar was the abbreviation the doctor used to describe her diagnosis. She had ALS.

ALS, or amyotrophic lateral sclerosis, is also known in the United States as Lou Gehrig's disease. It is a progressive and finally fatal disease that attacks the nerve cells that control the muscles and stimulate their movement. As the disease spreads, so does muscle atrophy. When, at last, it moves to the muscles that control swallowing and breathing, the patient dies. In some ways ALS is more frightening than some other debilitating and fatal diseases because the patient never loses her cognitive ability: the mind is effectively trapped in a body that so disintegrates that communication eventually becomes impossible. While some people with ALS live longer, the typical life expectancy of its victims is little more than five years.

Like so many others, Charlotte was shattered by the news, and it took some time to absorb the significance of the diagnosis. Disbelief, anger, and sorrow washed over her day after day. Eventually she and Jeff looked to the members of their church for help in facing the future. As is so often the case, the triage theology that shaped the advice of some friends was more painful than helpful. Some people were more anxious to silence their own sense of mortality than to help Charlotte face hers, and they offered easy comfort or told her they knew how she felt. Others were quick to defend God, suggesting that Charlotte search her life for some explanation of her untimely illness. And still others, who took comfort in the conviction that God is in control of everything that happens to us, argued that there had to be some hidden purpose behind her disease.

Fortunately, Charlotte had enough spiritual and emotional maturity to know that cold comfort of that sort lacked the staying power of a faith fit for winter. Instead, she sought out a small group of friends at her church who had faced trials of their own with greater candor. Margaret and Pam in particular were helpful. Content to sit with Charlotte through long, painful moments, they were convinced that faith in a God who is "in it with us, all the way," is a source of far greater comfort than belief in a God who knowingly subjects people to the kind of torment that Charlotte faced.

As a result of their friendship, Charlotte and Jeff found the spiritual and emotional space they needed to prepare for the inevitable physical challenges to come and to pray about the shape of the future. They had hoped to adopt a child in a year or two, but that no longer seemed wise or fair. So instead, they informally adopted two older teenagers who were members of their church's youth group. Eric and Tom were talented young musicians, but their single mother lacked the means to send them to a nearby arts magnet school. Jeff and Charlotte provided them with the tuition they needed to attend. They also opened their home to the boys, giving them a place to go after school when their mother was working, and they encouraged the boys to use their piano when they needed to practice.

They knew that it would be difficult, if not impossible, to continue participating in the mission trips they had taken to the Dominican

Republic. So instead, they combined their skills to create a small foundation that would provide the funds for others to continue the work they had contributed so much to in the past.

Just how much time Charlotte still has is difficult to say. Reflecting on their circumstances, Charlotte observed, "You know, in some ways life has changed completely, and the sense of loss can be overwhelming at times. In other ways the news has radicalized life. It has forced me to recognize a truth about life that was always there—that we have only this moment, and it is how we respond to Christ's presence in our lives in that moment that counts. The past is gone. The future isn't here yet. Do I think that God gave me ALS to teach me that truth? No. But in seeking God's will for me in the midst of my illness, that's a piece of what I've learned."

Real Life and the Will of God

The three composite stories I have told here represent only a few ways in which people look for an answer to the question, "What does God want for my life?" We could have easily explored other choices, or we could have drawn other comparisons. In putting it all together, however, the stories of Don, Stephen, Sara, Derrick, and Charlotte are suggestive of the diverse ways in which the search for God's will might unfold in our own lives. Each navigated the moment, as all of us triage theologians do, with the resources at hand. The search for direction is never marked by the same number of opportunities; the decisions we face are not always easy or pleasant; and the space we have in which to contemplate the choices is not always the same. There is no one right answer, and there are times in life when there is no "good" answer. What matters is the attention and time we give to asking the deeper questions that nurture the growth of God's life in ours.

Looking Back on the Invitation

Another means of putting it all together is to look back on the invitation I extended to you in the opening pages of this book and to surface the major elements of the invitation that lie at the heart of changing the way in which we seek God's will.

The story is told of a little boy who said, "I used to pray to God for a bicycle, but I realized that wasn't appropriate. So I stole a bicycle and prayed for forgiveness!" This is a perfect (well, maybe not *perfect*) example of "triage theology": reflecting on the experiences of life and how God intersects with those experiences and then deciding which of our deeply held convictions about God are likely to nurture us, and therefore survive, and which of those convictions will not survive. In a very real sense, then, the invitation I offered you at the beginning of the book was partly an invitation to do what you already do: triage theology.

Our focus, of course, has been just one part of that theology: the issues that revolve around finding and doing the will of God. Without a good deal of explanation, I would have been reticent to lift out the observations I have made in abbreviated form. But now you have a great deal of that explanation in hand, so it seems appropriate to highlight the progress we have made, revisit that conversation in slightly different terms, and make just a few closing observations. For the sake of clarity and as a means of providing you with something of an outline for further reflection, I'll cite the conclusions we have reached in an abbreviated, almost propositional form:

- The task of discernment entails asking three kinds of
  questions:
    God-questions
    We-questions
    I-questions

- People inevitably ask these questions in a different order from time to time.

- But the answers to I-questions are best sought in the light of the answers found to both God-questions and we-questions.

- The task of discernment is first and foremost a matter of identifying the work of God in the world.

- Finding the answers to our I-questions against the backdrop of an awareness of how and where God is at work in the world ensures not only better answers to our questions but spiritual health and balance as well.

- Thinking about the deeply formative names we give to God can be a useful strategy for getting started in asking God-questions, because the names we give to God both reveal and conceal certain things about how God works in the world.

- In living our lives, we consciously and unconsciously triage the ideas we hold to be true about God, prayer, and a host of other subjects, deciding which ones are likely to nurture our spiritual well-being.

  Triage theology is a process that is inevitable, healthy, and also—because it is often fixed on our own garden-variety lives—potentially limited for the same reason.

  The triage theology we practice needs to be shaped by a conversation with tradition, experience, and the larger realities of life.

  We are also more likely to reach better conclusions if we practice humility and if, freed from fear, we embrace the passion to understand how God is at work in the world.

With these observations in mind, I explored dimensions of the task that I hope will help you in shaping your own theology of discernment. This exploration led to the following conclusions:

- We look for signs and wonders in a quest to re-sacralize life and to reassure ourselves that everything will be all right and that we have made *the right* choice.

- Signs and wonders can misshape our spiritual lives, tying the will of God to only those efforts that are marked by success, closure, and expediency.

  We are and should be dependent instead on a relationship with God that transforms our hearts and minds.

  The transforming character of our relationship with God will change our perceptions.

  The key to seeing God at work in the world lies not with brute events themselves but with our transformed perceptions of those events.

- For many of us, the will of God is like a page from a Franklin Planner—a to-do list.

  Although we differ about the number and kind of things that appear on that list, we assume that there is a fixed character to the will of God for each of us.

  This list provides us with a sense of reassurance that offers us a sense of direction, diminishes our anxiety, and absolves us of responsibility for making choices in the face of complex circumstances.

  But we cannot have the certainty of a list.

- Authentic choice is ours.

  What we are invited to do is to probe, explore, and discover the will of God.

What we are offered as reassurance is the promise of love, support, and companionship on the way.

For that reason, discernment is not a matter of getting the right answer but an invitation to create an answer.

- The freedom to be creative is not an end in itself. It is, instead, the vehicle through which the life of God deepens in us. Or to put it another way, the choices we make are not as important as the fact that we make them in response to God's love.

  As such, the choices we make should be shaped by a love of God and others.

  Of course, knowing this does not preclude listening for the voice of God, and there is no formula that guarantees we will hear an answer.

- There are, however, ways of creating a space in which God can find us and we can listen adequately. And so we should:

  Listen to God like someone in love
  Listen to God for the sake of listening
  Listen holistically
  Listen with freedom
  Listen with our lives
  Find a way to listen here and now

- If God-questions and I-questions shape the more obvious tension in our quest to find and do the will of God, we-questions—the questions shaped in community—are all but invisible to us.

  These are questions that we need to reclaim because they are rooted in the deeper nature of our relationship with God and in God's triune nature.

In recognizing this truth, we reclaim our responsibility for
one another and enter more deeply into the nature of
what it means to be fully human.

We also receive the gift of being part of something larger
than ourselves.

Because none of us can be spiritual alone, asking we-
questions is both a privilege and an opportunity.

- When we finally do begin asking I-questions, the subject of
gifts and graces moves to the forefront.

  Defined here as talents and temperament, gifts and graces
  are not possessions but have been given to us by God to
  nurture and risk.

  Their proper use is found in realizing that, because of our
  fallen and flawed character, we can neither assume those
  gifts and graces are a sure sign of God's will nor ignore them.

  Instead, doing the will of God means embracing our
  "natural business": using the gifts and graces we have
  been given, while remaining open to risk and martyrdom
  at God's prompting.

- The most important I-question is therefore one of being, not
of doing—of making decisions that respond to the question,
"Who am I before God?"

If we are free to make choices and the process of finding and
doing the will of God is a matter of being and becoming, how will
you know that you have found God's will? We cannot be 100 percent
sure. What we can do is develop the disciplines and questions suggested here so that we can be relatively sure we are actually in conversation with God. The fact remains, however, that we live by faith
and we live encumbered by the limits of what an older generation
would have called our human condition.

What you will experience is joy. After we have set aside the mis-understandings that make the search for God's will burdensome, the challenges that continue to face us take on a completely different nature. And joy emerges as the natural outpouring of intimacy with God—that hand-in-hand exploration of what is "good and acceptable and perfect." The joy does not flow from the exploration alone, although that can be marked by a deep sense of satisfaction and delight. It flows from hearing God speak our name with delight and affection.

ACKNOWLEDGMENTS

No one can be spiritual alone. Even those who are supremely confident of their own strength of mind and vision are, in fact, the beneficiaries of a vast, gentle web of relationships that shapes us all. I am not burdened by that kind of confidence and in writing this invitation, I have had a great deal of help and counsel along the way.

Much of that help and counsel is woven into the fabric of my life and reading. There are teachers I have had along the way who are now so deeply a part of that fabric that I can no longer identify the threads they have contributed, nor completely distinguish those threads from what I might call the work of my own mind. I take comfort, however, in believing that they are, in some way, as aware of their contribution as I am of my debt to them. In Christ all things find their place and balance. I am inclined to believe that the gifts that we give to one another—sometimes without knowing—are eventually recognized and acknowledged as such in God's economy.

There are others that I can name and would like to name, acknowledging as much as possible the influence that they have had on my thinking and on the shape of this book. Among them are those who attended a variety of retreats and conversations held in recent years, including people at Bellaire United Methodist Church,

Houston, Texas; Centennial United Methodist, Roseville, Minnesota; Church of the Disciple in DeSoto, Texas; Church of the Incarnation, Dallas, Texas; First United Methodist, Dallas, Texas; First United Methodist, McKinney, Texas; Memorial Drive United Methodist Church, Houston, Texas; Park Place United Methodist, Houston, Texas; St. David's Episcopal Church, Ashburn, Virginia; St. Luke's Episcopal Church, Dallas, Texas; St. Martin's Episcopal Church, Keller, Texas; St. Michael and All Angels, Dallas, Texas; St. Paul's Episcopal Church, Cary, North Carolina; and University Park United Methodist, Dallas, Texas. Far-flung collegial relationships have also contributed to the shape of my thinking, including the clergy of the Episcopal Diocese of Oregon; the Episcopal Diocese of the Central Gulf Coast; the Kansas East Annual Conference of the United Methodist Church; and the staff of the College of Preachers and Washington National Cathedral, Washington, D. C. Throughout, of course, there have also been my students, who have listened, reflected, and sometimes differed, but have always clarified my thinking.

There have been others who have made a more direct contribution to the shape of the manuscript. Gary Stuard, a parishioner at the Church of the Transfiguration, Dallas, Texas, read the early drafts of chapters 1 through 3 and made valuable suggestions. Student assistants Lee Jefferson and David Whidden, as well as my administrative assistant Pam Goolsby, assisted with the research and proofread the text.

Two friends and colleagues had more influence than any others. The Reverend Dr. David Schlafer of Bethesda, Maryland, and the Reverend Canon Natalie Van Kirk of Dallas, Texas, gave generously of their time, listened attentively in ways that only good friends can, and offered suggestions that have made this a significantly better book than it would have been otherwise. Friendships marked by conversation of such depth are a grace.

I owe a special debt of gratitude to Marcus Borg who graciously contributed the foreword. A long-time friend and colleague, Marcus has been unfailingly generous with his time, even when there has been little of it to give; and he has been a valued partner in conversations touching on biblical studies, theology, and issues of spiritual formation. The foreword is one more gift born of the same generosity of spirit.

At Harper San Francisco there have been a number of people who have also given generously of their time and genius. Cindy Buck gave the job of copyediting the text careful and close attention. Terri Leonard shepherded the manuscript through the final stages. Mickey Maudlin and Gideon Weil read earlier drafts and gave me sound advice. Jim Warner designed the cover, which I needed to see only once to be delighted. Margery Buchanan found the image of the doors for the cover that so quickly captured the book's message in visual terms. And Miki Terasawa has done a wonderful job with publicity.

Above all, I want to acknowledge the great care that Roger Freet has given the book as senior editor. He has not only given attention to the words on the page, but to the logic and the shape of the conversation behind the words. As such, he has been all that one could hope for in an editor, offering sound advice, critical perspective, and encouragement when needed.

Of all the relationships that have influenced this book, the one that profoundly shapes it in both the particular and the general is the one that I share with my wife, Elaine. Those who have marriages that are deeply fulfilling know that it is difficult to describe the grace in it all in a way that does not sound either clinical or sentimental to others. Those who do don't need to be told.

NOTES

Credits for epigraphs that appear on page ix.

David Gilmour and Polly Samson, "High Hopes" (song), *The Division Bell* (New York: Columbia, 1994).

Simone Weil, *Waiting for God*, translated by Emma Craufurd (San Francisco: HarperSanFrancisco, 1951), 50

FOREWORD

1. From an interview in *The Christian Century* (Sept. 11–24, 2002), pp. 26–33. It is also a central theme of the introduction to his *The Sacred Journey* (San Francisco: Harper &Row, 1982).

INTRODUCTION

1. The inspiration is J. R. R. Tolkien's *The Fellowship of the Ring* (New York: Ballantine Books, 1982). The line I have cited appears in the film version (2001), but I have failed to find it in the novel.

2. By "baptized fatalism" I refer to the Christianized notion that everything that happens happens because it must or because God causes it to happen.

CHAPTER ONE

1. Martin Buber, *I and Thou*, translated by Walter Kaufmann (New York: Charles Scribner's Sons, 1970), 127–28.

2. The story is retold freely and quoted in part from John Cassian, *Conferences*, translated by Colm Luibheid, in *The Classics of Western Spirituality*, edited by John Farina (New York: Paulist Press, 1985), 61–62.

3. This is the difficulty with otherwise helpful and even thought-provoking definitions of discernment that stress I-questions or decisionmaking if the reader assumes that there is little more to the task. See, for example, Nancy Reeves, *I'd Say "Yes," God, If I Knew What You Wanted* (Kelowna, BC: Northstone, 2001), 17ff.; Anthony J. De Conciliis, *Every Decision You Make Is a Spiritual One* (New York: Paulist Press, 1995); and Parker Palmer, *Let Your Life Speak, Listening for the Voice of Vocation* (San Francisco: Jossey-Bass, 2000).

4. Don Henley and Stan Lynch, "They're Not Here, They're Not Coming" (song), *Inside Job* (Burbank, Calif.: Warner Brothers, 2000).

5. The language I use here to describe the prophetic task is an effort to sketch a picture of the challenges Jeremiah faced in categories that are easily recognizable to a modern audience. A historical description of the prophets would require many more distinctions and a much longer discussion than is possible here. For those issues, see, among others, Lester L. Grabbe, *Priests, Prophets, Diviners, and Sages: A Socio-historical Study of Religious Specialists in Ancient Israel* (Valley Forge, Penn.: Trinity Press International, 1995), 66ff. For a more overtly theological treatment of the same subject, see Walter Brueggemann, *Theology of the Old Testament: Testimony, Dispute, Advocacy* (Minneapolis: Fortress Press, 1997), 622ff.

6. William L. Holladay, *Jeremiah 1: A Commentary on the Book of the Prophet Jeremiah, Chapters 1–25: Hermeneia* (Philadelphia: Fortress Press, 1986), "Jeremiah," 33.

7. Holladay, *Jeremiah 1*, 1ff.

8. Jeremiah's language is tribal in character and not as individualistic as the language used in our own world. The I-questions asked by the prophets arise out of a much more immediate sense of responsibility to the communities of which they are a part. The language used is also stylized, and scholars rightly note that there was something of a formula at work in the way in which such stories were told. See Holladay, *Jeremiah 1*, 26ff.

9. Holladay, *Jeremiah 1*, 33. The language has little if anything at all to do with predestination. If that is on Jeremiah's mind, it is not the language of a philosophical commitment but the affirmation of faith that celebrates the confidence that comes with doing the right thing and making a choice that fits.

10. In the Old Testament, the "true prophet" is someone who not only is concerned with identifying the way in which God is at work in history but relies upon that conviction as affirmed in the covenant made by God with Israel. Expecting to see God at work in the world and looking for God at work in the world thus go hand in hand. See Martin McNamara, "True and False Prophets," in *Discernment of the Spirit and of Spirits*, edited by Casiano Floristán and Christian Duquoc, *Concilium* 119 (New York: Seabury Press, 1979), 12. In Paul's list of gifts (1 Corinthians 12:10), discernment is, as Enrique Dussel points out, "a gift of grace from the Spirit enabling us to distinguish clearly in actions and in person what is conducive to building the kingdom" (see his essay "Discernment: Orthodoxy or Orthopraxis?" in Floristán and Duquoc, *Discernment of the Spirit and of Spirits*, 48). But the citation in 1 Corinthians is so brief that it has generated a variety of interpretations; moreover, Paul may not be talking about the same kind of discernment to which we refer here. See, for example, Raymond F. Collins, *First Corinthians: Sacra Pagina*, vol. 7, edited by Daniel J. Harrington (Collegeville, Minn.: Liturgical Press, 1999), 455–56.

11. See also Charles Wood, *Vision and Discernment: Studies in Theological Education* (Atlanta: Scholars Press, 1985), 72ff.

12. Readers will recognize the influence of Marcus Borg's work in the foregoing description. See his *Conflict, Holiness, and Politics in the Teaching of Jesus*, Studies in the Bible and Early Christianity series, vol. 5 (New York: Edwin Mellen Press, 1984). Jon Sobrino observed: "For Jesus, discerning the will of God meant at first nothing other than clarifying for

himself who God really is." See his essay "Following Jesus as Discernment," in Floristán and Duquoc, *Discernment of the Spirit and of Spirits*, 15–16.

13. Ted Loder, *Guerrillas of Grace* (San Diego: Lura Media, 1984), 24.

14. Richard Rohr, *Everything Belongs: The Gift of Contemplative Prayer* (New York: Crossroad, 1999), 7.

15. Ruben L. F. Habito, *Healing Breath: Zen Spirituality for a Wounded Earth* (Dallas: Maria Kannon Zen Center Publications, 2001), 21.

16. Karen Armstrong, *Visions of God: Four Medieval Mystics and Their Writings* (New York: Bantam, 1994), 67.

17. Dag Hammarskjöld, *Markings*, translated by Leif Sjöberg and W. H. Auden (New York: Alfred A. Knopf, 1964), viii.

18. On the metaphors of seeking and dwelling as a means of characterizing the changes and tensions in American spiritual life, see Robert Wuthnow, *After Heaven: Spirituality in America Since the 1950s* (Berkeley: University of California Press, 1998).

19. Mary Strong, ed., *Letters of the Scattered Brotherhood* (San Francisco: HarperSan-Francisco, 1948), 7. I have been unsuccessful in locating the original source for White's observation, so I may be expanding on it in ways that differ from her original intention. The point here, however, remains the same, and the language is apt.

20. See Augustine, *City of God*, xv:5. I'm indebted to my colleague William S. Babcock for this observation, although the connection and inference drawn are mine. Not surprisingly, a similar notion is expressed in Jewish thought. In Kabbalistic thought, "*shepha* refers to the divine radiant energy of the unknowable, limitless Divine (*Ayn Sof*) that overflows and enlivens the configuration of God's personality, the Tree of Life (*Etz Chayyim*), and then brings vitality and blessing as it pours down upon our world. Rabbi Juda Loew of Prague . . . a prolific philosopher, Talmudist and legendary creator of the humanoid *Golem*, conceived of God as the ultimate *Mashpia* [spiritual guide], Who conveys goodness to the world. It then becomes the godly task of the righteous to place themselves consciously within the stream of blessing and channel divine goodness and guidance to others according to their needs." See Howard Avruhm Addison, "Reciprocal Grace: The Vocabulary of Jewish Spiritual Direction," *Presence* 10 (February 2004): 29.

CHAPTER TWO

1. Kenneth Cragg, *Faith and Life Negotiate: A Christian Story-Study* (Norwich, Eng.: Canterbury Press, 1994), 1.

2. Thomas Aquinas, *Collationes credo in deum* I. The translation is by Bruce D. Marshall and appears in an as yet unpublished paper, "Quod Scit Una Uetula: Aquinas on the Nature of Theology" (2004).

3. My thanks to Laurel New for permission to use her reflection.

4. Walter Brueggemann, *Genesis: Interpretation* (Atlanta: John Knox Press, 1982), 43–44.

5. One book that speaks directly to this tendency is Brian J. Mahan's *Forgetting Ourselves on Purpose: Vocation and the Ethics of Ambition* (San Francisco: Jossey-Bass, 2002).

6. To be precise, Professor Smith puts it this way in a recent interview: *"Why would you say that it's important to be organized when Jesus had just a couple of followers, and the Buddha*—SMITH: Because if he had not been followed by St. Paul, who founded the Christian Church, the Sermon on the Mount would have evaporated in a single generation. As it is, we have it today—and the same thing with Buddhism. It is the oldest institution surviving on our planet, twenty-five hundred years and still intact. Otherwise the Four Noble Truths [the basic teachings of the Buddha] and the rest of it would have evaporated with the Buddha's death. Institutions give traction, give spirituality traction in history." See Phil Cousineau, *The Way Things Are: Conversations with Huston Smith on the Spiritual Life* (Berkeley: University of California Press, 2003), 152.

7. My understanding of dialogue as used here is informed by the work of David Bohm, who writes: "I give a meaning to the word 'dialogue' that is somewhat different from what is commonly used. The derivations of words often help to suggest a deeper meaning. 'Dialogue' comes from the Greek word *dialogos*. *Logos* means 'the word,' or in our case we would think of 'the meaning of the word.' And *dia* means 'through'—it doesn't mean 'two.' . . . The picture or image that this derivation suggests is of a *stream of meaning* flowing among and through us and between us. This will make possible a flow of meaning in the whole group, out of which may emerge some new understanding. It's something new which may not have been in the starting point at all. It's something creative. And this shared meaning is the 'glue' or 'cement' that holds people and societies together." See David Bohm, *On Dialogue*, edited by Lee Nichol (London: Routledge, 1996), 6ff.

8. See Patrick D. Miller, *Deuteronomy: Interpretation*, edited by James Luther Mays et al. (Louisville: John Knox Press, 1990): 78–79, and Mark E. Biddle, *Deuteronomy: Smyth & Helwys Bible Commentary* (Macon, Ga.: Smyth & Helwys, 2003), 109ff.

9. William Barclay is right. The meaning of this beatitude plays against the double ancestry of the Greek word *praus* or "meek," one of which looks to God and the other to humankind. See William Barclay, *The Beatitudes and the Lord's Prayer for Everyman* (New York: Harper & Row, 1964), 38ff.; see also Alyce M. McKenzie, *Matthew: Interpretation Bible Studies* (Louisville: Geneva Press, 1998), 36–37.

10. See Alan Jones, *Living the Truth* (Cambridge, Mass.: Cowley Publications, 2000), 4ff. Jones, whose apt choice of words I echo here, refers more often to "pilgrims of the truth."

11. Source unknown.

12. Abraham Heschel, *The Prophets* (New York: Harper & Row, 1962), 308–9.

13. C. S. Lewis, *The Great Divorce* (San Francisco: HarperSanFrancisco, 1973), 41.

14. Source unknown.

15. See Jacques Barzun, *From Dawn to Decadence: 1500 to the Present: 500 Years of Western Cultural Life* (New York: HarperCollins, 2000), 200ff.; and Jennifer Michael Hecht, *Doubt: A History* (San Francisco: HarperSanFrancisco, 2003), 317.

16. Marcus Borg, *Reading the Bible Again for the First Time: Taking the Bible Seriously but Not Literally* (San Francisco: HarperSanFrancisco, 2001), 16.

17. Henri Nouwen, *The Road to Daybreak: A Spiritual Journey* (New York: Doubleday, 1988), 16–17.

18. Thomas Merton, *No Man Is an Island* (Garden City, N.Y.: Doubleday, 1955), 27ff.

CHAPTER THREE

1. Bono, "Crumbs from Your Table" (song), U2. *How to Dismantle an Atomic Bomb* (Los Angeles: Universal Music Publishing, 2004).

2. Used by and often attributed to Archbishop Oscar Romero, the prayer quoted here was originally drafted for John Cardinal Dearden in 1979 by Ken Untener. See *National Catholic Reporter* (March 28, 2004): 3.

3. The position I take here on Mark's gospel has wide support in the literature. See Frank J. Matera, *What Are They Saying About Mark?* (New York: Paulist Press, 1987), 1ff., and Dennis C. Duling and Norman Perrin, *The New Testament: Proclamation and Parenesis, Myth and History*, 3rd ed. (Fort Worth: Harcourt Brace College, 1994), 299ff.

4. Bruce K. Waltke, *Finding the Will of God: A Pagan Notion?* (Grand Rapids, Mich.: William B. Eerdmans, 1995), 121ff.

5. One of the perennial challenges facing interpreters of biblical texts is the fact that we have only one side of a conversation. That makes it tough enough to imagine what might have been happening, even when the author is writing a letter and filling in some of the gaps for us! But when the writer chooses to tell a story in order to address the issues faced by his or her readers, then the task of interpretation is even more difficult.

6. See 1 Thessalonians 4:13ff; see also Robert Jewett, *The Thessalonian Correspondence: Pauline Rhetoric and Millenarian Piety: Foundations and Facets* (Philadelphia: Fortress Press, 1986), 94ff.

7. A balanced description of the impact of the Temple's destruction on Judaism is given by Lee I. A. Levine, "Judaism from the Destruction of Jerusalem to the End of the Second Jewish Revolt," in *Christianity and Rabbinic Judaism: A Parallel History of Their Origins and Early Christian Development*, edited by Hershel Shanks (Washington: Biblical Archaeology Society, 1992), 125ff.

8. From time to time, however, apocalyptic enthusiasm has been more compelling. Consider, for instance, the influential book by Hal Lindsay, *Late Great Planet Earth* (New York: Bantam Books, 1970), and the successive waves of books written with every convulsion in the politics of the Middle East—for example, Charles H. Dyer, *The Rise of Babylon: Sign of the End Times* (Wheaton, Md.: Tyndale House, 1991).

9. Louis Menand, *The Metaphysical Club: A Story of Ideas in America* (New York: Farrar, Straus and Giroux, 2001), 75–76.

10. Nikos Kazantzakis, *The Last Temptation of Christ*, translated by P. A. Bien (New York: Simon & Schuster, 1960).

11. I owe the term, though not its application here, to Karen Armstrong, *The Battle for God* (New York: Ballantine Books, 2000), 370–71.

12. For an excellent and accessible description of that emptiness, see Ronald Rolheiser, *The Shattered Lantern: Rediscovering a Felt Presence of God* (New York: Crossroad, 2001).

13. Brother Lawrence of the Resurrection, *The Practice of the Presence of God*, translated by John Delaney (New York: Doubleday, 1977).

14. Source unknown.

15. Bruce H. Wilkinson, *The Prayer of Jabez: Breaking Through to the Blessed Life* (Sisters, Ore.: Multnomah, 2000), 21.

16. See, for example, Gerhard von Rad, *Old Testament Theology*, vol. 1, *The Old Testament Library* (New York: Harper & Row, 1962), 337.

17. As I noted earlier, for example, Bruce Wilkinson has shaped the triage theology of many Americans with the promise that you can say a "little prayer" and claim a "giant prize." See Wilkinson, *Prayer of Jabez*, 15. Coming from a very different perspective, Wayne Dyer makes much the same kind of claim in *Manifest Your Destiny: The Nine Spiritual Principles for Getting Everything You Want* (New York: Harper Torch, 1999). See also the analysis offered by Don Lattin, *Following Our Bliss: How the Spiritual Ideals of the Sixties Shape Our Lives Today* (San Francisco: HarperSanFrancisco, 2003), 209ff.

18. Sharon Welch accurately identifies the underlying assumption that drives even some of the most noble enterprises in American life: "Many activists in the United States are still propelled by a myth of social change similar to the comforting and illusory story of evolutionary progress. We work for justice in the hope that conditions will be better in the future; that our work, though partial, will not be in vain; that our children, that people in the future, will know more freedom, more justice, more peace." See Sharon Welch, *Sweet Dreams in America: Making Ethics and Spirituality Work* (New York: Routledge, 1999), xi. I disagree, however, with Welch's remedy, which she alternately describes as a postmodern or critical humanism (xix), and with her assertion elsewhere that "god" is not only "the source of our relational power" but "*is* that relational power." See Sharon Welch, *A Feminist Ethic of Risk* (Minneapolis: Fortress Press, 2000), 172ff.

19. I have heard that Alfred North Whitehead once observed: "The Worship of God is not a rule of safety, it is an adventure of the spirit. . . . Without the high hope of adventure, religion degenerates into a mere appendage of a comfortable life." The closest approximation to that statement I have been able to locate is found in his work *Science and the Modern World, Lowell Lectures, 1925* (New York: Macmillan, 1954), 269–70, in which Whitehead observes: "Religion is tending to degenerate into a decent formula wherewith to embellish a comfortable life."

20. At one point in reviewing the manuscript of this book, I wondered whether I was making too much of our preoccupation with success, expediency, and efficiency. It would be natural to ask, "So what is wrong with ambition and success?" The answer, of course, would be, "Nothing in and of itself." But elevated to the cultural supremacy it enjoys in our world, ambition and success can be very dangerous indeed. In a completely different connection, I came across some words from Jacques Ellul, who was a professor of law, a theologian, and a member of the French Resistance during World War II. Ellul saw firsthand the dangers of a world governed only by what works: "In this terrible dance of means which have been unleashed, no one knows where we are going, the end has been left behind. Humanity has set out at tremendous speed—to go nowhere. . . . Everything that 'succeeds,' everything that is effective, everything in itself 'efficient,' is justified." Quoted in Bill Wylie-Kellermann, "Jacques Ellul: A Hopeful Pessimist," *Sojourners* 23, no. 7 (August 1994): 11.

21. There are several full translations of *The Imitation of Christ*; see, for example, the one by Joseph N. Tylenda (New York: Random House, 1998). I prefer the translation of this particular passage found in J. Robert Wright, *Readings for the Daily Office from the Early Church* (New York: Church Hymnal Corp., 1991), 22–23.

22. I owe the succinct turn of phrase to my colleague, the Reverend Natalie Van Kirk, canon missioner for clergy formation in the Episcopal diocese of Dallas and a Ph.D. candidate at Perkins School of Theology.

23. I make this point elsewhere at greater length; see Frederick W. Schmidt, *When Suffering Persists* (Harrisburg, Penn.: Morehouse, 2001), 45ff.

24. Saint Francis de Sales puts it this way: "The pleasure we take in anything is a precursor that places in the lover's heart the qualities of the thing that pleases. Hence holy complacence [i.e., contentment] transforms us into God, whom we love, and the greater the complacence, the more perfect the transformation. Thus, having great love, the saints are very quickly and perfectly transformed, since love transports and translates the manners and dispositions of one heart into another. It is strange but true that when two lutes in unison — that is, with the same sound and pitch — are placed close together and someone plays one of them, although the other is untouched, it will not keep from sounding just like the one played on. The adaptation of one to the other is like natural love and produces this correspondence." See Saint Francis de Sales, *Finding God's Will for You* (Manchester, Eng.: Sophia Institute Press, 1998), 7–8.

25. Mary Poplin, "The Global Classroom of the 21st Century: Lessons from Mother Teresa and Imperatives from Columbine," *Educational Horizons* 78, no. 1 (Fall 1999): 37.

26. From William Butler Yeats, "A Prayer for Old Age," *A Full Moon in March* (London: Macmillan, 1935).

27. "Mitchell Sviridoff, 81, Dies; Renewal Chief," *New York Times*, October 23, 2000, A23.

28. The unknown author of *The Cloud of Unknowing* writes: "If you ask me when they should start work, I would reply, 'Not until they have purified their conscience of all the sins of their past life, according to the normal rules of Holy Church.'" See Armstrong, *Visions of God*, 87.

29. See, for example, Kallistos Ware, "The Way of the Ascetics: Negative or Affirmative?" in *Asceticism*, edited by Vincent L. Wimbush and Richard Valantasis (Oxford: Oxford University Press, 1998), 3ff.

30. It is the apt character of the comparison that has commended a number of allegorical interpretations of the Song of Songs. On the history of those interpretations, see Roland E. Murphy, *The Song of Songs: Hermeneia* (Minneapolis: Fortress Press, 1990), 11ff.; and Marvin H. Pope, *Song of Songs: Anchor Bible 7C* (New York: Doubleday, 1977), 89ff.

31. Taken to an extreme in the work of Augustine, the love of another human being is one and the same as a love for God. I am inclined to agree with Martha Nussbaum that as a result it is "unclear what role is left [in Augustine's thought] . . . for loving real-life individual people." But I am not convinced that Augustine's conclusion necessarily follows. Indeed, it could be argued that because God-in-Christ assumes a human form, the best of the Christian tradition endorses wholeheartedly a love for very real people in all their particularity. See Martha Nussbaum, *Upheavals of Thought: The Intelligence of Emotions* (Cambridge: Cambridge University Press, 2001), 549–50.

32. Mark MacIntosh summarizes the tradition succinctly: "In the tradition passing through Augustine (354–430) and Gregory the Great (c. 540–604), love and knowledge are

at the highest levels utterly coinherent: 'The soul wants to know God more and more because it loves him, and loves him because it knows that he is supreme Truth and Beauty. . . .' And this relationship came to be formulated in the tag from Gregory that 'love itself is a form of knowing' (*amor ipse notitia est*). Thomas Aquinas seems to have accepted this view as the correct one. For the angelic doctor *intellectus* does not, of course, equate to our usual modern understanding of 'intellection' or discursive rational analysis. It is, rather, a process of union between the knower and the known. Just as the will longs for the good, so the intellect longs for the true; and since the good and the true are identical in God, the highest form of knowing and willing (loving) coincide entirely." See Mark MacIntosh, *Mystical Theology: The Integrity of Spirituality and Theology* (Malden, Mass.: Blackwell, 1998), 70. In turn, the tradition found in Augustine and Gregory is rooted in the New Testament and in a Pauline passage discussed in the next chapter (Romans 12:1–2). Commenting on the passage, C. E. B. Cranfield observes that, according to Paul, the mind, "far from being an unfallen element of human nature, needs to be renewed, if it is to be able to recognize and embrace the will of God." See C. E. B. Cranfield, *The Epistle to the Romans: The International Critical Commentary*, vol. 2 (Edinburgh: T.&T. Clark, 1979), 609.

33.   Parenthetically, I might note that it is probably that preoccupation with our own feelings that weakens both our love of God and our willingness to honor the vows that we make to one another. Romance that is not grounded in love of another is a volatile and self-serving commodity.

34.   An argument that is made well and at length in MacIntosh, *Mystical Theology*.

35.   The origins of the shift can be traced to the Middle Ages and an emerging preoccupation with the individual, as over against the tribal or communal nature of life. Elements of Western culture have since accelerated the change. On the late medieval preoccupation with the individual versus the corporate dimensions of life, see Colin Morris, *The Discovery of the Individual, 1050–1200* (New York: Harper & Row, 1972). On the connection with spirituality, see MacIntosh, *Mystical Theology*, 64ff.

36.   Rightly, Martha Nussbaum argues that "emotions are appraisals or value judgments, which ascribe to things and persons outside the person's own control great importance for that person's flourishing" and, as such, contain "three salient ideas: the idea of a *cognitive appraisal* or *evaluation*; the idea of *one's own flourishing* or *one's important goals and projects*; and the idea of the *salience of external objects as elements in one's own scheme of goals*." She goes on to note, however, that breaking with the widely held assumption that emotions have no connection with our thoughts and represent "geological upheavals" in our thinking does not mean that our emotions necessarily reflect "the presence of elaborate calculation, of computation, or even of reflexive self-awareness." See Nussbaum, *Upheavals of Thought*, 1, 4, 23.

37.   The Rev. Dr. David Seamands, who at the time taught classes in supervised ministry for Asbury Theological Seminary.

38.   At its best, this examination of our emotions and the achievement of "indifference to all but God's will" is an important goal of preparation in the Ignatian approach to discernment. And rightly, some of the literature on the subject distinguishes between "indifference" and "affective deadness." But it is not always clear when some writers talk about our "emo-

tional duress" what, if any, role the emotions can play. See, for example, Jules J. Toner, "A Method for Communal Discernment of God's Will," *Studies in the Spirituality of Jesuits,* vol. 3 (September 1971): 128–29.

CHAPTER FOUR

1. Eugene H. Peterson, foreword to Stephen D. Purcell, *Even Among These Rocks: A Spiritual Journey* (Brewster, Mass.: Paraclete Press, 2000).

2. A similar debate shaped medieval Jewish philosophy. See Howard Avruhm Addison, "Reciprocal Grace: The Vocabulary of Jewish Spiritual Direction," *Presence* 10 (February 2004): 29.

3. Barry Schwartz, "When It's All Too Much," *Parade* (January 4, 2004), 5. See also his book-length treatment of the subject, *The Paradox of Choice: Why More Is Less* (New York: HarperCollins, 2004).

4. In my own work, I see this pattern play out over and over again in academic institutions, which, far from being ivory towers, are fully a part of the "real world." Thomas Greenfield, who studies leadership and schools, observes: "Organizations are the facade that covers individual intention and will; they are the marionette show that dazzles and deceives an audience—an audience of people who will themselves to believe the performance. But behind the facade are human actors who do what they want to do. As spectators we can choose to be enchanted or duped by the show or we can ask to see behind the facade and to discover who pulls the strings. Human effort creates organizations, but we usually choose to forget the effort and to focus on its outcome. We admire the achievement and deal with it as a detached, objective reality that is independent of the individuals who created it." See Thomas Greenfield, "Leaders and Schools: Willfulness and Nonnatural Order in Organizations," in *Leadership and Organizational Culture,* edited by Thomas J. Sergiovani (Champaign-Urbana: University of Illinois Press, 1984), 152.

5. This tendency can be traced to more than one cause: to confusion about what we mean when we refer to destiny or fate; to the mistake of equating God and fate; and to what might be described as the "dizziness of freedom." See Thomas H. Green, *Weeds Among the Wheat: Discernment, Where Prayer and Action Meet* (Notre Dame, Ind.: Ave Maria Press, 1984), 25; and Rollo May, *Freedom and Destiny* (New York: W. W. Norton, 1981), 83–101, 185–203. Using the metaphor of sailing in discussing the lifelong quest for identity, the poet David Whyte observes: "Sailing back to our anchorage in the midst of that silence set me to thinking of the edges and boundaries of everyday identity and especially the way that we live at the edges of our identity in work. Beyond the edge we have established for ourselves lies the unknown, where we often feel powerless and ready to blame. Above the throb of the engine, I was desperate to blame someone, crying out for someplace to lodge an ultimate sense of responsibility, and panicking a little because it came to rest nowhere but on my own shoulders. But how we long for that parental image of a captain or leader to carry the burden." See David Whyte, *Crossing the Unknown Sea: Work as a Pilgrimage of Identity* (New York: Riverhead Books, 2001), 44.

6. See, for example, Robert Jeffress, *Hearing the Master's Voice: The Comfort and Confidence of Knowing God's Will* (Colorado Springs, Colo.: Waterbrook Press, 2002). For a

more formal statement shaped by a Calvinist perspective, see Terrance Tiessen, *Providence and Prayer: How Does God Work in the World?* (Downer's Grove, Ill.: InterVarsity Press, 2000), 289ff.

7. To say that there is a "mountain" of literature on this subject borders on the literal rather than the metaphorical. For more academic treatments of these and related matters, see, for example, James Barr, *The Bible in the Modern World* (London: SCM Press, 1990), and G. B. Caird, *The Language and Imagery of the Bible* (Philadelphia: Westminster Press, 1980). For treatments that are accessible to a wider audience, see Marcus J. Borg, *Reading the Bible Again for the First Time: Taking the Bible Seriously but Not Literally* (San Francisco: HarperSanFrancisco, 2001), and Walter Brueggemann et al., *Struggling with Scripture* (Louisville: Westminster John Knox Press, 2002).

8. This very simplified description of the challenge originates with the work of Anthony C. Thiselton, *The Two Horizons: New Testament Hermeneutics and Philosophical Description with Special Reference to Heidegger, Bultmann, Gadamer, and Wittgenstein* (Grand Rapids, Mich.: William B. Eerdmans, 1980), 10ff.

9. Here again, I am using the language of David Bohm, but in a distinctly different way. Bohm was concerned with talking about dialogue with his contemporaries. I am using his description of dialogue to describe the conversation that takes place over time in a religious tradition. See David Bohm, *On Dialogue*, edited by Lee Nichol (London: Routledge, 1996), 6ff.

10. I have made this argument elsewhere. In *When Suffering Persists* (Harrisburg, Penn.: Morehouse, 2001), 103ff, I focus on the New Testament. See also the Jewish scholar Emmanuel Levinas, who observes much the same about God as described in the Old Testament: "The fact that kenosis, or the humility of a God who is willing to come down to the level of the servile conditions of the human (of which St. Paul's epistle to the Philippians [2:6–8] speaks), or an ontological modality quite close to the one this Greek word evokes in the Christian mind—the fact that kenosis also has its full meaning in the religious sensibility of Judaism is demonstrated in the first instance by biblical texts themselves. Terms evoking Divine Majesty and loftiness are often followed or preceded by those describing a God bending down to look at human misery or *inhabiting* that misery. The structure of the text underlines that ambivalence or that enigma of humility in the biblical God. Thus, in verse 3 of Psalm 147, 'He who healeth the broken in heart, and bindeth up their wounds' is the same one who, in the following verse, 'counteth the number of the stars and giveth them all their names'" See Emmanuel Levinas, *In the Time of the Nations*, translated by Michael B. Smith (Bloomington: Indiana University Press, 1988), 114.

11. Noting that the Jewish tradition takes the human responsibility for choice as a given, Walter Brueggemann observes, "This particular Jewish tradition of interpretation voices a countertheme to the predominant Christian inclination to accent in a singular way the tradition of sovereignty and deferential obedience. . . . What full humanness requires and expects in this tradition, moreover, is the *courage to assert* and the *confidence to yield*. Either posture by itself betrays both the tradition and the One with whom human beings are summoned to partner. . . . The high classical tradition of Christian interpretation has not paid significant attention to this latter aspect of Yahweh's fidelity, which issues in pathos and vul-

nerability to the human partner. Consequently and inevitably, that classical Christian tradition has not reflected sufficiently on the ways in which humankind is invited to assertion in
the face of Yahweh. As a result of that neglect, the dominant Christian tradition has not fully
appreciated the way in which *the dialectic of assertion and abandonment in the human person is a counterpart to the unsettled interiority of Yahweh's sovereignty and fidelity*. It seems to
me that the classical Christian tradition must relearn this aspect of the interaction of God
and human persons from its Jewish counterpart." See Walter Brueggemann, *Theology of the
Old Testament: Testimony, Dispute, Advocacy* (Minneapolis: Fortress Press, 1997), 458–59
(emphasis in the original).

12. Levinas, *In the Time of the Nations*, 125. Levinas goes on to observe that only
"simple pagans" do not have "cosmic responsibility. The evil or good they may do does not
yet have the significance of the human going beyond the human. They act only within the
limits of natural causality. Or, in an evocative phrase, 'they can only grind grain that has already been ground.'" By contrast, to be a child of God is of a completely different order.
"'Let the heart of the holy people tremble; it contains in its stature all the forces and all the
worlds'" (127). Brueggemann, who relies on Levinas as well, makes this observation about
the God of the Old Testament: "Human persons are, by the very inclination of Yahweh, provided a sure life-space in which to exercise freedom, power, responsibility, and authority, in
order to use, enjoy, and govern all of creation." See Brueggemann, *Theology of the Old Testament*, 456.

13. The New Revised Standard Version (NRSV) and the New English Bible (NEB) use
discern, but the word *prove* appears in the Revised Standard Version (RSV), the King James
Version (KJV), and the New American Standard Version (NASV). As a result, the word
prove continues to shape the way people understand Paul here.

14. I have intentionally changed the language. Ancient Judaism and early Christianity
were far more likely to ask: "How can we be the people of God?"

15. Robert Louis Wilken observes: "Christians found in Jesus 'something greater than
the temple.' Here is the source of conflict between Jews and Christians. It is not that Jews
had no place for mercy, justice, or love, or that Christians did not in time develop a body of
law to regulate the church's life, but that each started at a different point, subordinating the
one to the other. Once Christians dispensed with the authority of the Law, it was inevitable
that Jews, who continued to live by the Law, would be the object of criticism." See Robert
Louis Wilken, "Something Greater Than the Temple," in *Anti-Judaism and the Gospels*,
edited by William R. Farmer (Harrisburg, Penn.: Trinity Press International, 1999), 204ff.
Rightly, Wilken's respondent notes: "It worked the other way too: It was inevitable that Law-
observant Jews would be hostile to Christians." See Everett Ferguson, "Response to Robert
L. Wilken," in Farmer, *Anti-Judaism and the Gospels*, 206.

16. James D. G. Dunn, *Word Biblical Commentary: Romans 9–16* (Dallas: Word, 1988),
717; see also George Wolfgang Forell, *The Christian Lifestyle: Reflections on Romans 12–15*
(Philadelphia: Fortress Press, 1975), 5ff.

17. For simplicity's sake, I use the label "Christian," but on another level, of course, the
debate in the Epistle to the Romans, like the debates elsewhere in the New Testament, is a
family quarrel among Jews about Jewish institutions, not unlike the debates between Jews

and Samaritans, between Pharisees and Sadducees, and between Essenes and Pharisees. See Ferguson, "Response to Robert L. Wilken," 204f.

18. On Paul's dependence on the resurrected and glorified Christ as the starting point for the shape of the Christian life, see Hans Dieter Betz, "The Foundations of Christian Ethics According to Romans 12:1–2," in *Witness and Existence: Essays in Honor of Schubert M. Ogden*, edited by Philip E. Devenish and George L. Goodwin (Chicago: University of Chicago Press, 1989), 56–57.

19. Betz, "The Foundations of Christian Ethics," 61 (emphasis mine). See also Walter Grundmann, "*dókimos*, et al.," *Theological Dictionary of the New Testament 2*, edited by Gerhard Kittel (Grand Rapids, Mich.: William B. Eerdmans, 1964), 260.

20. As Betz observes, the absence of an existing pattern for addressing ethical issues forced Paul to "rethink and revise his ideas at several points before arriving at what he apparently regarded as the final version of his thought in his last letter, that to the Romans." See "The Foundations of Christian Ethics," 55. On the common thread linking Paul's thinking with Jewish mysticism, see Alan F. Segal, *Paul the Convert: The Apostolate and Apostasy of Saul the Pharisee* (New Haven, Conn.: Yale University Press, 1990), 63ff.

21. Quoted from the foreword to Elie Wiesel, *The Gates of the Forest*, translated by Frances Frenaye (New York: Holt, Rinehart and Winston, 1966).

22. Commenting on the parable, Bernard Brandon Scott writes: "The parable as a window onto the kingdom demands that the servant act neither as preserver nor as one afraid; but act boldly he must. If one is to act boldly, then the rules have been changed. They are no longer predictable." See *Hear Then the Parable: A Commentary on the Parables of Jesus* (Minneapolis: Fortress Press, 1989), 234.

23. Joan Chittister, *Illuminated Life: Monastic Wisdom for Seekers of Light* (Maryknoll, N.Y.: Orbis Books, 2000), 55.

24. Thomas Merton, *Thoughts in Solitude: Reflections on the Spiritual Life and the Love of Solitude* (New York: Image Books, 1958), 81.

25. Norman Juster, *The Phantom Tollbooth* (London: William Collins & Sons, 1962), 87–91. Juster loves puns and wordplay. In preaching a sermon some years ago that used this story to make much the same point, I discovered that some of Juster's relatives were in the congregation, and they seemed to think it coincided well with his intention.

26. Augustine, "Seventh Homily: I John 4:4–12," in *Augustine: Later Works*, Library of Christian Classics, vol. 8, edited by John Baillie et al., translated by John Burnabay (London: SCM Press, 1955), 316.

CHAPTER FIVE

1. Quoted in Michael Harter, ed., *Hearts on Fire: Praying with Jesuits* (St. Louis: Institute of Jesuit Sources, 1993), 9.

2. Belden C. Lane, *The Solace of Fierce Landscapes: Exploring Desert and Mountain Spirituality* (New York: Oxford University Press, 1998), 202–3.

3. Toner, "Method for Communal Discernment of God's Will," *Studies in the Spirituality of Jesuits*, iiiff., 139ff.

4. Rightly, David Lonsdale observes: "Decision-making on a particular occasion by discernment of spirits presupposes a living relationship with God and a background of daily life in which I am trying to be responsive and faithful to the Spirit's leading. That is the only context in which Ignatius' guidelines have meaning and use." See David Lonsdale, *Eyes to See, Ears to Hear: An Introduction to Ignatian Spirituality* (Maryknoll, N.Y.: Orbis Books, 2000), 109.

5. There is a vast literature devoted to the Church of the Holy Sepulchre. See, for example, Martin Biddle et al., *The Church of the Holy Sepulchre* (New York: Rizzoli, 2000).

6. I suspect, however, that my surprise at the degree of unanimity that can be found is a product of my own cultural context! People in many parts of the world where tribal and familial ties are stronger are no doubt scandalized by the individualism that marks North American life.

7. Commenting on Psalm 1, Peter Craigie notes: "The happy estate of the righteous is illuminated in v3 by the simile of the tree. A tree may flourish or fade, depending upon its location and access to water. A tree transplanted from some dry spot . . . to a location beside an irrigation channel, where water never ceases to flow, would inevitably flourish. It would become a green and fruitful tree. The simile not only illustrates colorfully the prosperity of the righteous, but also makes a theological point. The state of blessedness or happiness is not a *reward*; rather it is the result of a particular type of life." Peter C. Craigie, *Psalms 1–50: Word Biblical Commentary* 19 (Waco: Word Books, 1983), 60–61.

8. Roland Murphy observes: "To moderns steeped in the 'plain sense' of scripture and historical-critical methodology, allegorical exposition as practiced by patristic and medieval commentators may appear to be merely arbitrary, amusing, and even devious. In the particular case of the Song, it has been supposed that the physical language and explicitly amorous content were a major embarrassment to early Christian sensitivities and the device of allegory, by which Hellenistic authors had reinterpreted earlier Greek mythology, was ready at hand to provide a solution. . . . Such account of the matter is unfortunately one dimensional. A preoccupation with eroticism is rather boldly projected onto the ancient church, while allegory is reduced to a sort of exegetical alchemy for transmutation or spiritualization of the Song's ostensibly objectional sexual themes. There is no reason to deny that the values and goals of Christian asceticism contributed to and were significantly nurtured by a 'spiritual' understanding of the Song. But the actual course of Christian interpretation—from the complex exegetical achievement of Origen in the third century through the appreciative elaboration of it which continued for more than a millennium thereafter—cannot adequately be explained as an exercise in pathological rejection of human sexuality." Murphy goes on to note that Origen, for example, clearly recognized the "erotic 'plot' and imagery" of the Song, while arguing that "what is said literally about the outer, physical person should, if properly understood, apply in a figurative sense to the inner person, promoting the spiritual growth of the soul in its desire for communion with God (i.e., salvation)." See Roland E. Murphy, *The Song of Songs: Hermeneia* (Minneapolis: Fortress Press, 1990), 15ff.

9. Bernard of Clairvaux, *On the Song of Songs IV*, translated by Irene Edmonds (Kalamazoo, Mich.: Cistercian Publications, 1980), *Sermon* 79.1, 137–38.

10. Using another aquatic metaphor, Martin Marty describes the difference between a "moored" and "unmoored" spirituality. "'Unmoored' spirituality is entirely free-floating, directionless, enterprising, individualized. You make it up as you go along. You are purely eclectic. . . . 'Moored' spirituality does not mean being in dry dock or tied to the pier or safely anchored. In its case, you are also on the high seas, amid storms or afraid of being becalmed. But you know there is a destination and a source for further exploration." Quoted from the forward to Richard J. Foster, *Streams of Living Water: Celebrating the Great Traditions of Faith* (San Francisco: HarperSanFrancisco, 2001), xiff.

11. Robert Jay Lifton, *The Protean Self: Human Resilience in an Age of Fragmentation* (Chicago: University of Chicago Press, 1993), ix, 1, 4.

12. Lifton observes: "If the self is a symbol of one's organism, the protean self-process is by no means without confusion and danger, it allows for an opening out of individual life, for a self of many possibilities. As the poet Galway Kinnell tells us, 'Here I arrive there.'" Lifton, *Protean Self*, 5.

13. See the observations made in chapter 4. Lifton is aware of this, although he uses therapeutic categories. What he calls "negative proteanism" can lead us astray "in many different ways. There is the ever-present danger of diffusion, to a point of rendering the self incoherent and immobile: a 'chaos of possibilities.' The protean hunger for meaning can be fierce and ever unsatisfied. Endless forays into possibility can become endlessly superficial, leaving the self with a sense of diminished, rather than enhanced, meaning." See Lifton, *Protean Self*, 190.

14. See *The Oxford English Dictionary*, 2nd ed., s.v. "retreat."

15. Etched into the face of stone that belongs to a quarry dating back to the first century and beyond is a crude sketch of a ship and the words "Lord we went" in Latin. Scholars estimate that the message was left by a pilgrim who visited the site around 330 C.E. See Jerome Murphy-O'Connor, *The Holy Land: An Archaeological Guide from Earliest Times to 1700*, 3rd ed. (Oxford: Oxford University Press, 1992), 56.

16. Tom Wright, *The Way of the Lord* (Grand Rapids, Mich.: William B. Eerdmans, 1999), 1ff.

17. The phrase "tactile spirituality" is not original with me, but having heard it some time ago now, I am not sure about its origin.

18. Tom Wright, for example, who is bishop of Durham and a New Testament scholar, notes that there was a great deal in his religious upbringing that led him to believe that not only was pilgrimage unnecessary, but places could actually get in the way of hearing God. But, he notes, a number of changes in his theology and—significantly—in his experience of pilgrimage sites have led him to see things differently. Noting that he has been surprised on more than one occasion, he writes: "In the early 1980s when we lived in Montreal, my elder son went to a city school which a few years before had purchased from the United Church of Canada a redundant church right opposite the main school building. Being a modern structure, it didn't look much like a church, and they used it for very un-churchlike activities, rock concerts and so forth. The first time we went there, to a very 'secular' occasion, I was stunned. I walked in and sensed the presence of God, gentle but very strong. I sat through the loud concert wondering if I was the only person who felt it, and reflecting on

the fact that I had no theology by which to explain why a redundant United church should feel that way. The only answer I have to this day is that when God is known, sought and wrestled with in a place, a memory of that remains, which those who know and love God can pick up." See *Way of the Lord*, 5.

19. Source unknown.

20. See, for example, Jack Dean Kingsbury, *Conflict in Mark: Jesus, Authorities, Disciples* (Minneapolis: Fortress Press, 1989).

21. Douglas Jacobsen and William Vance Trollinger Jr., eds., *Re-forming the Center: American Protestantism, 1900 to the Present* (Grand Rapids, Mich.: William B. Eerdmans, 1998), 1ff. The term "hearing in halves" is mine, not theirs.

22. Christopher Lasch, who studied the influence of narcissism on American culture, observes that even social radicalism (as potentially one-half of a spiritual life) can and does become a substitute for unmet and deeper spiritual needs, which today are discussed in almost completely therapeutic terms. Writing of her experience during the 1960s as a member of a radical group called the Weathermen, Susan Stern remembered not the causes served and the risks taken in the name of a greater good, but, as Lasch points out, the excitement of working with brilliant people and the sense of physical and emotional strength she felt. Evidence of a commitment to causes and people beyond herself is all but missing from her memoir. Her failure to listen holistically to her spiritual needs is manifest in the imbalance captured by her version of the story of the sixties. See Christopher Lasch, *The Culture of Narcissism: American Life in an Age of Diminishing Expectations* (New York: W. W. Norton, 1979), 7–8.

23. Not surprisingly, it is a process that approximates some forms of therapy. See Martin Payne, *Narrative Therapy: An Introduction for Counselors* (London: Sage Publications, 2000).

24. David Lonsdale, *Eyes to See, Ears to Hear: An Introduction to Ignatian Spirituality*, Traditions of Christian Spirituality series, edited by Philip Sheldrake (Maryknoll, N.Y.: Orbis Books, 2000), 97ff.

25. See, for example, Robert C. Solomon, *Spirituality for the Skeptic: The Thoughtful Love of Life* (Oxford: Oxford University Press, 2002).

26. This misconception has been named over and over again in the theological literature of the last fifty years, and the stereotype lies at the heart of the critique lodged against theism by some theologians. As Marcus J. Borg notes, however, such assumptions about God are also rooted in some of our earliest and formative experiences. Reflecting on his childhood experiences, Borg notes that his own earliest visual image of God goes back to preschool memories of a Lutheran pastor who was "a finger-shaker" and who served as the perfect model for a "God of requirements." See Marcus J. Borg, "The God Who Is Spirit," in *The Changing Face of God*, edited by Frederick W. Schmidt (Harrisburg, Penn.: Morehouse, 2000), 33ff., 38–39; and Marcus J. Borg, *The God We Never Knew: Beyond Dogmatic Religion to a More Authentic Contemporary Faith* (San Francisco: HarperSanFrancisco, 1997), 15ff. It is important to note, however, that Trinitarian and theistic notions of God need not be construed in this fashion. On thinking theologically, see Gordon D. Kaufman,

In Face of Mystery: A Constructive Theology (Cambridge, Mass.: Harvard University Press, 1993), 46ff., 412ff.

27. Quoted in Donald Nicholl, *The Testing of Hearts: A Pilgrim's Journal* (London: Lamp Press, 1989), 306.

28. Mary Douglas, *Natural Symbols: Explorations in Cosmology* (New York: Pantheon Books, 1982), 31–32.

29. Jean-Paul Sartre, *The Words*, translated by Bernard Frechtman (New York: George Braziller, 1964), 30–31.

30. Ronald C. Arnett and Pat Arneson, *Dialogic Civility in a Cynical Age: Community, Hope, and Interpersonal Relationships* (Albany: State University of New York Press, 1999), xi.

31. John Cassian, *The Conferences: Ancient Christian Writers* 57, edited by Walter J. Burghardt et al., translated by Boniface Ramsey (New York: Newman Press, 1997), 92. Cassian uses the phrase in the story of Abba Serapion, who concealed the vice of gluttony; applied to the conscious duplicity of Serapion, it captures the nature of cynicism's knowing combination of deceit and contempt.

32. From a prayer by Dag Hammarskjöld, *Markings*, translated by Leif Sjöberg and W. H. Auden (New York: Alfred A. Knopf, 1964), 125.

33. Source unknown. Even if an urban legend, as some suppose, the story makes a point that is true nonetheless.

CHAPTER SIX

1. Thomas R. Kelly, *A Testament of Devotion* (San Francisco: HarperSanFrancisco, 1992), 59.

2. Robert N. Bellah et al., *Habits of the Heart: Individualism and Commitment in American Life*, updated edition (Berkeley: University of California Press, 1996).

3. Robert N. Bellah, "Finding the Church: Post-Traditional Discipleship," *The Christian Century* 107 (November 14, 1990): 1062.

4. See President Clinton's remarks at Robert Bellah's home page: http://www.robertbellah.com/biography.html.

5. Bellah et al., *Habits of the Heart*, 221, 235.

6. The play, which Bellah did not identify, is "The Just Vengeance," which appears in Dorothy L. Sayers, *Four Sacred Plays* (London: Victor Gollancz, 1948), 294–95.

7. Robert N. Bellah, "Habits of the Heart: Implications for Religion," lecture given at St. Mark's Catholic Church, Isla Vista, California, February 21, 1986.

8. Dorothy L. Sayers, "The Dogma Is the Drama," *Christian Letters to a Post-Christian World* (New York: Macmillan, 1978), 25.

9. As Nicholas Lash points out, "the God of the philosophers" has become the common way in which Christians and others talk about God. The philosopher Richard Swinburne, for example, defines God as a "person without a body (i.e. a spirit) who is eternal, free, able to do anything, knows everything, is perfectly good, is the object of human worship and obedience, the creator and sustainer of the universe." But as Lash observes, this is a worse than useless understanding of God, not just from a Christian point of view but

from a Muslim or Jewish point of view as well. All three faiths hold that "God cannot be divided, in the way that Swinburne does, into a 'central core' with variable penumbra, without doing fundamental violence" to the convictions of all three traditions. A belief in the Trinitarian nature of God is not, Lash observes, a "further belief" that may be "added to" a prior set of convictions concerning God, thus complicating those convictions. It is, for Christians, a part of "what might and might not be meant by 'godness.'" See Nicholas Lash, "Considering the Trinity," *Modern Theology* 2 (April 1986): 185–86.

10. Lash, "Considering the Trinity," 183.

11. Here and elsewhere I use the language of "relationship" and "relationality" to capture both the nature of God and the nature of our connection with God. For some, that language lacks the depth required. The theologian David Cunningham, for example, prefers the word *participation*, and certainly there is much to his approach that commends the use of that word. But Cunningham is forced to qualify the word *participation* in much the same way that the language used here requires qualification. See David S. Cunningham, *These Three Are One: The Practice of Trinitarian Theology: Challenges in Contemporary Theology* (Oxford: Blackwell, 1998), 25ff., 165ff.

12. Karl Rahner notes: "Despite their orthodox conversion of the Trinity, Christians are, in their practical life, almost mere 'monotheists.' . . . It is as though this mystery has been revealed for its own sake, and that even after it has been made known to us, it remains, *as a reality*, locked up within itself. We make statements about it, but as a reality it has nothing to do with us at all." See Karl Rahner, *The Trinity*, translated by Joseph Donceel (New York: Crossroad, 1997), 10, 14. On the lived relevance of doctrine in general, see Ellen T. Charry, *By the Renewing of Your Minds: The Pastoral Function of Christian Doctrine* (New York: Oxford University Press, 1997), viiff.

13. One example of this approach is Henry Blackaby and Richard Blackaby, *Hearing God's Voice* (Nashville: Broadman and Hollman, 2002). Rightly, I believe, Phillip Carey attributes this state of affairs to the influence of "the Calvinist penchant for a rhetoric of distance between us and God." By contrast, Carey notes, "it is an essential precondition for sound Trinitarian theology to dismiss such questions as 'How can the ontological gap between us and God be bridged?' as poorly posed. The transcendence of God imposes no sort of distance between God and us but rather implies that in him all creatures live and move and have their being. If God is closer to us than we are to ourselves, and equally and entirely close to every kind of creature from the highest angel to the lowest mud puddle, then it can no longer make sense to look for a mediator to meet us partway along the distance between God and us." See Phillip Carey, "On Behalf of Classical Trinitarianism: A Critique of Rahner on the Trinity," *The Thomist* 56 (1992): 404, cf. 402 and 405.

14. Raymond E. Brown, *The Gospel According to John XIII–XXI*, Anchor Bible 29A (Garden City, N.Y.: Doubleday, 1970), 747–48, 774ff.

15. Brown, *John XIII–XXI*, 775–76.

16. L. William Countryman observes: "The unity of believers with one another is nothing less than the unity of the father and son before the creation of the world. This is the unity alluded to at the very beginning of the prologue [John 1:1ff.], when John said both that the logos was with God and the logos was God. Such a unity does not submerge the

separate reality of the beings that enter into it; one can still speak of the logos as being *with* God. Yet this union overcomes all possibility of estrangement, so that, as our Gospel has repeatedly emphasized, Jesus and the father are really one. The unity into which the believers are now called is that of the primordial glory, the beauty and the power of the godhead, before the foundation of the cosmos. Yet it is not an unrelieved oneness that obliterates all distinctions, for even 'at first, there was the logos' (1:1)." See L. William Countryman, *The Mystical Way in the Fourth Gospel: Crossing Over into God* (Harrisburg, Penn.: Trinity Press International, 1994), 116.

17.　By becoming the "objects of God's love," we become "the subjects of that love" as well, and out of that experience, doing the will of God flows naturally and fluidly. See C. H. Dodd, *The Interpretation of the Fourth Gospel* (Cambridge: Cambridge University Press, 1970), 195ff. See also Gerard Rossé, *The Spirituality of Communion: A New Approach to the Johannine Writings* (Hyde Park, N.Y.: New City Press, 1998), 37. Commenting on John's theology, Rossé observes, "When believers draw near to Jesus, they encounter not one person but a 'we'; in this 'we' the divine persons manifest themselves in their intimate being and introduce human beings into the dynamic dialogue of love between the 'I' and the divine 'thou.'"

18.　Charry, *By the Renewing of Your Minds*, 121.

19.　Charry, *By the Renewing of Your Minds*, 19, 129–30. Charry cobbles the word together from two Greek words, *aréte* ("moral excellence or virtue") and *gennao* ("to beget").

20.　Oliver Clément, *The Roots of Christian Mysticism: Text and Commentary* (New York: New City Press, 1995), 58, 63, 64, 69–70.

21.　Julian of Norwich, *Revelations of Divine Love*, translated by Elizabeth Spearing (London: Penguin Books, 1998), 130.

22.　Henri J. M. Nouwen, *Behold the Beauty of the Lord: Praying with Icons* (Notre Dame, Ind.: Ave Maria Press, 1987), 22–23.

23.　This assumption is addressed with some success by Parker Palmer, *The Active Life: A Spirituality of Work, Creativity, and Caring* (San Francisco: Jossey-Bass, 1999).

24.　Even the quietist "heroes" of the Christian tradition (Saint Peter Domain, Saint Anthony, Lady Julian, Saint Bernard) all found that knowing God intimately called them back into the world of doing by bringing the world to their doorstep. To know God necessitates a life of service, teaching, and making God known. For that reason, life in the hermitage is an illusion.

25.　Sharon D. Welch does an excellent job of highlighting this challenge in *Sweet Dreams in America: Making Ethics and Spirituality Work* (New York: Routledge, 1999) and *A Feminist Ethic of Risk* (Minneapolis: Fortress Press, 2000).

26.　Contemplating Rublev's icon, Nouwen observes: "Through the contemplation of this icon we come to see with our inner eyes that all engagements in this world can bear fruit only when they take place within this divine circle. The words of the psalm, 'The sparrow has found its home at last. . . . Happy are those who live in your house' (Ps 84:3, 4), are given new depth and new breadth; they become words revealing the possibility of being in the world without being of it. We can be involved in struggles for justice and in actions for peace. We can be part of the ambiguities of family and community life. We can study, teach, write, and hold a regular job. We can do all of this without ever having to leave the house of love. 'Fear is driven out by perfect love,' says Saint John in his first letter (1 Jn 4:18). Rublev's icon gives us a glimpse of the house of perfect love. Fears will always assail us from all sides, but when we remain at home in God, these worldly fears have no final power over us. Jesus said it so unambiguously, 'In the world you will have trouble, but be brave: I have conquered the world' (Jn 16:33)." Nouwen, *Behold the Beauty of the Lord*, 21–22.

27. C. K. Barrett, *The Gospel According to St. John: An Introduction with Commentary and Notes on the Greek Text* (London: SPCK, 1958), 422.

28. Viktor E. Frankl, *Man's Search for Meaning: An Introduction to Logotherapy*, rev. ed., translated by Ilse Lasch (Boston: Beacon Press, 1962), 3–4.

29. David Whyte, *The Heart Aroused: Poetry and the Preservation of the Soul in Corporate America* (New York: Currency Doubleday, 1996), 47ff.

30. Whyte, *The Heart Aroused*, 52.

31. The description given here is based on the work of Robert Kegan, *The Evolving Self: Problem and Process in Human Development* (Cambridge, Mass.: Harvard University Press, 1982).

32. Kegan, *The Evolving Self*, 227.

33. Kegan, *The Evolving Self*, 107.

34. Augustine, *Confessions*, IV.8.9, translated by R. S. Pine-Coffin (New York: Penguin Books, 1961), 78–79.

35. For example, when Abba Arsenius pleads, "Lord, guide me so that I may be saved," the response he receives is, "Flee from humans, and you will be saved." See Kallistos Ware, "The Way of the Ascetics: Negative or Affirmative?" in *Asceticism*, edited by Vincent L. Wimbush and Richard Valantasis (Oxford: Oxford University Press, 1998), 3ff. To some degree this appears to have been the issue for Nikos Kazantzakis in *The Last Temptation of Christ*, translated by P. A. Bien (New York: Simon & Schuster, 1960).

36. Frederick W. Schmidt Jr., *When Suffering Persists* (Harrisburg, Penn.: Morehouse, 2001), 108. The phrase "radical simplification" is Henri Nouwen's. See *Letter of Consolation* (San Francisco: Harper & Row, 1982), 41, 52.

37. Gabrielle Bossis, *He and I*, translated by Evelyn M. Brown (Sherbrooke, Can.: Éditions Médiaspaul, 1985), 81.

38. See, for example, Wayne A. Meeks, *The First Urban Christians: The Social World of the Apostle Paul* (New Haven, Conn.: Yale University Press, 1983), 90. The body was a common image in Greco-Roman speeches and literature, and Paul's use of it as a metaphor was not unique. It has even found its way into the stock expressions of our own culture. We talk, for example, about the "body politic" to describe national life. In Paul's day the metaphor of the body was used to urge subordination and submission to political authorities, and by emphasizing an "inversion of prestige ('honor')," Meeks notes, Paul discourages the notion that one group at Corinth could claim a greater measure of the Spirit than another group.

39. See also Raymond F. Collins, *First Corinthians: Sacra Pagina* 7 (Collegeville, Minn.: Liturgical Press, 1999), 460.

40. Robert Barron, *The Strangest Way, Walking the Christian Faith* (Maryknoll, N.Y.: Orbis, 2002): 113ff.

41.   Commenting on Hillel's words, Yitzhak Buxbaum observes: "The first two lines of the saying cogently express the two sides of 'for oneself' and 'for others.' It is left to the wisdom of the listener to know the time for each and what the balance between them should be; that problem is not solved for him here. . . . The first two lines can work on all the levels of self, wherever a person is found. . . . Spiritually, a person has to save himself, but if he seeks to save himself alone, what is he? Thus, Hillel used to encourage scholars obsessed with their own spiritual progress to teach others, by quoting Proverbs 11:24: 'There is he who scatters and yet has more.'" See Yitzhak Buxbaum, *The Life and Teachings of Hillel* (Northvale, N.J.: Jason Aronson, 1994), 269–70.

42.   See Thomas A. Smail, *Reflected Glory: The Spirit of Christ and Christians* (Grand Rapids, Mich.: William B. Eerdmans, 1975), 131. Smail observes: "The fruit of the Spirit is less a catalogue of individual virtues, than the forms of relationship that bind together the Body of Christ; the gifts of the Spirit are less individual endowments, far less spiritual status symbols, than ways in which we work together within the Body of Christ." See also Siegfried S. Schatzmann, *A Pauline Theology of Charismata* (Peabody, Mass.: Hendrickson, 1987), 68.

43.   Sayers, "Just Vengeance," in *Four Sacred Plays*, 297.

44.   Sayers, "Just Vengeance," in *Four Sacred Plays*, 298.

45.   It might be worth noting that even the Lone Ranger had Tonto and Silver!

CHAPTER SEVEN

1.   Simone Weil, *Waiting for God*, translated by Emma Craufurd (San Francisco: HarperSanFrancisco, 1951), 51.

2.   The identification of gifts and graces is closely related to the task of discernment, but it is not one and the same. See *Discernment for Clergy* (Baltimore: Christian Vocation Project, 1993), 2.

3.   Plato, *Republic* X.620e. See Plato, *The Republic*, edited by G. R. F. Ferrari, translated by Tom Griffith (Cambridge: Cambridge University Press, 2000), 344.

4.   Plotinus, *Enneads*, translated by A. H. Armstrong (Cambridge, Mass.: Harvard University Press, 1967), II.3.15.

5.   See, for example, *King Lear*, IV.iii.35, and *Julius Caesar*, I.ii.139, in William Shakespeare, *Twenty-Three Plays and the Sonnets*, rev. ed., edited by Thomas Mark Parrott et al. (New York: Charles Scribner's Sons, 1953).

6.   James Hillman, *The Soul's Code: In Search of Character and Calling* (New York: Warner Books, 1996), 193.

7.   Hillman, *Soul's Code*, 7ff.

8.   Parker J. Palmer, *Let Your Life Speak: Listening for the Voice of Vocation* (San Francisco: Jossey-Bass, 2000), 3.

9.   John Hick, foreword to *Asceticism*, edited by Vincent L. Wimbush and Richard Valantasis (Oxford: Oxford University Press, 1998), ix.

10.   Wimbush and Valantasis, *Asceticism*, 7.

11.   In this respect, popular perceptions and actual reality do not line up very well. In the film *Monty Python and the Holy Grail*, monks walk around beating themselves on the head

with boards, and there are far too many people who mistake such a practice for reality rather than parody.

12. Kallistos Ware, "The Way of the Ascetics: Negative or Affirmative?" in Wimbush and Valantasis, *Asceticism*, 5.

13. Ware, "Way of the Ascetics," 5.

14. Karen Armstrong, *Through the Narrow Gate* (New York: St. Martin's Press, 1981), 135. See also John Dominic Crossan, *A Long Way from Tipperary: A Memoir* (San Francisco: HarperSanFrancisco, 2000), 53ff.

15. See Debra K. Farrington, *Living Faith Day by Day: How the Sacred Rules of Monastic Traditions Can Help You Live Spiritually in the Modern World* (New York: Berkley, 2000).

16. Marsha Sinetar, *Ordinary People as Monks and Mystics: Lifestyles for Self-Discovery* (New York: Paulist Press, 1986).

17. A list of such publications is virtually endless. It includes both stories of monastic life (for example, Benedicta Ward, ed., *The Wisdom of the Desert Fathers* [Oxford: Lion, 1998]) and books by monks (anything by Thomas Merton!).

18. Robert Bolt, *A Man for All Seasons: A Play in Two Acts* (New York: Vintage International, 1990), 126 (emphasis mine).

19. This, by the way, is the problem at the heart of the emotional and relational damage done by so-called midlife crises. Midlife crises have nothing to do with a chronological odometer that registers the mileage and shouts, "Crisis!" Far more often, such crises arise in lives lived incrementally and unreflectively. We follow our nose without paying attention to the shape of our lives, and when something happens to awaken our consciousness, we find ourselves living lives we didn't expect to live. And therein lies the stuff of crisis.

20. Paul Woodruff, *Reverence: Renewing a Forgotten Virtue* (Oxford: Oxford University Press, 2001), 6.

21. Anne Lamott, *Traveling Mercies: Some Thought on Faith* (New York: Anchor Books, 1999), 270–71.

CHAPTER EIGHT

1. Quoted in David Whyte, *The Heart Aroused: Poetry and the Preservation of the Soul in Corporate America* (New York: Currency Doubleday, 1996), 5.